Protestantism, Capitalism, and Social Science

PROBLEMS IN EUROPEAN CIVILIZATION

Under the editorial direction of
John Ratté
Amherst College

Protestantism, Capitalism, and Social Science

The Weber Thesis Controversy

Second Edition

Edited and with an introduction by

Robert W. Green
The Pennsylvania State University

D. C. HEATH AND COMPANY
Lexington, Massachusetts   Toronto   London

137111

Published simultaneously in Canada.

Printed in the United States of America.

International Standard Book Number: 0-669-81737-6

Library of Congress Catalog Card Number: 72-13639

CONTENTS

INTRODUCTION

Did the Protestant Reformation have a decisive influence upon the development of modern capitalism? Max Weber's resounding assertions concerning the positive influence of Puritanism on the growth and spread of capitalism have been at the center of a continuing controversy which began attracting widespread attention in the first decade of the twentieth century. At that time Weber published two articles: *Die protestantische Ethik und der Geist des Kapitalismus* ("The Protestant Ethic and the Spirit of Capitalism"), and *Die protestantische Sekten und der Geist des Kapitalismus* ("The Protestant Sects and the Spirit of Capitalism"). These articles with some additional footnotes were later included as the first part of Max Weber's collected essays on the sociology of religion (*Gesammelte Aufsätze zur Religionssoziologie*, 3 vols. Tübingen, 1920–1921).

In these articles Weber admitted his debt to the German economic historian Werner Sombart who, in his then famous study *Der Moderne Kapitalismus*, published in 1902, had stressed what he called "the spirit of capitalism" (*der Geist des Kapitalismus*) as a guiding force in the evolution of modern capitalism. Accepting Sombart's hypothesis that there was such a thing as a "spirit of capitalism" and that its role had been crucial to the development of the modern economy of the Western world, Weber then went on to speculate as to the origin or source of this special and essential "spirit." In his essay Weber proposed the thesis that this critical element had appeared as a kind of psychological by-product of the religious ethic of Calvinism.

That such assertions should arouse a storm of controversy was almost inevitable. In its various aspects the Weber thesis cut across the areas of a number of separate disciplines whose scholarly members employ different methods of investigation and who are often skeptical about methodologies other than their own. Historians, economic historians, sociologists, theologians, and psychologists usually do not approach research problems quite the same way. Nor is controversy among scholars of the same discipline an unknown occurrence. But scholarly controversies usually are resolved or abandoned long before the passing of the seven decades which not only have witnessed the survival of the Weber thesis controversy but also have observed its querulous growth to new depths of investigation and its insidious and insistent spread into areas it did not initially disturb. Probably the controversy owes its long life quite as much to what it implies as to what it states. By implication, the Weber thesis asks: what role did psychological attitudes play in the development of a capitalist civilization? The concern and activities of twentieth-century scholars make it clear they consider the question far too important to ignore; but, so far at least, widespread acceptance of any single answer has proven impossible to attain. Some scholars have attacked Weber's position; some have supported it; some seemed willing to accept a modified or carefully qualified version of it. Beyond that, however, if one may judge by what they have written, the authors commenting on Weber's work, either favorably or unfavorably, seem frequently to have misunderstood or misinterpreted either Weber's method or his conclusions, or both.

As a study of the present state of scholarly opinion on the questions raised and the answers given by Weber, clearly the first task of this volume is to present the Weber thesis; therefore the initial selection is Weber's own statement of the purpose of his study taken from his introduction to *The Protestant Ethic and the Spirit of Capitalism.* Space is lacking, of course, in a volume of this length, to include Weber's entire work; so the second selection, an article by Kemper Fullerton from the *Harvard Theological Review,* is included because it offers the reader an excellent summary of Weber's argument. The interested student, nevertheless, is urged to read all of *The Protestant Ethic and the Spirit of Capitalism;* and it is important that he realize that this most famous of Weber's works is but part of a larger study, *Gesammelte Aufsätze zur Religionssoziologie,* embracing the sociological roles of nonwestern as well as western religions. This longer study, not collected and published until the

1920s, is an attempt to understand the origins and development of nonwestern societies as an aid to explaining the unique development of occidental civilization and occidental capitalism. Since World War II the entire work has been published in translation (see the Suggestions for Additional Reading at the end of this volume); and an explanation and summary of Weber's sociology of nonwestern religion is provided by the third selection, R. Stephen Warner's article "The Role of Religious Ideas and the Use of Models in Max Weber's Comparative Studies of Non-Capitalist Societies."

Professor Warner, in explaining Weber's view of the sociological impact of Hinduism and Confucianism, emphasizes that those religions served the dominant economic and political establishments. The viewpoint and the conduct urged upon the believer, however, in the prevailing total environment, did not contribute to developing an economy similar to Western capitalism, nor did the Judaism of Biblical times, according to Weber. In addition, the article defends certain aspects of Weber's methodology, particularly his concept and use of ideal types. Warner insists Weber's ideal sociological type was not the usually accepted standard to which individual actions should be compared but a methodological device requiring the researcher consciously and explicitly to determine his own criteria and assumptions in constructing his research model or ideal type or standards for selection of evidence. Published in 1970, Warner's article presents a recent view of Weber's work and is also devoted in part to another aspect of the Weber thesis controversy— the compatibility of Weber's views with those of Karl Marx. The economic determinism set forth in Marx's works and insistently proclaimed by many twentieth-century Marxists had numbered them among Weber's critics almost from the beginning because Weber seemed to say that man's economic conduct was determined by a religious attitude rather than by material conditions resulting from the class struggle for control of the means of production. Warner argues that Weber extends rather than denies Marx's views by enlarging the range of social interests that have shaped religious history instead of limiting the motive power of historical change to class relationships. Making several additional points concerning Weber's views of the role of ideas in history, Professor Warner's article puts *The Protestant Ethic and the Spirit of Capitalism* in the context of

Weber's thought and, in discussing Weber's use of the "ideal type," introduces to this volume the methodological controversy to which Weber's work contributed.

As persuasive and perceptive as it is and well worth the careful reading it requires, Professor Warner's article includes such statements as:

> *Weber's preference for analyzing reality through the use of one-sided and isolating concepts . . . was based on a conviction that total societies are not the most useful units of analysis. . . . Weber typically used models . . . derived from their subjective meaningfulness . . . rather than "real types" of historical stages or styles . . . for the illumination of concrete historical situations, rather than to reconstruct and predict the movement of history or of the economy as a whole.*

Such a view of methodology is hardly likely to cause many historians to sigh in satisfied relief, confident that "the Truth" is being found and preserved. Among Weber's earliest critics had been historians and economists who asserted, among other complaints, that Weber's work was "constructional," not historical; he was theorizing about what should have happened instead of studying what did happen, selecting evidence to support his thesis and ignoring the data which suggested disagreement. The criteria Weber set were too narrow, they alleged; his ideal "capitalist" was "constructed" so that sixteenth-century Europe's greatest banking and mining families, the Fuggers and the Thurzos, did not qualify as "capitalists" by the Weber standard. Possibly the best known and most comprehensive study of this sort is H. M. Robertson's *Aspects of the Rise of Economic Individualism,* which first appeared in 1933 bearing the subtitle "A Criticism of Max Weber and His School," from which the fourth selection in this volume is taken. Like many fellow economic historians, Robertson asserts capitalism is a result of the material conditions of a civilization, not a creation of religious impulse. In a rather unusual answer to Weber's assertions about Puritan preaching, Robertson includes a lengthy, well-documented discussion of seventeenth-century Jesuit and Jansenist pamphlets and sermons, concluding that French Catholic preachers urged their audiences to live industrious and frugal lives just as Puritan congregations were admonished to do across the Channel.

Not all economists and economic historians were so opposed to

Weber's work as Professor Robertson, nor did they always agree as to which parts or conclusions were acceptable or unacceptable. Werner Sombart, who had furnished Weber the concept of a "spirit of capitalism," concluded in the second edition of *Der Moderne Kapitalismus* (1913) that capitalism had begun much earlier than he had previously thought, long before Protestantism of any sort had appeared. In *Die Juden und das Wirtschaftsleben* (translated into English as *The Jews and Modern Capitalism*) he argued that the social attitudes and economic practices associated with Judaism had been the primary source of the spirit of capitalism. As a result of this treatise, Sombart found himself the target of a critical barrage, one of the chief critics being Max Weber; but Sombart, undaunted, in 1913 published an entire book devoted to the study of the spirit of capitalism. This work, entitled *Der Bourgeois* was translated into English in 1915 with the title *The Quintessence of Capitalism.* Sombart gave heavy emphasis to the conservative theological side of Puritan preaching and practice, disagreeing almost completely with Weber's conclusions about the effect of Calvinist preaching in seventeenth-century Britain. It would appear that Sombart and Weber viewed the problem of the evolution of capitalism in much the same way, used the same or very similar methods to study it, and reached almost entirely different conclusions.

Another famous economic historian, R. H. Tawney, presents a view of the growth of capitalism less hostile to the Weber thesis than that of Robertson, but hardly similar to that of Sombart. *Religion and the Rise of Capitalism,* Tawney's unusually well-known scholarly work, is the source of the fifth selection in this volume. While Tawney accepted Weber's view that there was a causal relationship between the Protestant Reformation and the rise of capitalism, he nevertheless insisted that Weber's emphasis on the unique role of Calvinism in generating the new spirit of capitalism was inadequate to explain the broad overall relationship between Protestantism and capitalism. Tawney tended to place more emphasis on the causative roles of the whole Protestant movement and of general political, social, and economic conditions during the sixteenth and seventeenth centuries.

In the commentary of economic historians during the first half century of the Weber thesis controversy, quite possibly the most comprehensive critique to appear is the work of the Swedish economic historian and newspaper editor Kurt Samuelsson whose

Ekonomi och religion, first published in 1957, was translated into English and published as *Religion and Economic Action* in 1961. Samuelsson not only reviews the arguments of writers such as Tawney and Robertson but also provides one of the most perceptive published analyses of the methodological and statistical techniques employed by Weber and his partisans. *Religion and Economic Action* questions the writers who criticize Weber's theories at point after point and yet refuse to deny a certain plausibility to Weber's conclusions. Nor is Samuelsson satisfied with Weber's critics, such as Robertson, who have attempted to turn the argument around, alleging that economic activity produced religious change. Professor Samuelsson returns to the more fundamental question, not whether religion created attitudes affecting the growth of capitalism or vice versa, but whether any causal connection whatsoever exists between religion and economic action. Because such a host of writers have discussed the Weber thesis, it is perhaps imprecise to say Samuelsson was the first to ask some very basic questions about it; but surely he does emphasize some major points that the best known earlier participants in the controversy had largely ignored. Again, because space is limited in a volume this size, the selections used from *Religion and Economic Action* cannot cover the whole range nor really delve into the depth of evidence presented in Professor Samuelsson's treatise. The reader will notice that both Weber's and Tawney's assessment of the impact of Calvinist preaching is directly challenged: just how much effect did personal thrift and diligence have in producing great personal fortunes and accumulations of capital? It was not a clutch of painfully hoarded coppers, says Samuelsson, but fortunate speculation, vast risks and vast luck, enormous capital gains on unexploited or previously ill-exploited natural assets, and monopoly that produced a long line of great capitalists in the Western world. Using another approach to the problem, Professor Samuelsson compares the industrialization of Catholic Belgium with that of Protestant England. He explains why conditions make the comparison particularly equitable; and because Belgium was "anti-Jesuit Catholic," it does not fit the Robertson hypothesis, much less the Weber thesis. Then Professor Samuelsson turns his attention to an analysis of Weber's statistical methods with results hardly comforting to Weber's admirers. His view of Weber's "ideal types" agrees with neither Warner nor Robertson;

and he insists that however the Weber thesis is approached, almost all the available evidence contradicts Weber's theories.

The impact of *Religion and Economic Action* in academic circles was such that it was fairly frequently referred to as a definitive rebuttal of the Weber thesis. But Max Weber seems to have brought forth a Hydra-headed creation; and the pattern of the then half-century-old controversy remained true to form as Samuelsson's work took its turn as the target of the slings and arrows of academic outrage and exasperation. Professor Niles M. Hansen's "On the Sources of Economic Rationality," the seventh selection in this volume, asserts that Samuelsson's analysis is based upon a faulty appreciation of Weber's intentions. Only comparative history in the broad sense can answer questions concerning the emergence of economic rationality, and Professor Samuelsson fails to consider the essay in that larger context of Weber's thought, alleges Dr. Hansen. Nonwestern religions are still considered barriers to economic progress in underdeveloped countries, argues Hansen, and it is the effect of religious beliefs on economic behavior, not religious preaching per se, that concerned Weber. Protestant deemphasis or elimination of Roman Catholic sacraments, which Weber "held to be magical means of attaining the Grace of God," meant that the Protestant believer was compelled to plan his life in a systematic, rational order to convince himself of his own divine election. Hansen flatly rejects Samuelsson's view of Belgian industrialization and challenges his criticism of Weber's use of Benjamin Franklin's economic ethic as typical of capitalism. Once Calvinism has promoted a capitalist ethic, Professor Hansen alleges, the latter may well become self-sustaining, demanding no further religious activity or concern by its adherents. Like Professor Warner, Dr. Hansen is concerned with the relation of Marx's ideas to Weber's. Professor Hansen sees similarities between Soviet Marxism of the 1930s and Calvinism as sources of economic rationality: both responded to needs to create a new social system with a disciplined labor force who needed an ethical sanction for the perpetual routine of the working day.

By 1964, the centennial of Weber's birth and the sixtieth anniversary of the first publication of *The Protestant Ethic and the Spirit of Capitalism,* no five-foot shelf could have held all the works published on the Weber thesis controversy; but it was becoming apparent that the nature of the commentary was changing. The earlier stages of the debate tended to concentrate on rather specific questions of economics or theology, such as comparisons of the writings of Protestants and Catholics about usury or the history of economic behavior of various individuals or studies of early modern banking and commercial activity. Before all these specific economic or theological or historical disputes had been settled, a new focus began to appear in the controversy: Weber's method and his contribution to the methodology of the social sciences. The works of such scholars as Warner, Samuelsson, Hansen, and Hughes—all contributors to this volume— probably give as much or more emphasis to the debate about methodology than they do to the events Weber's thesis involves. As the realization became more widespread that Weber's contentions had as much or more to do with attitudes than with specific events or clearly quantifiable evidence, then quite naturally increasing attention was directed to finding and considering methods by which attitudes can be determined or measured. Long before this line of investigation led to a definitive set of conclusions, it branched again as some scholars shifted their chief concern from the attitudes of the people Weber had written about to Max Weber himself and, more precisely, to his intellectual development and the sources of his own attitudes toward the problems he had written about.

So, by the seventh decade of its existence, the controversy growing up around the Weber thesis had spread to three fronts: the pursuit of specific historical evidence about the growth of Protestantism and its relation to developing capitalism; the dispute over Weber's methods and his contribution to the methodology of social science; and, finally, the psychological and psychoanalytical studies of Weber's own life and attitudes and their effects upon his work. Pointing out three separate areas of study of the Weber thesis controversy, however, probably suggests a much neater scene than actually exists. Most of the contributors to the argument at least touch upon the methodology and then take up either the historical or the psychological aspect of the controversy. Complicating the picture further are the changes in Weber's ideas between 1904 and 1920 and the lack of clarity characteristic of some of Weber's writing. More than one debate has grown from disagreement about the precise meaning Weber assigned to various terms and concepts.

Combining a deep concern for Weber's methodology and the intellectual environment in which he worked, H. Stuart Hughes, author of *Consciousness and Society* from which the eighth selection in this volume is taken, presents a particularly persuasive analysis of Weber's work. Hughes sees Weber as one of the most important figures in the reorientation of European thought during the first third of the twentieth century. But Weber, almost intolerably burdened by his own psychological background, was a deeply troubled, self-divided man trying to reconcile a host of conflicting ideals. It was his search for a method to bring about a reconciliation between such ideologies as were expressed by nationalism and Marxism or by religion and economics, says Hughes, that drove Weber from his first appointment teaching law to conduct research in economic and social history and then to his first professorial chair, which was in economics. Only in the last few years of his life did he accept visiting professorships in sociology at Vienna and then Munich, where he died in 1920, still seeking an answer to the problem of rationality in Western society. Professor Hughes regards Weber's critique of Marxism as the most subtle and wide ranging of his generation. The relationship between Weber's work and Marxism, as Professor Hughes sees it, is more like Professor Warner's view than Professor Hansen's, but identical to neither. Weber's *Protestant Ethic,* says H. Stuart Hughes "remains one of the great works of social thought of our time—an almost unique combination of imaginative boldness in its central hypothesis and meticulous scholarship in its documentation. . . ." His critics, Professor Hughes insists, have overlooked or misunderstood Weber's definition of his purpose.

The last selection in this volume concerns a psycho-historical study of Weber, Arthur Mitzman's impressive work, *The Iron Cage: An Historical Interpretation of Max Weber,* published in 1969. To summarize Mitzman's arguments and provide informed commentary on this brilliant but tightly written book is the purpose of a searching review article by Professor Bruce Mazlish, an intellectual historian writing for the scholarly journal *History and Theory* in 1970. Professor Mazlish considers Mitzman's relating of Weber's psyche to his writings more convincing as a source of Weber's work than the generational conflict of the turn of the century which Hughes sees as the boiling retort in which Weber's works were distilled. Furthermore, Mazlish sees the enormous creative tension between passion and reason in Weber's life and thought as the characteristic which makes him so relevant to the present day. Agreeing with Hughes that Weber sought a creative synthesis for his times after 1902, Mazlish refuses to concede that Weber's personal motives wholly determined his findings. Instead, he asserts, they combined with his intellectual development and contributed to the drive he needed to continue his search for a rational synthesis. Whatever the psychological roots of Weber's behavior may have been, Professor Mazlish reminds the reader, they do not validate or invalidate Weber's studies or conclusions.

A volume of this length can do little beyond introducing the reader to the study of this controversy, if for no other reason than the number of writers who have taken part in the dispute. The selections offered here are an attempt to present the essentials of the Weber thesis and to provide a collection of writings representative not only of the different views of Weber's work and its context but of the developing and changing nature and the elusive focus of the controversy. The sheer mass of material published about the Weber thesis controversy is more than overwhelming; it is its own best evidence of the extensive and intensive research stimulated at least in part by the continuing debate. Recognizing the vital importance of both Protestantism and capitalism as forces shaping modern civilization, many thoughtful individuals have been led by the Weber thesis controversy to further reflection on the methods best suited to the study and analysis of this sort of phenomena. Not least important is the fact that this controversy highlights an even broader and more serious question: what is, or should be, the relation between man's moral philosophy and his economic behavior? The surviving documents of the sixteenth and seventeenth centuries decree that this was considered a question of compelling relevance then. Is it any less relevant in our own time?

Conflict of Opinion

In fact, the *summum bonum* of this ethic, the earning of more and more money, combined with the strict avoidance of all spontaneous enjoyment of life, is completely devoid of any eudæmonistic, not to say hedonistic, admixture. It is thought of so purely as an end in itself, that from the point of view of the happiness of, or utility to, the single individual, it appears entirely transcendental and absolutely irrational. Man is dominated by the making of money, by acquisition as the ultimate purpose of his life. Economic acquisition is no longer subordinated to man as the means for the satisfaction of his material needs. This reversal of what we should call the natural relationship, so irrational from a naïve point of view, is evidently as definitely a leading principle of capitalism as it is foreign to all peoples not under capitalistic influence. At the same time it expresses a type of feeling which is closely connected with certain religious ideas. If we thus ask, *why* should "money be made out of men," Benjamin Franklin himself, although he was a colorless deist, answers in his autobiography with a quotation from the Bible, which his strict Calvinistic father drummed into him again and again in his youth: "Seest thou a man diligent in his business? He shall stand before kings" (Prov. xxii. 29). The earning of money within the modern economic order is, so long as it is done legally, the result and expression of virtue and proficiency in a calling; and this virtue and proficiency are, as it is now not difficult to see, the real Alpha and Omega of Franklin's ethic.

MAX WEBER

But Weber's second criterion of the capitalist spirit is too narrow. It leads inevitably to the defect which I feel vitiates his whole argument; he hardly considers any capitalist other than the Puritan capitalist who seeks wealth for the fulfillment of his "calling."

This added refinement is quite superfluous. A realist like Marx, who originated the discussions on capitalism, would no doubt have been greatly astonished if he had been asked to consider only those whose money-making activities were promoted by religious or quasi-religious ends to be possessed of the true capitalistic spirit. This is what we are asked to do.

H. M. ROBERTSON

His [Weber's] gravest weaknesses in his own special field, where alone criticism is relevant, are not those on which the most emphasis has usually been laid. The Calvinist applications of the doctrine of the "Calling" have, doubtless, their significance; but the degree of influence which they exercised, and their affinity or contrast with other versions of the same idea, are matters of personal judgement, not of precise proof. . . . His account of the social theory of Calvinism, however, if it rightly underlined some points needing emphasis, left a good deal unsaid. . . . Though some recent attempts to find parallels to that theory in contemporary Catholic writers have not been very happy, Weber tended to treat it as more unique than it was. More important, he exaggerated its stability and consistency. Taking a good deal of his evidence from a somewhat late phase in the history of the movement, he did not emphasize sufficiently the profound changes through which Calvinism passed in the century following the death of Calvin.

R. H. TAWNEY

Our conclusion is that, whether we start from the doctrines of Puritanism and "capitalism" or from the actual concept of a correlation between religion and economic action, we can find no support for Weber's theories. Almost all the evidence contradicts them.

KURT SAMUELSSON

Weber, for all the intemperance of his polemical style, was hesitant, self-divided, and enormously troubled. . . . He stands at more decisive meeting points than any other thinker. . . . We may trace Weber's course from law through economic history to the general methodology of the social sciences, and then, after a series of preparatory labors in the sociology of religion, to systematic sociology itself. . . . This series of shifts . . . suggests his heroic efforts to bring his diverse interests into some sort of synthesis. For when we look at them more closely, we discover that all these concerns are dominated by one overriding problem—the problem of rationality in Western society.

H. STUART HUGHES

Mitzman's choice of Max Weber is unusually apt. For Weber not only is identified with the thesis of Western civilization's increasing rationality, but is intimately related to the concept of value-free research. If Weber can be shown as a man of subterranean passions flawing his rationality, and even more importantly, undermining his putative value-free work, then the "psychology of knowledge" will indeed have made a telling point. . . . Weber's theories have been placed in creative tension with his "agonizing personal pressures." . . . Mitzman has given us a Weber . . . truer to life, . . . a powerful instance of how intellectual history can be deepened and made animate with real life.

BRUCE MAZLISH

Max Weber
THE AUTHOR DEFINES HIS PURPOSE

Max Weber studied law as a young man and became a jurist. His career was altered, however, by the appearance of an article he wrote on German agricultural labor which led to his appointment to the faculty of political economy at the University of Freiberg. He began teaching at the University of Heidelberg in 1897 and later joined the faculty of the University of Munich. Early in the twentieth century he developed his ideas on the study of sociology. From Weber's point of view, the discovery of laws is an end in itself in the study of natural sciences; but in sociology, laws are only a means to aid in the study of the causal interrelationships of historical phenomena. The concepts which the sociologist uses to formulate his working hypotheses are "ideal types," such as the "capitalist" and the "Calvinist." Weber was also deeply interested in tracing what he maintained was the increasing rationalization of human activity. The Protestant Ethic and the Spirit of Capitalism is part of Weber's attempt to use his method to explain the causes and interaction of such seemingly diverse cultural phenomena as capitalism and Protestantism.

A product of modern European civilization, studying any problem of universal history, is bound to ask himself to what combination of circumstances the fact should be attributed that in Western civilization, and in Western civilization only, cultural phenomena have appeared which (as we like to think) lie in a line of development having *universal* significance and value.

Only in the West does science exist at a stage of development which we recognize today as valid. Empirical knowledge, reflection on problems of the cosmos and of life, philosophical and theological wisdom of the most profound sort, are not confined to it, though in the case of the last the full development of a systematic theology must be credited to Christianity under the influence of Hellenism, since there were only fragments in Islam and in a few Indian sects. In short, knowledge and observation of great refinement have existed elsewhere, above all in India, China, Babylonia, Egypt. But in Babylonia and elsewhere astronomy lacked—which makes its development all the more astounding—the mathematical foundation which

Reprinted by permission of Charles Scribner's Sons, New York, and George Allen & Unwin Ltd., London, from *The Protestant Ethic and the Spirit of Capitalism,* by Max Weber, translated by Talcott Parsons.

it first received from the Greeks. The Indian geometry had no rational proof; that was another product of the Greek intellect, also the creator of mechanics and physics. The Indian natural sciences, though well developed in observation, lacked the method of experiment, which was, apart from beginnings in antiquity, essentially a product of the Renaissance, as was the modern laboratory. Hence medicine, especially in India, though highly developed in empirical technique, lacked a biological and particularly a biochemical foundation. A rational chemistry has been absent from all areas of culture except the West. . . .

And the same is true of the most fateful force in our modern life, capitalism. The impulse to acquisition, pursuit of gain, of money, of the greatest possible amount of money, has in itself nothing to do with capitalism. This impulse exists and has existed among waiters, physicians, coachmen, artists, prostitutes, dishonest officials, soldiers, nobles, crusaders, gamblers, and beggars. One may say that it has been common to all sorts and conditions of men at all times and in all countries of the earth, wherever the objective possibility of it is or has been given. It should be taught in the kindergarten of cultural history that this naive idea of capitalism must be given up once and for all. Unlimited greed for gain is not in the least identical with capitalism, and is still less its spirit. Capitalism *may* even be identical with the restraint, or at least a rational tempering, of this irrational impulse. But capitalism is identical with the pursuit of profit, and forever *renewed* profit, by means of continuous, rational, capitalistic enterprise. For it must be so: in a wholly capitalistic order of society, an individual capitalistic enterprise which did not take advantage of its opportunities for profit-making would be doomed to extinction.

Let us now define our terms somewhat more carefully than is generally done. We will define a capitalistic economic action as one which rests on the expectation of profit by the utilization of opportunities for exchange, that is on (formally) peaceful chances of profit. Acquisition by force (formally and actually) follows its own particular laws, and it is not expedient, however little one can forbid this, to place it in the same category with action which is, in the last analysis, oriented to profits from exchange. Where capitalistic acquisition is rationally pursued, the corresponding action is adjusted to calculations in terms of capital. This means that the action is adapted to a systematic utilization of goods or personal services as means of acquisition in such a way that, at the close of a business period, the balance of the enterprise in money assets (or, in the case of a continuous enterprise, the periodically estimated money value of assets) exceeds the capital, i.e. the estimated value of the material means of production used for acquisition in exchange. It makes no difference whether it involves a quantity of goods entrusted *in natura* [in kind] to a travelling merchant, the proceeds of which may consist in other goods *in natura* acquired by trade, or whether it involves a manufacturing enterprise, the assets of which consist of buildings, machinery, cash, raw materials, partly and wholly manufactured goods, which are balanced against liabilities. The important fact is always that a calculation of capital in terms of money is made, whether by modern bookkeeping methods or in any other way, however primitive and crude. Everything is done in terms of balances: at the beginning of the enterprise an initial balance, before every individual decision a calculation to ascertain its probable profitableness, and at the end a final balance to ascertain how much profit has been made. For instance, the initial balance of a *commenda*[1] transaction would determine an agreed money value of the assets put into it (so far as they were not in money form already), and a final balance would form the estimate on which to base the distribution of profit and loss at the end. So far as the transactions are rational, calculation underlies every single action of the partners. That a really accurate calculation of estimate may not exist, that the procedure is pure guesswork, or simply traditional and conventional, happens even today in every form of capitalistic enterprise where the circumstances do not demand strict accuracy. But these are points affecting only the *degree* of rationality of capitalistic acquisition.

For the purpose of this conception all that matters is that an actual adaptation of economic action to a comparison of money income with money expenses takes place, no matter how primitive the form. Now in this sense capitalism and capitalistic enterprises, even with a considerable rationalization of capitalistic calculation, have existed in all civilized countries of the earth, so far as economic documents permit us to judge—in China, India, Babylon, Egypt, Mediterranean

---

[1] A *commenda* was a form of medieval trading association which usually was organized to carry out one sea voyage; when that voyage was completed, the profits were divided among the partners.—Ed.

antiquity, and the Middle Ages, as well as in modern times. These were not merely isolated ventures, but economic enterprises which were entirely dependent on the continual renewal of capitalistic undertakings, and even continuous operations. However, trade especially was for a long time not continuous like our own, but consisted essentially in a series of individual undertakings. Only gradually did the activities of even the large merchants acquire an inner cohesion (with branch organizations, etc.). In any case, the capitalistic enterprise and the capitalistic entrepreneur, not only as occasional but as regular entrepreneurs, are very old and were very widespread.

Now, however, the Occident has developed capitalism both to a quantitative extent, and (carrying this quantitative development) in types, forms, and directions which have never existed elsewhere. All over the world there have been merchants, wholesale and retail, local and engaged in foreign trade. Loans of all kinds have been made, and there have been banks with the most various functions, at least comparable to ours of, say, the sixteenth century. Sea loans,[2] *commenda,* and transactions and associations similar to the *Kommanditgesellschaft,*[3] have all been widespread, even as continuous businesses. Whenever money finances of public bodies have existed, money-lenders have appeared, as in Babylon, Hellas, India, China, Rome. They have financed wars and piracy, contracts and building operations of all sorts. In overseas policy they have functioned as colonial entrepreneurs, as planters with slaves, or directly or indirectly forced labor, and have farmed domains, offices, and, above all, taxes. They have financed party leaders in elections and *condottieri* in civil wars. And, finally, they have been speculators in chances for pecuniary gain of all kinds. This kind of entrepreneur, the capitalistic adventurer, has existed everywhere. With the exception of trade and credit and banking transactions, their activities were predominantly of an irrational and speculative character, or directed to acquisition by force, above all the acquisition of booty, whether directly in war or in the form of continuous fiscal booty by exploitation of subjects.

The capitalism of promoters, large-scale speculators, concession

[2] A method used in the Middle Ages to insure against loss at sea without violating regulations concerning usury.—Ed.
[3] A form of company between the partnership and the limited liability corporation. At least one of the participants is made liable without limit, while the others enjoy limitation of liability to the amount of their investment.—Trans.

hunters, and much modern financial capitalism even in peace time, but, above all, the capitalism especially concerned with exploiting wars, bears this stamp even in modern Western countries, and some, but only some, parts of large-scale international trade are closely related to it, today as always.

But in modern times the Occident has developed, in addition to this, a very different form of capitalism which has appeared nowhere else: the rational capitalistic organization of (formally) free labor. Only suggestions of it are found elsewhere. . . . Even real domestic industries with free labor have definitely been proved to have existed in only a few isolated cases outside the Occident. The frequent use of day laborers led in a very few cases—especially state monopolies, which are, however, very different from modern industrial organization—to manufacturing organizations, but never to a rational organization of apprenticeship in the handicrafts like that of our Middle Ages. . . .

And just as, or rather because, the world has known no rational organization of labor outside the modern Occident, it has known no rational socialism. Of course, there has been civic economy, a civic food-supply policy, mercantilism and welfare policies of princes, rationing, regulation of economic life, protectionism, and laissez-faire theories (as in China). The world has also known socialistic and communistic experiments of various sorts: family, religious, or military communism, state socialism (in Egypt), monopolistic cartels, and consumers' organizations. But although there have everywhere been civic market privileges, companies, guilds, and all sorts of legal differences between town and country, the concept of the citizen has not existed outside the Occident, and that of the bourgeoisie outside the modern Occident. Similarly, the proletariat as a class could not exist, because there was no rational organization of free labor under regular discipline. Class struggles between creditor and debtor classes; landowners and the landless, serfs, or tenants; trading interests and consumers or landlords, have existed everywhere in various combinations. But even the Western mediaeval struggles between putters-out and their workers exist elsewhere only in beginnings. The modern conflict of the large-scale industrial entrepreneur and free-wage laborers was entirely lacking. And thus there could be no such problems as those of socialism.

Hence in a universal history of culture the central problem for us is not, in the last analysis, even from a purely economic viewpoint, the development of capitalistic activity as such, differing in different cultures only in form: the adventurer type, or capitalism in trade, war, politics, or administration as sources of gain. It is rather the origin of this sober bourgeois capitalism with its rational organization of free labor. Or in terms of cultural history, the problem is that of the origin of the Western bourgeois class and of its peculiarities, a problem which is certainly closely connected with that of the origin of the capitalistic organization of labor, but is not quite the same thing. For the bourgeois as a class existed prior to the development of the peculiar modern form of capitalism, though, it is true, only in the Western hemisphere.

Now the peculiar modern Western form of capitalism has been, at first sight, strongly influenced by the development of technical possibilities. Its rationality is today essentially dependent on the calculability of the most important technical factors. But this means fundamentally that it is dependent on the peculiarities of modern science, especially the natural sciences based on mathematics and exact and rational experiment. On the other hand, the development of these sciences and of the technique resting upon them now receives important stimulation from these capitalistic interests in its practical economic application. It is true that the origin of Western science cannot be attributed to such interests. Calculation, even with decimals, and algebra have been carried on in India, where the decimal system was invented. But it was only made use of by developing capitalism in the West, while in India it led to no modern arithmetic or bookkeeping. Neither was the origin of mathematics and mechanics determined by capitalistic interests. But the *technical* utilization of scientific knowledge, so important for the living conditions of the mass of people, was certainly encouraged by economic considerations, which were extremely favorable to it in the Occident. But this encouragement was derived from the peculiarities of the social structure of the Occident. We must hence ask, from *what* parts of that structure was it derived, since not all of them have been of equal importance?

Among those of undoubted importance are the rational structures of law and of administration. For modern rational capitalism has need, not only of the technical means of production, but of a calculable legal system and of administration in terms of formal rules.

Without it adventurous and speculative trading capitalism and all sorts of politically determined capitalisms are possible, but no rational enterprise under individual initiative, with fixed capital and certainty of calculations. Such a legal system and such administration have been available for economic activity in a comparative state of legal and formalistic perfection only in the Occident. We must hence inquire where that law came from. Among other circumstances, capitalistic interests have in turn undoubtedly also helped, but by no means alone nor even principally, to prepare the way for the predominance in law and administration of a class of jurists specially trained in rational law. But these interests did not themselves create that law. Quite different forces were at work in this development. And why did not the capitalistic interests do the same in China or India? Why did not the scientific, the artistic, the political, or the economic development there enter upon that path of rationalization which is peculiar to the Occident?

For in all the above cases it is a question of the specific and peculiar rationalism of Western culture. Now by this term very different things may be understood, as the following discussion will repeatedly show. There is, for example, rationalization of mystical contemplation, that is of an attitude which, viewed from other departments of life, is specifically irrational, just as much as there are rationalizations of economic life, of technique, of scientific research, of military training, of law and administration. Furthermore, each one of these fields may be rationalized in terms of very different ultimate values and ends, and what is rational from one point of view may well be irrational from another. Hence rationalizations of the most varied character have existed in various departments of life and in all areas of culture. To characterize their differences from the viewpoint of cultural history it is necessary to know what departments are rationalized, and in what direction. It is hence our first concern to work out and to explain genetically the special peculiarity of Occidental rationalism, and within this field that of the modern Occidental form. Every such attempt at explanation must, recognizing the fundamental importance of the economic factor, above all take account of the economic conditions. But at the same time the opposite correlation must not be left out of consideration. For though the development of economic rationalism is partly dependent on rational technique and law, it is at the same time determined by the ability and disposition of men to adopt certain types of practical rational conduct. When these types have been obstructed by spiritual obstacles, the development of rational economic conduct has also met serious inner resistance. The magical and religious forces, and the ethical ideas of duty based upon them, have in the past always been among the most important formative influences on conduct. In the studies collected here we shall be concerned with these forces.

Two older essays have been placed at the beginning which attempt, at one important point, to approach the side of the problem which is generally most difficult to grasp: the influence of certain religious ideas on the development of an economic spirit, or the *ethos* of an economic system. In this case we are dealing with the connection of the spirit of modern economic life with the rational ethics of ascetic Protestantism.

Kemper Fullerton

CALVINISM AND CAPITALISM: AN EXPLANATION OF THE WEBER THESIS

Kemper Fullerton was a theologian and a specialist in the study and teaching of the languages of the Old Testament. As a student in both United States and Germany, he held degrees from Princeton University (A.B., M.A., D.D.), was a graduate of Union Theological Seminary in New York, and for several years was a fellow of Union Theological Seminary at the University of Berlin. The year before he published the article from which this selection is taken, he received an honorary Doctorate of Theology from the University of Tübingen. For many years he was a professor (and later professor emeritus until his death in 1940) of Old Testament Languages and Literature at the Oberlin Graduate School of Theology.

Perhaps in nothing, not even in scientific outlook, is the contrast between the Modern Age and the Middle Ages more striking than in the changed attitude toward money and money-making. In the Middle Ages trade was frowned upon and the moneylender despised. In this attitude church and society generally agreed. The church was

From Kemper Fullerton, "Calvinism and Capitalism," *The Harvard Theological Review* 21 (1928): 163–191. Used by permission of Harvard Divinity School. Footnotes omitted.

always castigating the sin of avarice. The making of money was designated by Thomas Aquinas as "turpitudo," even though he admitted its necessity. The thesis that the shopkeeper could only with difficulty please God was introduced into canon law. Usury, which meant not only extortionate interest but interest of any kind, was prohibited by several councils of the church, and to a usurer the privileges of the sacraments were often denied. Even in those days there were, to be sure, practical qualifications of these theoretical judgments, due to the need of money—a need often as keenly felt by the lords spiritual as by the lords temporal. Nevertheless the generalization is safe that money-making was regarded as socially degrading and morally and religiously dangerous. Today all this is changed. Money-making has become the chief aim of modern civilization. In countless ways, gross or subtle, it determines our lives and thinking. It entices into its service many of the best minds of our college graduates. Even our professions, law, medicine, the ministry (witness the vast development of ecclesiastical advertising), are more and more entangled in its net, while the commercialization of amusements, including our college sports, is notorious.

But at this point a distinction is necessary. The change between the present and the past is not primarily in the greater love of money in the present. In all ages avarice has been found in all classes. Whether it is now more widespread than heretofore is not the important question. That difference, if it exists, would be only quantitative, not qualitative. Nor is the change in the method of money-making, its technology, the distinguishing characteristic. Capitalism has existed in one form or another in every age. The real difference, which it is Professor Max Weber's aim to point out and more closely examine in the essay which the present article discusses, is found in what he calls "the spirit of modern capitalism." The difference is psychological, or, more precisely formulated, it is found in a new "ethos" of money-making. What is meant by this spirit of modern capitalism and, an even more interesting question, what is its origin?

Before attempting to answer these questions Weber makes a preliminary historical observation of great interest. He notes that the great trading classes of the bourgeoisie have been chiefly found in the ranks of Protestantism. The proportion of leading industrialists, traders, financiers, technical experts, is greater among Protestants than among Catholics. The latter have always been more inclined to the handicrafts. The Spaniards early recognized this. They said that heresy (that is, the Calvinism of the Netherlands) furthers the spirit of trade. More specifically, these same classes in the sixteenth and seventeenth centuries were mainly found not merely among the Protestants, but among the Protestants of Calvinistic or Calvinistically allied churches—the Huguenots of France, the great Dutch traders, the Puritans of England. In other words, the growth of capitalism in its modern expression coincided to a remarkable degree with that form of Protestantism which, as contrasted with Lutheranism, Weber calls the "ascetic" form. Montesquieu seems to have recognized this singular coincidence when he said of the Protestant English that "they are superior to all other peoples in three things, piety, trade, and liberty." Is this coincidence merely an historical accident, or is there some inner organic connection between these two phenomena, the rise of modern capitalism (or rather of the spirit of modern capitalism) and the great Protestant "ascetic" movement, dominated very largely by the Calvinistic theology? At first sight the two seem quite unlike each other and in their existing forms they really are unlike. In order to answer this question Weber next seeks to define more nearly what he means by the spirit of modern capitalism.

He chooses as the starting point in his analysis of the spirit of modern capitalism Benjamin Franklin's "Advice to a Young Tradesman":

> *Remember that time is money. He who could make ten shillings a day through his work, but goes walking half the day or idles in his room, even if he spends for his amusement only a sixpence, may not count this alone [as a loss], but he has, in addition, given up five shillings, or rather thrown it away. Remember that credit is money. If anyone leaves money with me after it falls due, he makes me a present of the interest. This amounts to a considerable sum if a man has good credit and makes good use of it. Remember that money can beget money [a theory the reverse of Aristotle's!]. Five shillings turned over become six . . . and so on till they are a hundred pounds sterling. He who kills a sow destroys its progeny till the thousandth generation. He who wastes five shillings murders [note the unconscious choice of an ethical term here!], all that might have been produced by it, whole columns of pounds sterling.*

It is not simply the saving of money for the use to which it can afterwards be put that Franklin has in mind. The idea which really lies back of it is that of making money as an end in itself, as a profession, as a "calling," in which all one's best capacities are to be engaged. Franklin quotes Prov. 22, 29, "Seest thou a man diligent [note the word!] in business? he shall stand before kings." Here it is not so much the reward of efficiency as diligence, or the duty of efficiency, in which Franklin is interested. He means to enjoin not the love of money but the obligation to make money. But where an obligation exists, there an ethical element enters in. It is this feeling of responsibility to make money which Weber finds the most significant difference between modern capitalism and the forms of capitalism current in past ages. In other words, the difference lies in the spirit, the peculiar ethos of modern capitalism, defined as a sense of obligation in money-making. When one seriously examines this sense of obligation, the question at once arises, Why does it exist? A reason can be seen for making money in order to provide for a man's family, or to secure prestige and power, or even to lead a life of self-indulgence. But there would seem to be something irrational in a ceaseless drive to make money and ever more money. It is not a native instinct in man. In fact, it has to assert itself against his native instincts. One of the greatest difficulties which capitalism in its modern forms has had to contend with is the frequent lack of this feeling of responsibility among workmen. For the intensification of production a sense of responsibility on the part of workmen is absolutely necessary. But if in an emergency higher wages are offered for increased exertion, workmen will indeed work harder, but are apt to work for only half the time; they prefer to halve their time rather than double their wages. The opposite method, that of starving workmen into harder work by reducing their wages, is even less successful in stimulating productivity. (But Weber notices, in passing, that among working people of pietistic circles in Germany this feeling of obligation is often highly developed!) This indifference to the obligation to make all the money a workman possibly can is called by Weber "traditionalism," as opposed to the spirit of modern capitalism. Before the modern era this traditionalism prevailed not only among the working classes but among the employing classes as well, and Weber draws a picture of the easy-going life of the trader in earlier times. He felt no particular obligation to increase his trade. He felt no anxiety lest, if his trade did not increase, it would dry up. He did not feel it necessary to turn most of his profits back into his business instead of enjoying himself. An excellent example of the spirit of traditionalism is a bazaar-keeper in Damascus of whom I was told when I was in the Near East. My informant said he always liked to trade with this particular dealer. But there was one difficulty. You never could tell when he would be in his shop. It was his custom in the morning to go to his little booth, but he would shut up shop, no matter what the hour, whenever he thought he had made enough metallik for the day, and would then go home to smoke his narghile and enjoy himself. The mediaeval man, even a man engaged in capitalistic enterprises, would have understood this Damascene shopkeeper's intermittent trading far better than he would the ceaseless drive of my poor friend. He would probably have thought the oriental mode of life much the more rational of the two.

But there is another element in the spirit of modern capitalism upon which Weber comments, besides this feeling of obligation to make more profits. Those who are most permanently successful in modern business life are usually marked by a certain quality of self-discipline or "asceticism." They are not the spenders and wastrels of the world. They live moderate and abstemious lives. They do not seek display. They must, if they are to be permanently successful, win the confidence of their workmen and customers. They must be trustworthy. Though Weber does not refer to them, John D. Rockefeller and Russell Sage are excellent examples of the type he has in mind. Such men must pass self-denying ordinances upon themselves. Free indulgence in ordinary pleasures and recreations is not for them. A measure of rigid self-discipline is necessary to ultimate success. Thus, in addition to the feeling of obligation, Weber's analysis of the spirit of modern capitalism includes this tinge of "asceticism." Sacrifices are entailed. And for what? In order to make ever larger and larger profits! Again the question must be raised: Is there not an element of irrationality in all this, if it be judged by the usual standards of what makes life worth living? How can this curious phenomenon be explained?

It might be thought that because this spirit of capitalism is at present so necessary in carrying on the capitalistic processes it is therefore a result of these processes, and the explanation might be given that this feeling of obligation is an adjustment of men's minds to the new economic era that was ushered in by the great discoveries of the fifteenth and sixteenth centuries with their stimulation of trade. But Weber points out that capitalistic forms and capitalistic spirit, which so naturally go together, by no means always coincide. The capitalistic spirit, the feeling of obligation in one's business or calling, was prevalent in seventeenth-century New England, which was founded by preachers and university men in the interest of religion, but wanting in the Southern states, which were developed in the interests of business. The same spirit was wanting in Florence in the fourteenth and fifteenth centuries, in spite of a highly developed form of capitalism, but present in the Pennsylvania backwoods of the eighteenth century amid such primitive economic conditions that, because of the lack of gold, trade was almost reduced to barter and banks were in their infancy. Under such conditions Franklin emphasized the moral obligation of making money. Could there be a greater contrast than in this differing attitude toward money-making? Instead of being "turpitudo," money-making is now itself almost a religion. A religion! Might it be that this strange irrational feeling of obligation to make money, though now unconnected with any religious interest, once had a religious sanction which gave it meaning and support?

The reader will recall the observation that the great trading classes arose and became most fully developed among Protestants rather than Catholics. Is there not here a hint of some strange elusive connection between the Protestant form of religion and money-making?

We have now reached a point where we must embark with Weber on a voyage of rediscovery to a world that for most of us has sunk as completely as Atlantis beneath the waves of the sea. His account of this rediscovered world, and the connection which he establishes between it and the life of our capitalistic culture today, form the most fascinating part of his essay.

In casting about for a clue to the possible solution of the interesting question just raised, Weber lights upon a curious philological fact. He notes that Luther used the German word *Beruf* ("calling") in a sense which it had never before possessed. Nor is there any precise equivalent for it either in antiquity or Catholicism. It appears in Luther's translation of Ecclesiasticus 11, 21, "Trust in the Lord and abide in thy *Beruf*." From this translation and from Luther's use of the word elsewhere it became a standing word in the vocabulary of the Protestant peoples. Now the Greek word which Luther translates "calling" is πονός, "toil." But to translate this by "calling" is evidently an interpretation rather than a strict translation. What did Luther mean by it? From his use of the term elsewhere it is clear that he is here thinking of the labor of the secular, everyday life as a God-appointed task, a calling. By means of this word a religious significance thus comes to be attached to the secular life, even down to its humblest details. "God accomplishes all things through you," he tells us, "through you he milks the cow and does the most servile works." But more especially still, this conception of the secular life as a God-appointed task necessarily involves the idea that the proper performance of such a secular task is a religious obligation; and the idea of the obligation to live a religious life within the sphere of the secular which is found in Luther's use of the word "calling" is one of the most momentous contributions which the Reformation made to social theory. How significant it is can be fully appreciated only when the Catholic theory is understood which Luther was attacking through the use of this word. One of the fundamental doctrines of Roman Catholicism is the sharp distinction between the laity and "secular" clergy on the one hand and "religious" orders on the other. The adjective, "religious," was applied, not to the former but to the monks and the nuns. The latter were "religious" in a sense in which others could not be. A different standard of morals was enjoined upon them. The general obligations of a Christian were comprised in what were known as *praecepta evangelica,* or the morals of the Decalogue, which were in turn practically identified with natural-law morality, or the law written upon the conscience of mankind of which St. Paul speaks in the first chapter of Romans. The religious orders, on the other hand, were obligated to follow the *consilia evangelica,* the higher morality of the gospels, specially expressed in the vows of obedience, poverty, and chastity. This latter morality was impossible of fulfillment in the secular life; in order to practice it, men must withdraw from the world. "Come out from among them and be ye separate," is the motto of monasticism. Thus what may be called a double standard of morality came to exist within the church itself.

Luther's conception of the secular life as a "calling" involved a complete break with this theory. For him no distinction was permissible between two standards of morality, *praecepta evangelica,* to be performed within the world, and *consilia evangelica,* which can be fulfilled only apart from the world. All men are equally obligated to fulfill both the commands and the "advices" of the gospel. And this fulfillment is to be accomplished, not in the cloister, apart from the world, but in the sphere of the secular life itself. This does not mean that Luther's attitude was essentially a "world-affirming" attitude. It was not. He was to a very large degree inwardly estranged from the world. His view, as distinguished from the monastic view, may be summed up in the words, "Be ye in the world but not of it." Nevertheless Luther's conception of "calling" was the first and most important step toward a new appraisal of the secular life. For the Catholic, "calling," or "vocation," was to live the religious life apart from the world. "Calling" for Luther was to live the secular life religiously, to serve God within one's calling (*in vocatione*). The final step remained to be taken, namely, to serve God by one's calling (*per vocationem*). This step Luther does not seem to have taken in any decisive way. In his earlier writings he had a Pauline indifference to the secular life; it was morally and religiously neutral like eating and drinking. Later, through his opposition to monasticism, which he repudiated as egoistic and an evasion of the duties of love to one's neighbor, he came to look upon the secular life as affording opportunities to express this love. Through the various secular activities of our lives we are to serve others.

But as Luther came more and more under the domination of the predestinarian idea, he began to look on "calling" as an opportunity given to man primarily for the purpose of obeying God by humbly and cheerfully acquiescing in that lot in life to which God had assigned him. Not what a man could accomplish through his calling (*per vocationem*) but the spirit of obedience or resignation which he could exhibit within it (*in vocatione*) was Luther's controlling thought in his conception of the secular life. Thus it came to pass that while Luther opened the way for a new appraisal of the secular life by breaking down the Catholic distinction between it and the religious life, he did not himself develop the vast economic possibilities latent in this new appraisal. As a matter of fact he remained a "traditionalist" in his attitude toward money-making, untouched by the spirit of modern capitalism. Through this new estimate of the secular life we begin dimly, though only dimly, to see how it may possibly have come about that Protestants rather than Catholics have been the chief traders and industrialists; the Protestant religion begins to invade the sphere of the secular. But it is yet a far cry from the religious value which Luther set on the sphere of the secular and the utterly irreligious spirit of modern capitalism. Is there any middle term between these two extremes? The Protestants of Calvinistic origin have been the most conspicuous exponents of successful trade. Is the middle term to be found in this branch of Protestantism? To the examination of the great Calvinistic movement, or, more generally stated, of the disciplinary, or "ascetic," movement in Protestantism as distinct from Lutheranism, we must now turn.

While Luther started from the experience of justification by faith, that is, from the human side of experience, Calvin's attempt to restate the Christian religion as against Rome starts from the conception of God. In his view God is absolute Will, and the only absolute that exists. Hence God is the only being who is perfectly free. Therefore what God wills is right, and must be accepted whether we can understand it or not (which is a fundamentally irrational conception of God). This free and righteous will of God expresses itself in Scripture, according to Calvin, in the double decree of election and reprobation. Calvin's treatment of this doctrine is thoroughly intellectualized; its implications are drawn out by logical processes; experience and emotion play little part in his deductions. In other words, Calvinism as a system, though it starts from an irrational conception of God, is worked out in a thoroughly rationalistic way, and this rationalistic note in the system must be constantly borne in mind as we study its practical consequences.

The first great consequence is what may be called an intellectual as well as practical other-worldliness. Man is not the center of the system, nor is even Christ, but God. In the words of the famous answer to the first question of the Westminster Shorter Catechism, "Man's chief end is to glorify God and enjoy him forever." This aim gives to life its reason, its *rationale*. Anything that diverts the mind from this one supreme aim is a species of idolatry, a worship of the creature rather than the creator. Out of this suspicion of the creature arises the "ascetic" view of life, so characteristic of Calvinism and of the Puritan movement generally, which continued to prevail even after the dogmatic system of Calvinism became seriously impaired. Again, since the individual is elected by the eternal decree of God, all intermediaries between God and man are, at least theoretically, excluded. No sacramental grace, no priesthood which controls it, no church, no human help of any kind avails here. The soul stands in the presence of its God in awful isolation. Weber calls this the "disenchantment of the world," that is, its emancipation from sacramental magic, begun by Old Testament prophecy, supported by the scientific movement of Hellenism, and now culminating in the Calvinistic polemic against Rome. It is at this point that Calvinism distinguishes itself most sharply from Rome.

Because of the elimination of all intermediaries between God and man there arises at the very heart of the Calvinistic system a tremendous emphasis upon individualism. That this individualism has played a noble part in the cause of human liberty is too often forgotten, but logically it is antisocial. It concentrates the attention upon the self, even at times to the extent of avoiding too intimate friendships as a worship of, or reliance upon, the creature. The gentle Baxter warns us that "it is an *irrational* act and not fit for a *rational* creature to love any one farther than *reason* will allow us. . . . It very often taketh up men's minds so as to hinder their love of God." This intense preoccupation with oneself is effectively illustrated in the opening chapter of the Pilgrim's Progress, where the Pilgrim's flight from the City of Destruction is described:

> *So I saw in my dream that the man began to run. Now he had not run far from his own door when his wife and children, perceiving it, began to cry after him to return; but the man put his fingers in his ears and ran on, crying, "Life! life! eternal life!"*

On the other hand, in sharp contrast with this emphasis upon the individual, Calvinism has shown a much greater genius for social organization than Lutheranism, and with its intense individualism has been able to combine an equally intense social activity. The Pilgrim, in order to get to heaven, does not flee to the desert as an anchorite. His way lies, as Weber points out, through Vanity Fair. Not withdrawal from the world, as in monasticism, but struggle with the world is the Calvinistic idea of life. Not, "Come out from among them and be ye separate," but, "Be ye in the world but not of it," is the new battle cry. Weber points out the striking contrast between the Divine Comedy, which closes with the contemplation of the vision of God, and Paradise Lost, at the end of which Adam and Eve go forth, in a kind of triumphant resignation, to battle with the world. In the Puritan poem, what has been called the "mysticism of action" has been substituted for the mysticism of contemplation. And this action is

within the world, within society. But how can the intense individualism of Calvinism and its equally intense social activity be combined?
The middle term is here the glory of God. That is the aim of society
as well as of the individual. Through the improvement of society
God is also glorified. And how is this improvement to be accomplished? Through faithfulness in one's calling. This world of ours
was so arranged by God as to serve the needs of mankind. In our
calling we too are to follow this cosmic hint of God and serve our
fellow men.

But at this point Luther's conception of "calling" undergoes in
Calvinism a significant transformation. It will be remembered that
Luther considered our calling to be the means of expressing either
love to our neighbor or our acquiescence in the divine will concerning our lives. In the former case a personal, humane interest in our
neighbor was the natural result; in the latter case there develops a
rather quietistic attitude toward life. But by the introduction of the
greater glory of God as the supreme and absorbing motive of all
human endeavor, both these consequences of Luther's conception
of calling become modified in very important ways. In the first place,
since the work for the regeneration of society is now to be done
primarily for the glory of God, the emotional, humanitarian element
in what we today call the "social-service ideal" is largely eliminated.
The general good of the many takes the place of personal interest in
the individual. Social service becomes, to use Weber's term, "depersonalized." It is social only because it is performed within society.
It ministers, indeed, to the good of society, but it is not done primarily for the sake of society. It is done for the glory of God. If it
were done for the sake of the individual alone, that would set the
creature in place of the creator, and so be a species of idolatry. Two
illustrations will make clear what Weber means by a depersonalized
social activity. In the life of Adoniram Judson his reflections are
recorded after he had tried to evangelize the city of Proom in Burmah
and was stoned out of town. His sad comment was that its inhabitants
would have the chains of hell fastened upon them more tightly
because they had heard the gospel message and refused it. If the
purely personal and humanitarian interest had been uppermost, it
would probably have prevented Judson from exposing the people of
Proom to such a dreadful risk. But as it was, he felt that he was dis-
charging the will of God: "Go ye into all the world, and preach the

gospel to every creature." In 1915 the present writer was ordered out of Palestine by the Turks and left the country in company with many members of the religious orders and Protestant missionaries. One of these, a member of the Christian and Missionary Alliance, was asked if he expected to return after the war. He was doubtful about it, and gave as his reason that he had already preached the gospel in all the villages of Palestine and had thus fulfilled the will of God. The heroic but in fact absurd slogan of the Student Volunteer Movement in its earlier stages, "The Evangelization of the World in this Generation," springs from the same depersonalized conception of the social activity of the missionary. The evangelization of the world because God wills it takes the place of the salvation of the world for its own sake. Contrast the appealing close of the book of Jonah.

In the next place, though work for the good of mankind is in a certain measure depersonalized when the motive of love to our neighbor is modulated into the motive of God's glory, there is no lessening of the pressure of work. If God has ordered and arranged this great physical universe for the good of man and through this manifests his glory, it is supremely important to correlate society to the same great end, and this is done through the fulfillment of such duties in our calling as are imposed by the laws of nature. No mere quietistic acceptance of the universe is possible here. The tremendous drive of God's will and God's glory lies back of all work in our calling. The normal result is a tense and ceaseless activity. Thus the new motive of life, to glorify God and enjoy him forever, this completely other-worldly orientation of our existence, leads to a rationalized and a quasi-ascetic view of life in general (we are to enjoy forever God, not creature pleasures), a depersonalized and therefore rationalized view of love to our neighbor, and ceaseless activity within the sphere of the secular in order to bring the secular within the final aim of life, the glory of God. But this drive toward activity in one's calling which, along with the rationalizing of life, Weber wishes especially to emphasize, is intensified even more directly by another consideration which originates in the heart of the Calvinistic system, namely in the doctrine of election.

The great question for every nonsacramental religion is, How can I be sure that I am saved? or, in the Calvinistic formula, How can I be sure that I am one of the elect? In Roman Catholicism the church could mediate to the believer this assurance through the sacraments, especially the sacrament of penance, but in Calvinism, as we have seen, all authoritative intermediaries are swept aside and the soul is left alone in the presence of its Maker. And its Maker's will is inscrutable. How, then, is the soul to be assured of its election? At first the question was not so insistent in Calvin's own thinking. The promises of God in Scripture and Calvin's own unwavering faith in Christ made doubt impossible. But as Calvinism developed, the question pressed more and more for an answer. Two answers were given. Assurance can be obtained either from the *testimonium Spiritus Sancti,* the inner consciousness of the individual that the power of God is *in* him, or from the ability consistently to perform good works, the consciousness of the individual that the power of God is working *through* him. In the first case he is conscious that he is a vessel, in the second that he is an instrument. While the first method of assurance was undoubtedly emphasized by Calvin himself and always played, at least theoretically, a part in Calvinistic theology, the second method became the more important in practice. And it is at this point that one of the main differences between Calvinism and Lutheranism emerges. Lutheran piety is more of the passive, contemplative, mystical type. It shares with Catholic mystics the idea of the mystical union with God, in which God enters into the soul, or, rather, in which the soul becomes absorbed in God and thus finds assurance. But Calvinism had a highly transcendentalized conception of God to which the idea of the mystical union was inwardly alien, and, as a highly rationalized system of thought, it was suspicious of the emotional life favored by the idea of the mystical union. Emotions can deceive. For these reasons both the logic and the philosophy of Calvinism worked more and more away from the idea of assurance based upon inward experience, in which there was an important point of contact with the Lutheran conception of the mystical union, and came to rest for the assurance of election upon the outward sensible signs of a pious life. Certitude is to be preserved not so much through the feelings as in action. It is interesting to notice that whereas the Westminster Confession of Faith still relies on the promises of Scripture and the Testimony of the Spirit as the formal grounds of Assurance in the section devoted to that subject (section 18), it is held in section 16, on Good Works, that these *strengthen assurance.* Similarly the Savoy Declaration maintains that

Christians are saints "by effectual calling visibly manifested by their profession and walking.' Objective, recognizable signs in the Christian's mode of life are now required in addition to inward feeling in order to give assurance. The great scriptural support for this idea is 1 John 2, 3: "Hereby we do know that we know him, if we keep his commandments." Thus once more we arrive at the emphasis upon action which is so characteristic of Calvinism. The will of God, God's own glory which is at the same time the chief end of man, combined with the soul's necessity of gaining an assurance of election, produces a tremendous drive toward action, as contrasted with the contemplative life.

We have now reached the point where the bearing of all this upon the peculiar Calvinistic conception of "calling" may be seen, and at the same time the similarities and differences between Calvinism on the one hand and Roman Catholicism and Lutheranism on the other are most clearly revealed.

(1) Both Calvinism and Catholicism lay great emphasis upon works. Lutheran theologians often twitted the Calvinists with this romanizing insistence upon works. But there was a sharp distinction between the Romanist and the Calvinist doctrine of works. In the former, works are the means of salvation; in the latter, the means of assurance. By faith alone could men be saved—the Calvinist held fast to this great Reformation principle.

(2) But Calvinism followed Luther in ignoring the Catholic distribution of good works between *praecepta evangelica* and *consilia evangelica*. The former, as we have seen furnished the standards for the laity and secular clergy, the latter for the religious orders. In the case of the laity, Mother Church mercifully took account of the weakness of the flesh. Any defective performance of the "precepts," due to the corruption of man's nature, could be made good by sacramental grace (penance). The consequence was that Catholic lay morality took on, in the Protestant view, a certain casualness. Lapses were easily made good. It was far otherwise with the performance of the *consilia*. Within the secular life these could be performed only to a limited degree; and so life withdrawn from the world now becomes necessary. But within this withdrawn life itself the sternest self-discipline is required. The whole of it is subjected to the strictest and most constant regulation. The "ascetic" ideal, the necessity of which was waived for the laity, is reserved for the religious orders,

and for them not even the sacraments could ameliorate its severity. It is true that here also lapses could be made good by the sacraments, but if "merit" were to be gained, the number of lapses must be reduced as much as possible. Hence the whole monastic life had to be rationalized upon the basis of the "ascetic" ideal. Now when Luther broke down the distinction between the life of the laity and the life of the monks, and contended that the full Christian life could be lived within the sphere of the secular, he did not work out the final consequences of his new position. He did not introduce the rationalized, "ascetic" ideal of monasticism into the secular life. We have seen how in Luther's idea of "calling," that is of the Christian life in the secular sphere, there is expressed either a quietistic acquiescence in the will of God or love to our neighbor. He laid little emphasis on works, much less on a systematized and rationalized life of action. "Tears," he said, "precede works and suffering surpasses doing." His experience of forgiveness and of justification by faith led him to emphasize the inner life of the Christian rather than his outer life. Thus Lutheranism in its main tendency was never ascetic. The piety of the Lutheran was more like the casual piety of the Catholic layman. It was a piety dominated by emotion rather than by reason, and this characteristic was favored also by the considerable measure of sacramentarianism which Luther took over from Catholicism. But in Calvinism all this is reversed. By the ideal of man's chief end as the glorification of God, an ideal that is God-willed, and by the practical necessity of having some means of assurance, a necessity that springs from the doctrine of election when the sacramental approach to God is abandoned, the basis is furnished for a new conception of the secular life. The ideal of discipline, or "asceticism," proper to Catholic monasticism is now transferred to the secular life. Within the sphere of this life lies one's calling (so Luther), but calling now becomes the means of moral discipline (so Calvin). Just as the monk apart from the world must subject the whole of his life to the severest regulation, so now the Calvinist within the world must rigorously discipline himself. His life is to be a rationalized life of systematic self-control. The monk did this to secure a reward. It was a work of supererogation. The Calvinist did it not for reward—that would be to deny the grace of God in election, but in order to secure the sense of assurance that he was elect. Yet this statement is not quite exact. The Calvinist practiced self-discipline not even to secure assurance; he practiced it for the glory of God, and in the practice of it assurance came. Assurance itself was not the aim but the consequence of this discipline, a kind of by-product, though a by-product of immense importance.

(3) But further, as merit was not secured by the Catholic except through extraordinary effort, through works of supererogation, so *full* assurance did not come to the Calvinist except through perseverance. He must continue in good works if he is to continue in assurance. Thus the Calvinist, as contrasted with the Lutheran, was led again to transfer the Catholic monastic ideal of strict discipline to the secular life, the life of "calling." According to Sebastian Franck the significance of the Reformation is just this, that "every Christian must be a monk *his whole life long."* Instead of the spiritual aristocracy of the monks apart from the world, we now have, as Weber puts it, "a spiritual aristocracy of the elect within the world." We can now understand what the Calvinistic or, more generally, the Puritan conception of "calling" is, and in what respects it resembles or differs from Catholicism and Lutheranism. It is the life of strict discipline (an idea borrowed from Catholic monasticism) lived in the secular sphere (an idea borrowed from Luther) with the sole intent of glorifying God and with the blessed sense of assurance of election as its reward (the special contribution of Calvinism). We have thus finally arrived at the idea of the service of God through one's calling (*per vocationem*) as contrasted with Luther's idea of this service in one's calling (*in vocatione*). This life of calling must be quasi-ascetic, for the secular life tempts to the worship of the creature and so would detract from God's glory. This "asceticism" takes the form of the strictest regulation of the whole of life, as in monasticism. Assurance is attained only through perseverance. Life thus becomes thoroughly rationalized, Calvinistic piety at this point contrasting with Lutheran piety. It is rationalized by its aim, the glory of God, and by its method, a life of ceaseless watchful self-control. All this led practically to the development of an immensely intensified moral activity within the sphere of the secular life as the most noticeable characteristic of the Calvinistic churches and of similar Protestantism generally, a moral activity which has probably never been equalled before or since. It is (a) this rationalized theory of life, (b) this intensified mood for work, and (c) the quasi-ascetic discipline which accompanies both theory and mood that have immediate interest for Weber. Such an

immense output of spiritual energy could not fail profoundly to influence subsequent generations. Can it be that these three factors,
which grew directly out of the Calvinistic theology in its distinction
from Rome on the one hand and from Lutheranism on the other,
furnish the key to the development of the spirit of modern capitalism?
Do these aspects of Calvinism furnish the middle term between
Luther's conception of "calling" performed in the secular life and
that conception of money-making as in itself a "calling" which in
part constitutes the spirit of modern capitalism?

In the last main section of his essay Weber undertakes to show
how this rationalized, strenuously active, methodically "ascetic"
mode of life, represented by the Puritan conception of "calling,"
furnishes the religious basis of capitalism, without which capitalism
would never have attained the control which it now exercises over
the minds of men. After all, however blind economists may be to the
fact, metaphysical convictions are the only ones which have the
power absolutely to dominate men's lives. Economic reasons alone
cannot account for the extraordinary power in the Western civilization of today which the money-making motive exerts. The whole
point of Weber's essay is to show that something deeper, more
transcendental, more idealistic, is at work here, and must be
reckoned with if the psychology of capitalism, its spirit or temper, is
to be adequately explained.

If one looks into Baxter's "The Saints' Everlasting Rest" or his
"Christian Directory" or similar pastoral works of the Puritan divines
(and it is such practical works rather than the more theoretical dogmatic discussions which reflect the real moral interests of the
masses), one is at first sight struck by the suspicious attitude
toward riches expressed in all these writings, in full harmony with
the similar warnings of the mediaeval church. The possession of
riches is regarded as dangerous, and equally so the pursuit of them.
Riches tempt to confidence and contentment therein, to laziness and
sensuality. The pursuit of them diverts from the main object of life,
the glory of God. But in conjunction with all these warnings, and
unconsciously confusing them, another note is sounded by these
writers. They are constantly exhorting to industry. The saints' everlasting rest is a rest in the next life, not in this one. Here it behooves
man to work, and ever more to work.

There are two chief motives given for work. Work is still, as it always has been in the Western church, a means of discipline. It is the best prophylactic against what the Puritan called the "unclean life," against the sloth and sensuality which riches so often engender. Work in one's calling is Baxter's prescription against sexual temptation as well as against religious doubts. Again, work is to be done because God commanded it, in other words for his glory. This meant that utilitarian motives were disregarded or at least subordinated. So far as this life is concerned, work becomes an end in itself. It gains a meaning beyond itself only when looked at *sub specie aeternitatis,* from a religious and otherworldly point of view.

> *It is for action [says Baxter] that God maintaineth us and our activities. Work is the moral as well as the natural end of power. . . . It is action that God is most served and honored by. . . . The public welfare or the good of many is to be valued above our own.*

This last sentence sounds like an expression of our own social-service ideal. It must be understood in the light of what has already been said as to the religious, depersonalized interest in public welfare, yet it does form, as Weber suggests, the point of transition from the motive of the glory of God to the utilitarianism of the later liberal theology.

Again Baxter says:

> *Will not wealth excuse [from work]? Answer: It may excuse you from some sordid sort of work, by making you more serviceable to another, but you are no more excused from the service of work . . . than the poorest man. . . . Though they [the rich] have no outward want to urge them, they have as great a necessity to obey God. . . . God has strictly commanded it [work] to all.*

Even Zinzendorf says: "One does not work simply to live, but one lives to work." The great scriptural warrant for the exhortation to work is 2 Thess. 3, 10, "that if any would not work, neither shall he eat." This passage emphasizes not the reward, but the duty, of work. The Puritan will make the most of his calling. A bee-like industriousness is enjoined.

> *God hath commanded you [urges Baxter] some way or other to labor for your daily bread and not to live as drones of the sweat of others.*

And again:

> *Be wholly taken up in diligent business of your lawful callings when you are not exercised in the more immediate service of God. . . . Labor hard in your calling. . . . See that you have a calling which will find you employment for all the time which God's immediate service spareth.*

The terrific Puritan drive toward intense activity is illustrated in various ways in Baxter's writings. For example, it leads him to elaborate the reasons for various callings. Specialization in callings educates and trains the skill of the laborer, and so enables him to increase his output quantitatively and to better it qualitatively. It thus makes for the common good, which is the good of the most people— ideas these which, as Weber reminds us, strikingly resemble the economic principles of Adam Smith. But it cannot be too often repeated that this apparent utilitarianism of Baxter is not in his case real utilitarianism. It springs out of religious interests, not out of humanitarian or economic interests. It is, so to speak, the "ascetic" rather than the economic use of "calling." Industry in one's calling is the expression of the methodically disciplined life devoted to the glory of God. But, and this is to be remembered in view of what follows, the mood for work in such an "ascetic" Protestantism, although engendered by religious considerations, may easily become diverted to a purely economic interest when once the otherworldly point of view is abandoned.

Again, the emphasis upon activity is indicated by what is said by Baxter and others on the use of time:

> *Keep up a high esteem of time and be every day more careful that you lose none of your time than you are that you lose none of your gold and silver. And if vain recreations, dressings, feastings, idle talk, unprofitable company or sleep be any of them temptations to rob you of your time, accordingly heighten your watchfulness.*

With these warnings of Baxter may be compared that of Matthew Henry: "Those who are prodigal of their time despise their own souls." Sloth becomes one of the deadly sins. It is, so to speak, a continuous sin, and thus interferes in the most dangerous way with the methodically disciplined life. To sleep more than six or at most eight hours is, according to Baxter, morally reprehensible. "Sloth," he says, "destroys the state of grace." We have not yet reached Franklin's "Time is money," but we have arrived at its religious counterpart. Time is infinitely valuable, for every lost hour detracts from the glory of God.

Now all this emphasis upon industry and efficiency in a man's calling insensibly leads to a new attitude toward riches, in sharp contrast with the warnings against them already cited. As a matter of fact, the religious and disciplinary use of one's calling has much the same result as the directly economic exploitation of it. It inevitably leads to the accumulation of riches. It is permissible to change one's calling if the glory of God can be better subserved. Practically this means, if the new calling is a more useful one; and the standards for judging its usefulness are first, its moral character, secondly, the importance of the goods to be produced, and thirdly, its profitableness, for if God who orders our lives provides a chance for profit, he has his own purposes in this, and therefore the chance of profit must be accepted. Thus Baxter says:

> When God shows you a way in which you can lawfully make more without danger to your soul or to others than you can in some other way, and when you reject this way and follow the way that brings in less, then you cross one of the purposes of your calling. You refuse to be God's steward and to accept his gifts in order to use them for others when he so demands. Of course [Baxter continues, as though aware of the danger of this advice] you are not to labor to be rich for the purposes of fleshy indulgence, but for God's sake.

To strive for riches as an exercise in one's calling is thus not only permissible, but commendable.

> You may labor in that manner that tendeth most to success and lawful gain. You are bound to improve your talents.

It was frequently argued that to wish to be poor was as absurd as to wish to be sick. As scriptural warrant for all this the parable of the talents did yeomen's service. Thus arises the strange anomaly that the pursuit of riches, which is such a danger to the soul, since it tends to divert it from doing all things to the glory of God, has become, from the standpoint of magnifying one's calling, not only permissible but a duty, and the possession of riches, which tempts to sensuality and sloth, has become a mark of faithfulness in the discharge of one's calling. It is clear that in this whole development the decisive thing is the idea of "calling," that is, of the methodically disciplined mode of life within the sphere of the secular. The more intense the life of calling, the more God is honored; the more consistently such a life is lived, the more sure one can be of salvation. All this works out into an intensified industriousness, into the mood for work, and the natural economic result is riches. The most earnest adherents of the disciplinary ideal of Protestantism thus come to serve the interests of capitalism. This result must now be studied more in detail.

The direct economic effects of the Puritan mode of life in calling are manifested in two ways. In the first place the "ascetic" mode of life worked powerfully toward the limitation of consumption. The Puritan looked, for example, with suspicion upon fine clothes. He looked with suspicion upon all the enjoyments of the senses as inclining to the worship of the creature. As a protest against the extravagant life of the feudal nobility the Puritan exalted the idea of stewardship. Enjoyment must not cost anything. To spend money upon one's self leads to unfaithfulness in stewardship. Frugality comes to be a cardinal virtue. Baxter says:

> *Every penny which is paid upon yourselves or your children or your friends must be done by God's own appointment, and to serve and please him [the glory of God motive]. Watch narrowly, or else that thievish, carnal self will leave God nothing.*

Accordingly, what is spent upon oneself must be strictly limited. It also follows that the more property one has, the greater the sense of stewardship. It must be kept unimpaired and even increased, as Jesus taught in the parable of the talents, for this redounds to the glory of God.

In the second place, the intensified activity in one's calling which Puritanism encouraged led to a vastly increased production. Money-making was now freed from the traditional opprobrium which had attached to it. Profits had already been legalized. Calvin himself had seen to that, when, for the first time in history, he had advocated the permissibility of usury (interest). But now profits were looked upon as willed by God, as a mark of his favor and a proof of success in one's calling. The Puritans continued to wage war against the dangers of riches, yet this was not in opposition to rational business, but, as Weber puts it, to irrational consumption, to the extravagance and dissipation which wealth might encourage. Their attack was directed against indulgence in all the external forms of luxury which characterized the feudal aristocracy as a worship of the creature and as opposed to the rational, God-willed use of possessions for the good of the individual and the community. The limit of the permissible in consumption is defined by the word comfort. It was extravagance, display, that was sinful. The ideal of the home takes the place of the feudal ideal of the palace. So far as production was concerned, Puritanism fought against injustice in money-making, against hoarding, against mammonism, the love of riches for their own sake.

But at this point Puritanism found itself in a dilemma. On the one hand the pursuit of wealth for its own sake was sinful. On the other the religious value set upon constant, systematic, efficient work in one's calling as the readiest means of securing the certainty of salvation and of glorifying God became a most powerful agency in economic expansion. The rigid limitations of consumption on the one hand and the methodical intensification of production on the other could have but one result—the accumulation of capital. But the Puritan attitude to calling, with its almost automatic result in accumulation of riches, was destined to become more influential than the Puritan fear of riches. To a very large extent the disciplinary rationalization of life as "calling" accounts for the spirit of modern capitalism. It is not the accumulation of capital in itself that is the decisive thing, but rather a methodical accumulation of it which is a chief characteristic of modern capitalism. And this methodical accumulation has at least one of its main motives in the Calvinistic conception of life as calling. Wherever the Puritan theory of life was held, it strengthened the tendency toward a rationalized, bourgeois, economic mode of life. The Puritan, as Weber expresses it, "stood at the cradle of the economic man." Weber clinches his argument by the following remarkable paragraph from one of John Wesley's sermons:

I fear whenever riches have increased, the essence of religion has decreased in the same proportion. Therefore I do not see how it is possible in the nature of things for any revival of true religion to continue long. For religion must necessarily produce both industry and frugality, and these cannot but produce riches. But as riches increase, so will pride, anger, and love of the world in all its branches. How then is it possible that Methodism, that is, a religion of the heart, though it flourishes now like a green bay tree, should continue in this state? For the Methodists in every place grow diligent and frugal. Consequently they increase in goods. Hence they proportionately increase in pride, in anger, in the desire of the flesh, the desire of the eyes, and the pride of life. So, although the form of religion remains, the spirit is swiftly vanishing away. Is there no way to prevent this continued decay of pure religion? We ought not to prevent people from being diligent and frugal; we must exhort all Christians to gain all they can and to save all they can, that is, in effect, to grow rich. What way can we take that our money-making may not sink us to the nethermost hell? There is one way, and there is no other under heaven. If those who gain all they can and save all they can will also give all they can [the 'ascetic' motive], then, the more they gain the more they will grow in grace and the more treasure they will lay up in heaven.

To this passage I would add another taken from one of the last sermons preached by Wesley before his death:

After you have gained all you can and saved all you can, spend not one pound, one shilling, one penny, to gratify either the desire of the flesh, the desire of the eyes, or the pride of life, or for any other end than to please and glorify God [note the usual motive]. Having avoided this rock on the right hand, beware of that on the left. Hoard nothing. Lay up no treasure on earth; give all you can, that is, all you have. I defy all men upon earth, yea all angels in heaven, to find any other way to extract the poison from riches. . . . You who receive 500 pounds a year and spend only 200, do you give back 300 to God? If not, you certainly rob God of that 300. . . . Nay, may I not do what I will with my own? Here lies the ground of your mistake. It is not your own. It cannot be, unless you are lord of heaven and earth.

In these citations we have in a nutshell most of those fundamental ideas of Protestant "asceticism" which Weber has been describing. Wesley correctly foresaw the dangers which would befall the church through the very virtues which Puritanism emphasized. What he did not foresee was the cosmic extent of these dangers. He did not foresee a world so dominated by money-making that its whole organization is determined by this one great aim. And now we are prepared to understand the way in which Protestant "asceticism" became transformed into the spirit of modern capitalism.

As the great economic movements of the seventeenth, eighteenth, and nineteenth centuries developed through the increasing exploitation of the New World, Africa, and Asia, through the consequent growth of foreign trade, and through the rise of industrialism, the making of profits became an end in itself. *But before this was accom-*

plished religion had consecrated money-making. As Weber says, "What the great religious epoch of the seventeenth century bequeathed to its utilitarian heir was above all else a gloriously, one might even say a pharisaically, good conscience in money-making."

> *Is it merely a coincidence [asks the Quaker Rowntree] or is it a consequence that the lofty profession of spirituality made by the Friends has gone hand in hand with shrewdness and tact in the transaction of mundane affairs? Real piety favors the success of the trader by insuring his integrity [faithfulness in calling] and fostering habits of prudence and forethought, important items in obtaining that standing and credit in the commercial world which are requisite for the steady accumulation of wealth.*

The relationship of the Puritan self-disciplined and methodical life, as seen in the words "integrity," "prudence," "forethought," to the methodical life of business, as seen in the phrase, "the steady accumulation of wealth," could not be more tellingly, because unconsciously, expressed. Every vestige of the old ecclesiastical theory that a tradesman could scarcely please God now disappeared, and the specifically bourgeois ethic represented in Franklin's maxims arose. No longer was money-making a means, by which the assurance of salvation could be secured or God be glorified. It had become an end in itself. The methodical "asceticism" of the Puritan, his thrift and frugality, are now employed in a business interest. Baxter and Wesley exhorted their hearers to save in order not to rob God, and the habit of frugality was established; Franklin exhorts his young tradesman to save in order to accumulate capital. Puritanism had led to the rationalization of life as calling. Then a tragic thing happened. Capitalism saw the business significance of calling, removed the transcendental, otherworldly motive, and transformed "calling" into a job. . . .

R. Stephen Warner

WEBER'S SOCIOLOGY OF NONWESTERN RELIGIONS

Like many scholars interested in the history of sociological thought, Dr. Warner has closely studied the life and work of Max Weber. Few, however, have subjected Weber's methodology to such close scrutiny as has Professor Warner, who has been particularly concerned with Weber's comparisons of Western and nonwestern civilizations as a means to gain a better understanding of our own society. Dr. Warner earned all his degrees at the University of California at Berkeley where he also served as a teaching assistant, as a research assistant, and as an acting assistant professor of sociology before he accepted a position on the faculty of the Department of Sociology at Yale University in 1970. He has received a distinguished succession of fellowships and is the author of a series of professional papers and scholarly articles in English, German, and Italian. The aspect of Weber's work upon which Professor Warner's research is currently focused is the conception of ideas as potentially controllable resources. The reader particularly interested in Dr. Warner's work will be well rewarded to turn to the following selection in its originally published form in The Journal of Economic History. *There, he will find the extensive documentation, much of it expository, nearly equals in length the entire text of the selection.*

The theme of this conference, "The Organizational Forms of Economic Life and Their Evolution," implies a concern for specifying the limits of the applicability of classical and neoclassical economic theory. Presumably because we sociologists have been in the forefront of those who insist on the recognition of these limits, I have been asked to present a paper from the viewpoint of historical sociology. Now I suppose that your field and mine are alike in at least one respect: the infrequency of finding any *one* view on a broad and significant question. I am sure you will understand, therefore, my concentration on some lessons to be learned from the work of one of the heroes of my discipline, Max Weber (1864–1920). Weber, as you may know, was, among his other titles, a professor of economics and avoided the epithet of "sociologist." Yet because sociol-

From R. Stephen Warner, "The Role of Religious Ideas and the Use of Models in Max Weber's Comparative Studies of Non-Capitalist Societies," *The Journal of Economic History* 30 (March 1970): 74–99. Used by permission of the author and the publisher. Footnotes omitted.

ogy has changed since his day, largely under his influence, and because he was also a professor of law and of political science, we sociologists have now claimed him. Nevertheless, many of the issues that informed his massive scholarly research were and are issues central to both your field and mine.

In this paper I shall focus on two of these issues—the usefulness of the concept of values in social explanation, and the use of models in historical research—both for their intrinsic interest and because they are two issues on which much energy has been wasted in polemics based on misunderstandings of Weber's position. By the "use of values" I refer not to the never-ending debate on the role of the scientist's value judgments in research, but to the usefulness of identifying the analytical category of human values as an ingredient in the understanding of human action. Most sociologists, especially those in the fields of cross-cultural analyses, insist that understanding values as a *variable* element in action is crucial to adequate sociological interpretation; yet that insistence remains at issue. Max Weber made a great contribution to our understanding of religious ideas as an element of the sphere of values, and yet his contribution is still not fully appreciated. Similarly, Weber's category of the "ideal type" has been widely discussed and nearly as widely misunderstood. By presenting his analysis of the ideal-typical method, Weber had in mind to mediate the antagonism between economic historians and economic theorists, but his message has been lost. In restating his positions on these issues, I hope, on the one hand, to make clear what contributions he made and, on the other hand, to focus the continuing debate on Weber on Weber himself. Because many of the misinterpretations of Weber have been made hand in hand with overdrawn comparisons to Karl Marx, I shall have occasion to refer frequently to Marx as well.

The text for the analysis I shall present here is Weber's collection of comparative essays in the sociology of religion, one of which is the famous work, *The Protestant Ethic and the Spirit of Capitalism.* Partly in order to present negative experiments to the occidental case and partly to examine the general interrelationships of religion and society, Weber undertook a series of comparative studies of the economic ethics of the world's religions. His early death allowed him to publish only three of the intended essays: those on China, India, and Biblical Judaism. These are studies of noncapitalist societies, undertaken with an aim of unaerstanding the genesis of the unique development of occidental civilization as well as of occidental capitalism. They are crucial for the understanding of Weber's approach to the analysis of religious ideas and are extremely suggestive of further research. For another reason as well shall I focus on these essays: the discussion of Weber's methodology has largely lacked relevance for practicing researchers because of its abstract character. By turning to the major empirical research effort of Weber's maturity, we shall be able more nearly to identify his own practice.

Religious Ideas and Social Action

No one view of Weber is more widespread nor more mistaken than that which characterizes him as an "idealist" or "value-determinist" in contrast to the "economic determinist," Marx. If it is true that careful scholarly work has corrected these stereotypes, shorthand expressions in textbooks and review articles continue to reinforce them. In part this is due to the history of the translation of Weber's writings into English, the most well-known being that of the *Protestant Ethic* (English translation, 1930), whereas his comparative and political studies have received later and less widespread attention. Weber did of course emphasize the role of values and ideas as one factor among many in sociological and historical explanation, and much of the critical attention that has been devoted to his empirical claims has been worthwhile. We seem, however, to tire easily of Weber's qualifications and, basing our judgments on the sheer volume of attention that Weber devoted to the problem, to then slip into the grossly misleading characterization of Weber's work as a claim that values determine economic life. Charles Tilly, a sociological historian whose work on the counterrevolution in the Vendée has been misinterpreted as a statement that urbanization *caused* the counterrevolution, has given an example of the way in which the identification of one factor in a causal configuration of several can be distorted. He writes,

A geographer might well show us how erosion had washed rich soil from unwooded hillsides to be captured by streams which then carried the soil down to a splendid delta. He might point out how a new rainstorm would impoverish the uplands and nourish the delta. If he then declared that

erosion had caused *plantations, he would have his fingers slapped. But he certainly could tell us that erosion had shaped the possibilities for agricultural enterprise in the region.*

To no avail would Weber complain that he was more of a "materialist" (a term always to be read with quotation marks) than his critics gave him credit for being; the distortions continued. The result of a careful study of Weber's work, however, shows that his mode of sociological analysis is less an *alternative* to the Marxian than a *supplement* to it. Let us proceed in detail.

We can summarize the place of religious ideas in Weber's comparative studies in the following way: The sphere of religious ideas is (1) an *analytically independent* factor with (2) its own *internal dynamic* and which (3) must be considered along with many other factors in complex relationships of *empirical interdependence*. While it is true that the religious ideas of a social stratum, for instance, are most often functional for its position, these ideas cannot be deduced from or reduced to that position. At some point in an investigation that claims to have adequate social understanding as a goal, they must be considered *as if* they were independent factors; only in this way can the extent of their often considerable empirical dependence on extra-religious factors be determined. Note, however, that even in a case where, say, economic factors had contributed to the rise and dominance of a religious idea to the extent that that idea were in a relation of complete functionality to the economic situation—the limiting ideal type of the Marxist "superstructure"— Weber would still insist on the analytical independence of the religious sphere. This is so because among the processes contributing to the development of religious ethics is the specific quest of intellectuals for rationalization itself.

Weber thus rejects from the outset any emanationist explanation of religious ideas. This is, indeed, an a priori research injunction, which, however, does leave open the question of conclusions. It does not force Weber to see religion as always the key factor, or even an important one; it was not such, according to his brief survey, in the case of Japan. Moreover, Weber accepts the burden of proof in the investigation of the independent role of ideas. Finally, he rejects any one factor as the "ultimate" historical cause. In his own words,

For those to whom no causal explanation is adequate without an economic (or materialist as it is unfortunately still called) interpretation, it may be remarked that I consider the influence of economic development on the fate of religious ideas to be very important and shall later [i.e., in the comparative studies—RSW] attempt to show how in our case the process of mutual adaptation of the two took place. On the other hand, those religious ideas themselves simply cannot be deduced from economic circumstances. They are, in themselves, that is beyond doubt, the most powerful plastic elements of national character, and contain a law of development and a compelling force entirely their own. Moreover, the most important differences, so far as nonreligious factors play a part, are, as with Lutheranism and Calvinism, the result of political circumstances, not economic.

How do religious ideas come to have their effect on social action? Although in his methodological writings Weber called for rigorous conceptualization, the processes through which these effects occur are not rigorously and systematically spelled out in Weber's empirical studies. Nonetheless, Weber undoubtedly had in mind as he did the research for these studies a number of embryonic conceptualizations of typical social processes involving the effect of religious ideas on conduct. These can be reconstructed through analysis, and I shall deal here with three, in an ascending order of complexity.

The first is the patently *direct impact* of religious prescriptions and proscriptions of conduct which we shall call the *"ritualistic."* Specific antichrematistic regulations, such as the Roman Catholic prohibition of usury, are of dubious causal significance, but other more strongly enforced and internalized ritualistic demands have occasionally proved to be considerable obstacles to economic and social change. Hinduism, according to Weber, is very tolerant on matters of doctrine and philosophy, but very rigid on matters of ritual duty. Explicit codes and strong sanctions are present to determine conduct in many detailed ways. The worship of the cow prevented the development of rational animal husbandry by requiring the feeding of cattle well past their prime of economic usefulness. The worship of tools as quasi-fetishes was a strong handicap to technological development. The prescription of occupation by caste position and the ritual degradation resulting from change of occupation were hindrances to the development of industrial capitalism. In the case of China, particular religiously inspired codes of conduct were less directly antipathetic to technological and occupational enterprise, yet even there the Taoist cultivation of magic and Confucian tolerance of it, according to Weber, contributed to a magical stereotyping of science and technology which precluded the indigenous development of certain types of modern enterprise. Such effects, however, should not be overestimated. Religious prescriptions of conduct without powerful sanctions behind them are merely literary constructions. Moreover, such direct hindrances to enterprise are the common property of every great religious system. More important to Weber, true to his love of complexity and the paradox of unintended consequences, are the less patent effects of religious ideas.

A second and more profound level of Weber's interest in the role of religious ideas is their function in the *legitimation of social and political institutions* which themselves have in turn an impact on economic conduct. Every structure of political and social domination seems to require legitimation, both because of the need on the part of those in privileged positions to feel that their good fortune is justified, and because of their need to pacify the masses below them. Often religious intellectuals have, in effect, cooperated with political rulers to the mutual benefit of both. In the case of India, for example, the propagation of Hinduism and its caste system was furthered by the Brahmins who stood to gain materially through believers' use of their ministerial services, and by conquering princes whose position of superiority could be justified by the Brahmins' provision of the necessary "proofs" of their genteel ancestry. In China, the Confucian ethic protected the intellectual property of the literati stratum at the same time that its doctrine of ancestor worship was an ideological buttress of the patrimonial regime. In each case, the legitimated institutions had important economic effects. Thus, in India, the caste system prevented the development of a "citizenry"—a factor identified by Weber as crucial in the economic development of the West—and, in China, the familial piety inculcated by Confucianism hindered the development of the impersonal economic ethic so necessary to rational calculation in business affairs. Although the connection between the legitimating religious ideas and the interests they served is typically an intimate one, here again the conceptual independence of ideas is necessary to adequate analysis. The usefulness of their philosophy for their own and for their political allies' interests cannot diminish the intellectual achievement of the Brahmins, their theodicy, which Weber appraises as a work of genius. It was the "construction of rational ethical thought and not the product of any economic 'conditions.' " The Confucian literati, for their part, were prevented from engaging in an all-out struggle with their Taoist rivals, partly because of the very animistic beliefs which were an aspect of their otherwise "utilitarian" philosophy. In Biblical Israel, the underdog ethic, once so useful for a people dependent on the tolerance of powerful neighbors, became a constraint on the rulers of those same people when the economic and political situation had altered considerably. Now the legitimating role of ideas and its political and economic consequences is the subject of much of Weber's work in the comparative sociology of religion; yet it is the special concern of another major part of his work in *Economy and Society*. The central concern of the comparative studies is with a third and still more profound level of the role of ideas; to that we shall now turn.

In a now-famous aphorism, Weber stressed the *role of ideas as "switchmen."* Here are his words:

> Not ideas, but material and ideal interests, directly govern men's conduct. Yet very frequently the "world images" that have been created by "ideas" have, like switchmen, determined the tracks along which action has been pushed by the dynamic of interest. "From what" and "for what" one wished to be redeemed and, let us not forget, "could be" redeemed, depended upon one's image of the world.

Herein lies the specific supplement that Weber makes to Marxian analysis, and indeed to economic analysis in general. Of course neither Marx nor institutional economists hold a simple view of the operation of the dynamic of interests. For them, as well as for Weber, interest-oriented action is mediated through the particularities of social institutions. To Weber, however, we owe the formulation and the sustained demonstration of the proposition that *the social nature of "interest" is a variable.* Weber, for example, provides us with an explanation of the phenomenon of cross-societally variable supply curves of labor. His conception enables us to understand how the choice between labor and "leisure" is not a matter of individual idiosyncrasy but a matter of cultural determination.

Weber's identification of this third rule of ideas (which I will call, following a suggestion of his, *"refraction of interests"* is no mere opening up of theoretical possibilities. Recognizing the limits imposed by the unfinished state in which his ideas have come down to us and by his general lack of passion for systematization, it is nevertheless true that Weber went beyond mere suggestions in this regard. The first step is to identify the typical interests whose dynamic is refracted by ideas of the world, or, in other words, to determine what it is that individuals typically desire. So Weber constructs a common-sense psychology. Man, as Weber sees him, is motivated by the needs for material security, status acceptance and social honor, power over others, assurance of his salvation (*certitudo salutis*), and a sense of order in the cosmos. It is by defining what *is* security, what *is* honor, power over *what,* the *nature* of salvation, and, more generally, by *defining* the cosmos that ideas have come to have the great effect that many before and many after Weber saw them as having. Weber did not invent the notion that religion has been a powerful factor in history; he regarded it as his special contribution to show "the manner in which ideas become effective forces in history." He specifically denied that ideas have any motivating force.

The second step is to identify, in each case, those elements of religious systems which are relevant to the pursuance of these relatively universal psychological needs. Thus in the case of each of the great world religions (Weber had projected studies of Islam and early Christianity in addition to the studies of Confucianism, Hinduism, Buddhism, and Judaism which he published), Weber deals at length with their "metaphysical" presuppositions; for example, the Calvinist doctrine of predestination, the Confucian doctrine of cosmic harmony, the Hindu doctrines of ethical compensation and reincarnation, the Hebrew conception of a supra-mundane personal deity, and so on. This point bears repeating, since the most widespread sociological conception of the role of religious ideas and religious "values" is that they serve as a fundamental motivating force, the major premise, as it were, of action. For Weber, the most powerful effects of the world images provided by religion have been as a *condition* of action: salvation as an end is, relatively speaking, a given; *from what, for what,* and *how* it is *possible* to be saved have been determined by world images often the inventions of religious thinkers.

The third step is then to put the two—interests and world images —together to understand the direction in which interest is directed.

Now economic interests play a major role in Weber's sociology, but the economic ethics inculcated by religious ideas are only in part the result of the refraction of these economic interests. It has been the paradox of the history of religious ideas that they suggest, in a fashion usually not anticipated by the prophet, ways in which the others of man's interests may be directed into economic action. Weber's favorite example, of course, is the Protestant ethic and its contribution to the spirit of capitalism. The Calvinist minister Baxter's own hostility to wealth and acquisitiveness pales beside the psychological impact of his mentor's doctrine of divine election. A powerful answer to the intolerable insecurity fostered by this conception is that one's election may be manifested in the success of his worldly activities. Lacking any access to a human agent with the power to forgive and redeem, warned to avoid personal contact with those who might be among the damned, standing alone before his God whose decision to damn him or save him had already been made, promised that his election would be manifested in his worldly good works, the Calvinist had the strongest of motives to adopt methodical and impersonal means to worldly success. "The religious valuation of restless, continuous, systematic work in a worldly calling, as the highest means to asceticism, and at the same time the surest and most evident proof of rebirth and genuine faith, must have been the most powerful conceivable lever for the expansion of that attitude toward life which we have here called the spirit of capitalism."

In China, by contrast, Confucianism was the religious ethic of the traditional vested interests, the literati and the patrimonial state. Its organic view of the world, its stress on the sacredness of tradition, its denial of a transcendental God, its belief in ancestral spirits, and its conception of education as cultivation rather than expertise all bear witness to this fact. With no world-transcending deity to turn to, the Confucian "never bothered about the beyond."

The cultured Confucian's one interest beyond death was that his name be honored; to protect this honor he had to be prepared to endure death. . . . The strongest motive for highminded deportment known to Confucianism may well have been this specific sense of honor, which characterized a cultured man and was linked essentially to a man's accomplishments not to his birth. In this way the Confucian way of life was oriented to status and not to "bourgeois" values in the sense of the Occident.

Like Puritanism, Confucianism was an ethic emphasizing worldly conduct; unlike Puritanism, its conception of the world was a thoroughly traditionalist one. The basic presuppositions of Indian religion put a premium on other types of conduct. The belief in the principles of *samsara* (the transmigration of souls) and of *karma* (ethical compensation for worldly acts) was universal to all Hindus as well as to adherents of other religions. The additional Hindu conceptions of caste position and caste duty *(varna* and *dharma)* meant that one's interest for a better life in the next cycle of rebirth was furthered by rigid adherence to the prescription of caste obliqations, including occupational ones. The result was a reinforcement of the fetters of the traditional economy. "Absolute prerequisites" for the betterment of life chances "were strict fulfillment of caste obligations in this present life [and] the shunning of ritually sacrilegious yearning for renouncing caste. . . . Hinduism did not join occupational stability to teachings of the moral nature of the person's vocational stability and humble modesty, as do patriarchal forms of Christendom, but to the individual's very personal interest in salvation." The very *idea* of the "accident of birth" was almost completely absent. Those privileged strata with the leisure to reflect upon this picture of the social cosmos might well be repelled by the senselessness of such a cycle of ever-renewed birth and ever-repeated death to no end. But the individualistic salvation religions which sought to escape from this wheel of rebirth did so in a manner which accepted the basic presuppositions of the Hindu world-view. To escape from the cycle it was necessary to break the chain of *karma* causality, and Buddha identified the belief in the soul as the fundamental barrier to salvation from the senseless unrest of existence. The result is a flight from the world in the direction of mystic meditation. Like Puritanism, the doctrine of Buddha provides an incentive for individualism; unlike Puritanism, its individualism is one of a psychic state remote from activity. "Indeed, in terms of the 'how,' 'from what,' 'to what end' of salvation, Buddhism represents the most radical form of salvation-striving conceivable." Its lack of incentive toward rational economic action is clear.

The refractive effect of religious ideas is not limited to the adherents of the religion in question. A common objection to Weber's propositions is that he takes too seriously the ethical teachings of religious innovators and fails to take into account the extent to which the mass of men are indifferent to such questions. Yet Weber is fully aware of the gap between what he calls elite and mass religiosity. No doubt the mass of Chinese were unmoved by the Confucian conception of the cultivated man. No doubt the mass of Hindus know nothing about salvation. Yet Weber holds that the development of capitalism requires a qualitative break with the traditionalism in which most of the world's peoples have been enmeshed. In this respect the social, political, and intellectual dominance of the great religions of Asia has been an obstacle to economic development in the negative sense. In China, the dominance of Confucianism inhibited the development of heterodox prophetic innovation and orgiasticism which might have performed these revolutionizing functions. In India, the hard-won dominance of the Hindu metaphysic directed intellectual salvation-striving in asocial directions and left the plebeian masses to their magic and domination by *gurus.* The heterodoxy of Buddhism only increased the gap between the laity and the monastery. The former were required to remain in their economic roles in order to support a monastic stratum prohibited from work. "The later soteriology fashioned for the laity, therefore, could not follow the course of an inner-worldly puritanical asceticism, but only that of a sacramental, hagiolatrous, idolatrous, or logolatrous, ritualistic religion." For the fashioning of an economic ethic conducive to qualitative change, the sins of such religious ideas have been as much of omission as of commission.

In my focusing on these three types of effects that religious ideas have on conduct—the ritualistic, the legitimating, and the refractive —I am giving only a few examples, and abbreviated ones at that, from Weber's wealth of detail. Of these propositions, as well as the many more I have not the space to consider, no doubt some are plainly wrong and others are oversimplified. Only specialists—if, alas, specialists could agree among themselves—can pronounce on their empirical adequacy. What I want to suggest to you is the affinity of Weber's type of analysis to economic thought and its contribution to it. What others may dismiss theoretically as irrational patterns of action not assimilable to rational analysis, Weber tries to "understand" as intelligible action in terms of a *structure of incentives.* No theological determinist, he insists that sanctions—social, political, economic, and psychological—are the key to the effectiveness of religious ideas in ways often not anticipated by their inventors. And it is the variation in the ways that such sanctions impinge on relatively common types of individual interest that is the key to their understanding.

My purpose to this point has been to suggest to you the ways in which religious ideas influence conduct. In doing so, not only have I stated propositions in a far more categorical manner than was Weber's wont, but I have also isolated these propositions from a series of studies that, with the exception of *The Protestant Ethic,* in principle consider the *inter*-relationships of religion and society. In his studies of China, India, and Ancient Judaism, Weber was equally, if not to an even greater extent, concerned with the effect of social action in its many forms upon religion. Thus Weber does not take a position opposite to that of Marx; he extends Marx by enlarging the range of social interests that have shaped religious history. With Marx, religion as an element of the superstructure was anchored in *class* relationships. With Weber, social strata (not necessarily defined by the Marxian relationship to the means of production) and political rulers play the dominant role. Yet interest remains the key; as Guenther Roth formulates Weber's position, "There are no historically effective ideas and ideals without social interests backing them. . . ."

Having isolated certain effects of religious ideas, the next question becomes that of determining how they gain currency. We have already hinted how a conjunction of interests between privileged intellectual strata and patrimonial princes contributed to the successes of both Confucianism and Hinduism. In similar and complex ways does Weber see the religions with which he deals in relations of "elective affinity" to social interests. On the one hand, the needs of those in privileged positions to justify themselves and those in subordinate positions for answers to their condition; on the other hand, the requirements of social viability imposed on religious organizations in a competitive ideological world—these and other factors combine to compromise the autonomy of religion in society. This, however, takes us from the realm of economic history and into that of the sociology of religion, and for want of space I must conclude this aspect of our discussion.

Ideal-Typical Methodology

Polemics against a non-existent Max-Weber-the-idealist have, if indeed they have been misdirected, at least had the merit of grappling with empirical questions. The same, unfortunately, cannot be said for much of the polemic literature focused on Weber's ideal-typical methodology. My competence as a sociologist does not extend to profound questions of philosophy; yet it is clear enough to me that much effort has been wasted. In his discussion of John Stuart Mill and mid-Victorian economics, Joseph Schumpeter distinguishes between their "Scope and Method: What Economists Thought They Were Doing," on the one hand, and "What Mill's Readers Actually Got," on the other. Cautioning that "We are all of us bad interpreters of ourselves and untrustworthy witnesses to the meaning of our practice," he then goes on to an examination of the methodology of the period in order to clear up misunderstandings based on a too literal reading of it. It is in this same spirit that I wish to examine Max Weber's methodology.

A vigorous and never-ending controversy has been occasioned by Weber's writings on the methodology of social science. Let us examine its inception. In 1904, Weber published an essay identifying an ideal-type methodology as the specific means used in the social sciences toward the attainment of objective results. He characterized the marginal utility theory of the Austrian school, as well as Marxian theory and interpretive concepts in general, as "ideal type" constructs. Economic theory, he wrote,

> . . . *offers us an ideal picture of events on the commodity market under conditions of a society organized on the principles of an exchange economy, free competition and rigorously rational conduct. This conceptual pattern brings together certain relationships and events of historical life into a complex, which is conceived as an internally consistent system. Substantively, this construct in itself is like a utopia which has been arrived at by the analytical accentuation of certain elements of reality. . . . [I]t is no "hypothesis" but it offers guidance to the construction of hypotheses. It is not a description of reality but it aims to give unambiguous means of expression to such a description.*

Weber went on to claim that this procedure applies also to concepts of a more "historical" character. The ideal type of economic theory

. . . is developed for us by quite the same logical principles as are used in constructing the idea of the medieval "city economy" as a "genetic" concept. When we do this, we construct the concept "city economy" not as an average of the economic structures actually existing in all the cities observed but as an ideal type. An ideal type is formed by the one-sided accentuation of one or more points of view and by the synthesis of a great many diffuse, discrete, more or less present and occasionally absent concrete individual phenomena, which are arranged according to those one-sidedly emphasized viewpoints into a unified analytical construct. In its conceptual purity, this mental construct cannot be found empirically anywhere in reality. It is a utopia. Historical research faces the task of determining in each individual case, the extent to which this ideal-construct approximates to or diverges from reality, to what extent for example, the economic structure of a certain city is to be classified as a "city economy." . . . [The ideal type] has the significance of a purely ideal limiting concept with which the real situation is compared and surveyed for the explication of certain of its significant components.

Weber was not a man to avoid controversy (he specifically repudiated the *via media* as a means to scientific objectivity) and he knew full well that such terms as "ideal," "one-sided accentuation," "conceptual purity," "logical," and "utopia" were sure to arouse the ire of historians. They did. Gustav Schmoller, the dean of the German "Historical School" of Economics, took umbrage at Weber's inclusion of his concept of the mediaeval city economy in the same logical category as the "utopia" of the Manchester school. Arthur Spiethoff, a student of and successor to Schmoller, took up the battle in his opposition of "real types" to Weber's "ideal types." He argued for concepts that would "reflect economic reality," to be constructed not according to arbitrary selection and logical consistency imposed by the researcher, but according to the essential features of the phenomena in question. We need, he maintained, not utopias to compare with reality, but real types of the historically occurring economic styles as summations of regularly appearing phenomena. The procedure recommended by Spiethoff is as follows:

. . . first, statements must be as close to reality as possible, so that hypothetical elements and imaginary constructs are excluded; second, selective choice is not permissible, all important [or "essential," as Spiethoff puts it elsewhere] elements must be taken into consideration. It does not matter whether or not the elements, put together, form a logically consistent body of knowledge. The ideal of consistency plays no

role in the selection of what appear to be the characteristics of a style. A spirit of realistic accuracy must determine the selection. The combination of those elements in a model will nevertheless appear meaningful when those characteristics go together in reality.

Spiethoff, then—and his position is not idiosyncratic—expresses skepticism of the usefulness of Weber's type of concept and offers his own sharply distinguished alternative.

I want to suggest, however, that the alternative is not as sharp as it is claimed to be. To be sure, there are true differences between Weber and the historical school as represented by Spiethoff, differences stemming from basic philosophical presuppositions as to purpose, epistemology, and ontology. Yet some of the continued debate might be unnecessary if we were better able to understand Weber's message and his own practice.

To do that, it is necessary first to consider the intellectual context of Weber's methodological articles. He wrote them as an attempt to clarify and supersede the famous *Methodenstreit,* or battle of methods, between the Historical School, in one corner, and abstract marginal utility theory, in the other. The battle was initiated by Carl Menger in 1883 in a treatise attacking the views of the dominant Historical School in order to vindicate his own vocation of theoretical analysis. Schmoller responded with an unfavorable review in his *Jahrbuch.* Menger entered a rebuttal, and so on. It is beyond the limitations of this paper to review this controversy in detail; for our context, the following arguments of the historical school will suffice. (1) The "laws" of economic theory should not be hypostatized, said the historical school. They are reflections of only a transient historical situation; moreover, they deal with only isolated aspects of that situation. (2) Adequate understanding of a historical economic situation requires the consideration of the full range of human motivation, not simply the narrow self-interest psychology presupposed by classical theory. (3) The deductive method must not be abused. Abstract deduction from false premises, argued Schmoller, leads to a caricature of reality. Menger responded by accusing the historical school of naive realism and of a devaluation of that art of abstract thinking so necessary to scientific accomplishment in any field. The debate petered out when each of the schools went its separate way. However, with the recent incursion of abstract model building into "traditional" economic history, the old issues have reappeared in newer dress.

Weber's position in the controversy was to attempt a polemical synthesis. He considered himself to be an offspring of the historical school, but argued, in common with the theoretical school, for a Kantian view of science. On the one hand, he agreed with the reservations of the historical school about the historically relative and provisional character of economic theory, and with the insistence on the study (within the discipline of economics) of "economically relevant," and "economically conditioned," as well as purely economic, phenomena. On the other hand, however, he sided with the *logical* objections phrased by the theorists against the attempt of the historical school to "analyze reality 'without presuppositions.' " Following Kantian epistemology, he argued that what is "significant," "real," or "essential" is never to be found by a purely inductive analysis, but that the researcher exercises his own criteria of selection in the assessment. What he emphasized in this context was that those criteria—including implicit constructs of ideal-typical form—be made clear and explicit. He was not so much recommending a new procedure as calling for a better justification of an old one.

Weber's *"Wissenschaftslehre,"* thus, was primarily an attempt to clarify the logical basis of the historiography he so greatly admired. Since, however, it was his pedagogical practice to point out "inconvenient facts" to his particular audience, and since that audience happened to be composed of the historical school in this instance, it was the logical position of the historical school that was his primary target. For that reason, he argued that the one-sidedness, abstraction, and utopian character that the historical school rejected in economic theory were essential to all attempts at interpretive or genetic concept formation, even those used by the historians themselves. He did *not,* however, intend to invite undisciplined theoretical speculation or a merely logical analysis masquerading as science. His ideal-typical method involves an intimate relationship between concepts and empirical data.

This relationship of concepts and data can be seen if we return to an analysis of the way in which he practiced his method in his empirical writings. Weber's ideal-typical methodology involves reasoning similar to that used in the construction of models and theories and in the writing of interpretive history. It stresses that the historian's or theorist's *necessary act of selection* of the empirical material with which he deals be done consciously according to an explicit criterion of selection. The days are gone when the political historian, for instance, could naively assume that no such act is necessary. Weber's own primary criterion, which he repeatedly if not always consistently asserts, is the relation of religious ideas to economic ethics. The objection that such selection does violence to the historical data is true (if overstated) of any attempt at analysis of a world which does not explain itself.

Those empirical data are organized in part through the use of empirical generalizations or "rules of experience." Weber's comparative studies of religion are scattered throughout with observations such as the tendency of religious doctrines to be adjusted to the emotional needs of the laity, the typical tendency of priests to appropriate monastic prebends as hereditary possessions, the practices of political rules of leveling the status of their subjects and of allying themselves with priests. The "ritualistic" and "legitimating" functions of religious ideas, discussed above, are other examples. Now the identification of such rules of experience is not a matter of pure induction, as any practicing historian should know; it is based on a wide knowledge and a sharp insight as well as on careful investigation of the facts at hand. It is not in this respect that Weber's method becomes controversial, since even Schmoller was willing to speak of "regularities" and "persistent directions of development."

Weber's emphasis, and the methodological bone of contention, is the "logical" ordering of such observations. Yet this is often forgotten: the ideal-typical methodology begins with such *empirical* "events and relationships." So much is true of any scientific model; it is true of the Keynesian model with its empirical assumptions concerning savings behavior, and it is true of Weber's ideal types. Part of the "coherence" of the best-known of these, his ideal type of bureaucracy, is based upon empirical, even common-sense rules of experience. The fact that the components of that model include the separation of office and incumbent along with the use of written documents is neither fortuitous nor a matter of pure logic. It is based upon the observations that officials tend to appropriate their offices as personal property unless checked from doing so and that the necessity to record transactions in written form is one such check. The "logic" of the concept is the organization of the components according to a principle or a number of principles—in the case of "bureaucracy," the maximization of the strict performance of the superior's orders—designed to give them coherence. Similarly, the "logical principle" of the ideal type of the Protestant ethic, discussed above, is that behavior is rationally directed toward the maximization of *certitudo salutis.*

Thus Weber's ideal type reasoning incorporates and attempts to "make sense of" empirical data by means of empirical rules of experience and an organizing principle. Let us examine his use of one of these in the comparative studies, the ideal type of patrimonial domination, which plays a large role since it is his purpose to examine the genesis of the world religions as well as their effects on economic ethics. Patrimonialism is a form of traditional domination in which the ruler makes use of a personal staff to maximize his appropriation of power as a personal privilege. Insofar as a number of concrete historical phenomena can be regarded as being used for the purposes of such maximization, they are rendered meaningful. Thus Weber can say that conquering patrimonial rulers "naturally" sought to undermine the leading strata of the conquered peoples. Thus he finds tax farming in India "characteristic" of patrimonial logic, and can say that the use of princely relatives and parvenus of lower caste origin rather than the traditional knighthood as officials "corresponds" to the nature of patrimonial bureaucracy. Finally, the spread of apolitical and contemplative religions, Weber suggests, may in large part be due to the interests of patrimonial rulers in the pacification of their subjects in order to increase the scope of their arbitrary rule.

Such a model of patrimonialism is not a hypothesis; it suggests, however, abundant hypotheses for further research. Nor is it a description; it rather suggests a compelling means for ordering a number of descriptions. But neither is it an artifact of logic; and here, I am afraid, Weber's programmatic expressions have been most troublesome when taken out of context. The full elaboration of the ideal type of patrimonialism involves many concrete individual observations, a number of empirical generalizations, and an ordering principle. The model is, in fact, most useful when that principle converges with the actual orientation of the regime in the particular case, as is true *mutatis mutandis* for any model. The present-day

(Weber was writing in 1908) significance of abstract economic theory is bound up with the fact that the empirical approximation to the theoretically established principles is increasing around the world. The concept of the state derives some of its significance from the fact that it abstracts ideas already held in the minds of individuals. And part of the reason that Weber presents consistent, ideal-typical pictures of religious doctrines is that the logical consistency of an ethical system has a certain "power over man," especially over intellectuals.

The construction and use of ideal types, therefore, is *both* a deductive *and* an inductive process: inductive, insofar as it is based upon empirical knowledge of various kinds and insofar as an ideal-typical construction may be empirically improved upon; deductive, insofar as this empirical knowledge is ordered according to logical —or better yet, *psycho*-logical and *socio*-logical—principles and insofar as the ideal-type is used as an explanatory or *verstehende* device. Since the deductive aspect is the specifically theoretical aspect the worth of which remains to be assessed through the deduction of and testing of hypotheses, Weber was quite right to insist on the principle of the "utopian" nature of ideal-type models. Let it not be thought, however, that he or any other model builder *celebrated* their divergence from reality nor that such models are devoid of empirical content or empirical implications. The notion that the sole use of ideal types lies in their "measuring" or being "compared to" reality as a "yardstick" in order to determine the degree that reality diverges from the ideal type—a notion that Weber unfortunately lent himself to—misses their true significance. It would be quite simple deliberately to construct an "ideal type" that could be shown through "comparison" to diverge radically from reality; having done that it would be easy to lay aside that particular ideal type and construct a new, equally useless one. And so on, *ad infinitum*. Such a *reductio ad absurdum* has the merit of highlighting the fact that good models have empirical content and that we attempt always to improve them, *both* in their relation to reality and in their logical consistency. They have the function, as Weber put it, of making features of reality "pragmatically *clear* and *understandable*"; we use them as "flashlights" for the "illumination" or "explication" of some of its components, and for the identification of new research problems. If not made into ideologies, such models as neoclassical theory and Marxian theory (its sociological aspects) as well as "bureaucracy" and "refraction" have the function of reducing the strangeness of the empirical world.

To best serve that purpose, not one model but several should be brought to bear on a given empirical situation. Since Weber's models were typically conceptualizations of the maximizing activity of individuals, social strata, social organizations, and political regimes, and since these activities conflict in the real world, we must expect that the empirical implications of even the best of such models will not in fact correspond to the totality of a situation. In China, the use of patrimonial means by the emperor was not always successful. For India, Weber finds that a combination of the centrifugal implications of the ideal type of feudalism together with the centripetal implications of patrimonialism could be fruitfully used in historical interpretation. He warned, however, that the concrete historical reality in which he was interested could not be deduced from even the most complete theoretical system.

In conclusion, I have emphasized that ideal-typical constructs as Weber understood them and used them do not fall under the usual nominalistic dictum that concepts as pure definitions are not subject to empirical criticism; Weber's ideal types are so subject, and they gain by it. Yet this qualification on Weber's nominalism should not obscure his methodological message. He warns theorists lest they forget the abstracted and historically relative nature of the premises and logical principles on which their constructions are based. On behalf of theorists, he tells the historian that every attempt at explanation or interpretation—even through the use of a genetic concept such as mediaeval city economy—involves the selection and the arrangement of the data. References to the inherently "essential" nature of the selection and the emergent "meaningfulness" of the constructed concept will not substitute for the explicit statement of the criteria of selection and arrangement. Far from inviting distortions of reality, he was demanding clarification of background assumptions so that historical objectivity could be better approximated.

One final issue: it may be somewhat of a disappointment that I have yet to address myself in this paper to the question of the "forms" of economic life and their "evolution." The reason is that Weber is specifically skeptical of stage concepts and their arrangement in evolutionary sequences. Herein lies the crux of his disagreement with Schmoller and Spiethoff, as well as that with Marx. Insofar as the debate between Weber and the historical school was based on real differences rather than on misunderstandings, it was based on the disagreement Weber expressed with the perfection of "stage" and "style" concepts as the goal of economic history. While recognizing the usefulness of such concepts as "nomadic," "agrarian," and "'feudal" for the purposes of outlining the distinctiveness of particular historical situations, he nevertheless held that they were misused when applied in anything more than this preliminary fashion. His own preference was to use such concepts as comprehending *aspects* or *tendencies* within a given social situation. "Feudalism," for Weber, was used as a tendency concept in opposition to patrimonialism to conceptualize the power arrangement resulting from the ability of landed notables to raise private armies; it did not refer to any historically existing total society. Similarly, he used Toennies' famous contrast to *Gemeinschaft* and *Gesellschaft* to express differences in tendency and orientation rather than differences in societies, thus changing it to *Vergemeinschaftung* and *Vergesellschaftung.* His specific demurrer from Marxian theory was entered whenever the Marxian "laws" of the total economy were taken to be "effective forces" which determined history.

Weber's preference for analyzing reality through the use of one-sided and isolating concepts rather than through attempting to construct concepts of total societies was not, however, based on a rejection of scientific determinism, quite the contrary. It was based on a conviction that total societies are not the most useful units of analysis, a conviction stemming from his philosophical pluralism, sociological pluralism, and orientation toward foreign policy, as well as from his conviction that individuals have played crucial historical roles. In the modern world, moreover, social change occurs on a world-historical scope. For these reasons as well as the requirements of conceptual nominalism, Weber typically used models whose coherence was derived from their subjective meaningfulness—for example the previously mentioned models of interest-refraction, bureaucracy, and patrimonialism—rather than models or even "real types" of historical stages or styles. It was his goal to use such models for the illumination of concrete historical situations, rather than to reconstruct and predict the movement of history or of the economy as a whole. In the nature of the case, that method prevents him from handling social systems, but it may bring him closer to social reality than the methods presented as alternatives.

H. M. Robertson
A CRITICISM OF MAX WEBER AND HIS SCHOOL

The first version of Aspects of the Rise of Economic Individualism *was written in 1928–1929 as a dissertation for the Ph.D. degree at Cambridge University. Mr. Robertson had collected most of the material for the study while a research student at Emmanuel College, Cambridge, and actually wrote the greatest part of it while he was a lecturer at the University of Leeds. When the book appeared in 1933, Dr. Robertson was Senior Lecturer in Economics at the University of Cape Town. His study was welcomed by many historians as an historical, rather than psychological or sociological, study of an historical problem. Robertson was sharply criticized for his assertion that the Roman Catholic Church and the Protestant churches stressed the same economic precepts in the sixteenth and seventeenth centuries, but his work remains one of the most impressive to emerge from the Weber thesis controversy.*

Max Weber is responsible for the opinion, widely held today, that Protestantism, especially in its Puritan form, has had a very great influence in forming the "spirit of capitalism," and, therefore, in forming capitalism itself. In 1904–1905 he published two articles under the title of *Die protestantische Ethik und der Geist der Kapitalismus* in which this thesis was maintained. They not only inaugurated a whole literature, they gave a new direction to the whole of modern thought on a fundamental problem of economic history. I claim that they directed it on to the wrong lines.

It is not hard to understand why these theories should have been adopted so widely. They are the type of generalization that would obviously have a popular appeal; and they can be made to form a

From H. M. Robertson, *Aspects of the Rise of Economic Individualism* (Cambridge, 1933). Used by permission of the Cambridge University Press. Footnotes omitted.

convenient and serviceable weapon in religious controversy. They have been accepted in many cases because of their utility to the propagandist. Many writers have taken advantage of an unpopularity of capitalism in the twentieth century to employ them in attacks on Calvinism, or on other branches of religion. But the theories have also been accepted in other and less likely quarters.

It is remarkable that historians should have been so ready to accept the arguments of this piece of dialectic. For the reasoning employed is not that of the historian. Despite a wealth of references, its foundations have not been laid on a sound historical analysis. A philosophy of historical development which has been fashioned in the "constructional"[1] method of the sociologist might have been expected to have met with more opposition.

Weber attempted to establish a reverse chain of causation from that advanced by Marx in the economic interpretation of history. He sought a psychological determination of economic events. In particular he saw the rise of a "capitalism" as the result of the rise of a "capitalist spirit." What was this capitalist spirit?

To Weber it was hardly more than bilateral. It consisted first in a rationalist as opposed to a traditionalist outlook. It consisted also in the desire to seek profit continuously (by means of the rational organization of free labor) for its own sake—even as a duty—and not for the purpose of enjoying the fruits. It cannot be denied that the ideal capitalist mentality is rational, if the spirit of capitalism is to mean anything more than that of acquisitiveness. It is probable, also, that Calvinism, created by a man whose favorite idea was considering "things in themselves, not words," has led to the expansion of a rational methodizing of life. It may be admitted at once that to this extent Calvinism has been favorable to the growth of a spirit of capitalism. But Weber's second criterion of the capitalist spirit is too narrow. It leads inevitably to the defect which I feel vitiates his whole argument; he hardly considers any capitalist other than the Puritan capitalist who seeks wealth for the fulfillment of his "calling."

This added refinement is quite superfluous. A realist like Marx, who originated the discussions on capitalism, would no doubt have been greatly astonished if he had been asked to consider only those whose money-making activities were promoted by religious or quasi-

---

[1] "Constructional" because it constructs abstract ideal types instead of accurately describing facts.

religious ends to be possessed of the true capitalistic spirit. This is what we are asked to do. The great renaissance financier, Jakob Fugger, a good Catholic, was urged by his nephew, Georg Thurzo, to retire from business on account of the involved state of the family affairs. He rebuked his nephew for his faint-heartedness and said that he "had quite another disposition, he would make money as long as he could." This is disregarded as an expression of the capitalistic spirit, as it had no ethical tinge. Yet it was an example of precisely the type of "worldly asceticism," making earning an end in itself, which is put forward as the great contribution of the Calvinists and the Puritan sects to the rise of the spirit of capitalism.

To most people today the typical "capitalist" is a purely secular creature who, far from regarding his daily occupation as a religious calling, sees no reason for religion to meddle with business affairs at all. He was the same in previous ages. Perhaps he resented the claims of religion to act as a moral witness in the affairs of everyday life, like the merchant Gromelgayner in Dr. Wilson's *Discourse of Usury:*

> *Merchants doings must not thus be overthwarted by preachers and others, than can not skill of their dealings. And thys over great curiositie of some to meddle in other mens matter, I muste tel you plaine, it is even the verie right waye to undoe al in the ende.*

Or perhaps he behaved like the typical capitalist whom Milton described in *Areopagitica:*

> *A wealthy man addicted to his pleasure and to his profits, finds Religion to be a traffic so entangled, and of so many piddling accounts, that of all mysteries he cannot skill to keep a stock going upon that trade. What should he do? fain would he have the name to be religious, fain would he bear up with his neighbours in that. What does he therefore, but resolves to give over toiling, and to find himself out some Factor, to whose care and credit he may commit the whole managing of his religious affairs; some Divine of note and estimation that must be. To him he adheres, resigns the whole Warehouse of his Religion, with all the Locks and Keys into his custody; and indeed makes the very person of that man his Religion; esteems his associating with him a sufficient evidence and commendatory of his own Piety. So that a man may say his Religion is now no more within himself, but is become a dividual moveable, and goes and comes near him, according as the good man frequents the house. He entertains him, gives him gifts, feasts him, lodges him; his Religion*

comes home at night, prays, is liberally supt, and sumptuously laid to sleepe; rises, is saluted, and after the malmsey or some well-spic't bruage, and better breakfasted, than He whose morning appetite would have gladly fed on green figs between Bethany and Jerusalem; *his Religion walks abroad at eight, and leaves his kind entertainer in the shop trading all day without his religion.*

Nothing could be further from the Puritan than either of these two types. In neither case was the conception of the "calling" of any influence; in neither case did it stir the merchant to activity. Neither fits in with a Puritan setting. The second, indeed, would be much more at home among the Jesuits with their system of expert casuistry. Yet Milton described him as a typical possessor of the commercial spirit—a man who was not interested in religion, but was in business. And Wilson's Gromelgayner was intended to be the typical merchant of 1569.

A quite unnecessary element has, then, been introduced into the definition of the capitalist spirit. Men do not need to be "called" to riches to devote themselves whole-heartedly to their pursuit without stopping to enjoy them. When King Pippin asked Alcuin, "Of what have men never enough?", he received the reply, "Of gain." If men have the appetite for riches without a "call," they require no "calling" to organize a continuous striving after them.

The survey of the capitalist spirit inaugurated by Max Weber has also been unduly limited by a definition which excludes "Jewish pariah-capitalism" as something entirely alien to the real, respectable "bourgeois-capitalism." This narrowness of definition, which dismisses every manifestation of the speculative or entrepreneur spirit from consideration, seems hardly suitable as a method of approach to the understanding of that frequently very eclectic person, the capitalist.

I do not, however, propose to press this line of criticism very far. To do so would involve me in a wider discussion of the growth of capitalism and the capitalist mentality than I am prepared to undertake. Though I criticize the theories connecting Protestantism with capitalism on account of the narrowness of their scope, I cannot do more than indicate alternative ways of approach to the subject of the rise of the spirit of capitalism. In the main, my criticisms will touch these theories on their own grounds.

My criticism must concern itself very largely with Max Weber's celebrated essay on *Die protestantische Ethik und der Geist des Kapitalismus.* It is a topic which he made peculiarly his own; and as I am concerned with the repercussions of his theories I must often refer to their origin. I hope to show that owing to Weber's adoption of a sociological, and not a historical, approach to the subject, his main argument, which deals with the Puritan doctrine of the "calling," cannot be sustained. I hope to show also that secondary considerations make it impossible to accept the argument that the capitalist spirit is a product of the Protestant Ethic. I hope briefly to indicate, therefore, another approach to the problem of the rise of the "spirit of capitalism," which takes into account factors which religious sociologists have ignored, and gives a truer explanation of the formation of the psychological elements in the historical development of economic forms, which I believe have been rightly (though over-) emphasized, but wrongly explained. I wish to show that the spirit of capitalism has arisen rather from the material conditions of civilization than from some religious impulse.

According to Weber, the influence of Protestantism was not merely negative, in permitting the exercise of practices forbidden by the Catholic Church, but also positive, turning religion to capitalistic ends. The chief instrument of this he considered to be the doctrine of the "calling" which came in with Luther and introduced the ideal of an asceticism incumbent upon the laity as well as the religious; an asceticism not of the cloister, but practiced in the affairs of everyday life, by the utter sacrifice of any self-indulgence, by unremitting industry in one's "calling," which was thus promoted to the quality of a religious exercise. He asserted, moreover, that on the Calvinists taking over this doctrine they made success in one's "calling" an outward and visible sign of the acquisition of spiritual grace.

He employed philological arguments to bring out the importance of the doctrine of the "calling." He pointed out that there are no equivalents in the Romance (and Catholic) languages to the Protestant-German *Beruf,* the Protestant-Dutch *beroep,* the Protestant-English "calling," in the sense of "a life-task," "a definite field in which to work." He contended that Luther's reformation introduced both the word and the concept.

Luther is said to have written *Beruf* quite gratuitously in two places in his translation of Ecclesiasticus where the Septuagint gave in the one case *ergon* and in the other *ponos,* and where the Vulgate gave *opus* and *locus.*

This contention was strongly denied by Brentano, who pointed out that the Vulgate has not merely *work* but *work of the calling* (or *thy commissions)*—"et in opere *mandatorum tuorum* veterasce." He also asserted that "calling" *Beruf* had its exact equivalent in the Latin of the Vulgate version of the passages of I Corinthians vii, 20–24, from which the Puritan use of the word "calling" was derived.

> *Unusquisque in qua vocatione vocatus, in ea permaneat. Servus vocatus es? non sit tibi curae; sed et si potes fieri liber, magis utere. . . . Unusquisque in quo vocatus est, fratres, in hoc permaneat apud Deum.*[2]

There seems to be little doubt that Brentano's criticisms have value. It is not proved that Luther introduced both word and concept. It is true that the Vulgate versions do not express the modern conception of the "calling." But, on the other hand, it is also true that the early Protestant conceptions of the "calling" were different from those of the present day and nearer those of the Vulgate.

There is one noteworthy feature of Weber's philological argument. Apart from this discussion of Luther's *Berufskonzeption,* Weber has made practically no use of Lutheran Protestantism in advancing his views, as he found himself unable to trace the spirit of capitalism in Lutheranism, but only in Calvinism, and among the Baptists and some Puritan sects. But Genevan Calvinism shared the use of a Romance tongue with French Catholicism, and therefore there is no contrast between Catholic and Calvinist phraseology.

To destroy the philological argument it is only necessary to quote the Calvinist version of the passage in Ecclesiasticus:

> *Demeure en ton rang et t'exercise en celui, et veille en faisant ton* office. *Ne t'émerveille point des oeuvres du meschant; fie toi au Seigneur, et continue en ton* labeur.

Here we find *office* taking the place of *Beruf,* and are reminded that it very often did so. The French *office,* the Spanish *oficio,* the

---

[2] "Let every man abide in the same calling wherein he was called. Art thou called being a servant? care not for it: but if thou mayest be made free, use it rather. . . . Brethren, let every man wherein he is called, therein abide with God." See Brentano, *Die Anfaenge des modernen Kapitalismus,* pp. 136 ff.

Italian *officio* all of them bring to mind a similar identification of the worldly and the religious (for instance the French *office* means both "employment" and "worship") and are frequently used by Catholics in a way not radically different from the Protestant-English use of "calling" or German use of *Beruf.*

Weber's case for asserting, on philological grounds, that Luther had introduced a novel conception of the "calling," bringing with it a new ideal of worldly asceticism, is not established. It seems on other grounds to have been an unnecessary innovation. The doctrine of Work has at any rate as old a history in the Christian *mores* as St. Paul's—"we commanded you, that if any would not work, neither should he eat." Mediaeval Catholicism had recognized that the deadly sin of Accidia must be combated with work as well as watchfulness. This recognition had taken form in the Augustinian and Benedictine rules, the foundations of all monastic disciplines. The asceticism of which an essential element was a divinely ordained worldly toil was not, then, foreign to mediaeval Catholicism. And Luther had been an Augustinian monk.

But it is argued, this asceticism was in the Middle Ages confined to the cloister. It had no part in the lives of any of the laity. To say that is to ignore the part which the friars were sent out to play—to take religion from the cloister into everyday life. It is to ignore the motives which led to the foundation of third orders. (It is not sufficient excuse for ignoring them to say that it was not considered to be as meritorious to be a member of a third order as to be a full religious; Calvinists do not consider the butcher's "calling," even if the butcher is an elder of the Kirk, to be as honorable as the minister's.) The Franciscan Order of Penitents, as befitted an order founded in the thirteenth century, was in some ways very similar to a religious guild. But it was more than this. It called for an asceticism exercised in the world not in the cloister, and it cultivated some of the bourgeois virtues—the same virtues which Weber stressed so much when he indicated the importance of Benjamin Franklin's worldly creed, his insistence that time is money and not to be wasted, his love of detail and exact reckoning. To the members of the Franciscan third order extravagance was forbidden; also, as with the Puritans, wasting one's time at feasts or masques or dances. It was recognized that the Brethren and Sisters of Penitence had worldly matters to which they had to attend. They had, for instance, to go to Mass during the Lent of St. Martin and the Greater Lent "nisi personarum vel rerum incommoditas immineret"—their worldly duties had, in some measure, precedence over their duties of church attendance, which might perhaps have proved to be a greater concession to the commercial spirit than was allowed to the Puritans. Yet nobody has thought of pointing to Franciscan Puritanism as a breeding ground for the spirit of capitalism. Weber has indeed confessed that the preaching of the friars, and especially of the Franciscans, had anticipated very markedly the teaching of the Baptists (a sect in which he affirms the encouragement of capitalism through worldly asceticism was very strong) in attempts to impose an ascetic rule on the laity. But this, he said, can be accounted for first by the fact that all asceticism based on Biblical commands would tend to be similar, and secondly by the general tendency to reach the same results in all systems of mortifying the flesh. This is probably very true; yet the fact remains that if the teaching of the Baptists and of the friars was so similar one should only guardedly employ the teaching of the Baptists as a means of proving that the spirit of capitalism was a product of the Protestant sects.

The great objection to all the arguments based on the Puritan doctrine of the "calling" is, however, that it has not always had the content so constantly ascribed to it. Even if Weber is correct in his interpretation of the doctrine in its eighteenth-century manifestations, he is incorrect in projecting this back into the sixteenth century, when the doctrine wore an entirely different aspect.

At the beginning it was nothing but a new expression of the old belief in the existence of divine and natural distributive justice, a belief that different men were "called" to their several occupations and estates by a divine providence—as a result of which it was flouting providence to exhibit capitalistic enterprise!

There seems to be no essential difference between the doctrine of the Catholics and the Puritans on this point. St. Thomas Aquinas' teaching on distributive justice was that:

This . . . division of men in different occupations occurs in the first place through divine providence, which distributes the condition of men in such a way . . . and also in the second place from natural causes, as a result of which it happens that there are different aptitudes for different occupations amongst different men.

Despite the assertion that Aquinas has set his conception on an entirely different plan from the Puritans' by the stress laid upon natural causes in determining the choice of an occupation, this seems to contain much the same idea as the doctrine of the "calling" in the sixteenth and seventeenth centuries. The practical lessons which the Puritans derived from their doctrine were also on the whole merely the same as those taught to the Catholics who were brought up to avoid the deadly sin of ambition.

Nothing expressed the early doctrine of the "calling" more succinctly than Robert Crowley's verse:

> *Fyrste walke in thy vocation*
> *And do not seke thy lotte to chaunge;*
> *For through wycked ambition,*
> *Many mens fortune hath ben straynge.*

Yet nothing could be further from the truth than to suggest that this verse introduced a new doctrine favorable to the rise of a "spirit of capitalism," or that the "calling" was an invitation to amass and continue to amass great riches.

When we remember the great use Max Weber has made of the doctrine of the "calling," it seems important that evidence should be accumulated to demonstrate what the earlier Puritan conception of the "calling" really was.

. . . In the sixth of Hugh Latimer's sermons preached before King Edward VI he reminded his congregation that:

> *Our Saviour Christ before he began his preaching, lived of his occupation, he was a carpenter, and got his living with great labour.*

He did not say this with any intention of encouraging the capitalistic spirit. It was with the intention of condemning idleness indeed; but to Latimer as to many another reformer, the capitalists were the idle rich, battening on surplus value. He was concerned with the dignity of labor, not with gain and ambition.

> *Therefore let no man disdain, [he continued] or think scorn to follow him in a mean living, a mean vocation, or a common calling and occupation. For as he blessed our nature with taking upon him the shape of man, so in his doing he blessed all occupations and arts. . . .*

It is lucre enough, it is advantage enough to be content with that, that
God sends. The faithful cannot lack, the unfaithful is ever lacking, though
he has never so much.

Once more we find the "calling" employed to combat capitalistic
ambition.

The "calling" was man's earthly state, allotted to him by God,
and his opportunity for Grace. As a gift from God, it was a gift with
obligations. Weber has stressed the point that the doctrine of the
"calling" caused the Puritans to be diligent in their application to
business, to the greater glory of God. But it was not only in a sober
application to worldly toil, it was in every department of life that their
acts were designed *ad majorem Dei Gloriam.* It was from this broader
conception of the "calling" that Latimer derived his saying:

For God gave never a gift, but he sent occasion at one time or an-
other to show it to God's glory. As if he sent riches, he sendeth pore men
to be helped with it.

and it was with disregarding one's "calling" that such an opportunity
was missed:

But now must men occupy their goods other ways. They will not look
on the poor, they must help their children, and purchase them more land
than ever their grandfather had before them.

Nothing could be further from the truth than to suppose that the
"calling" was an invitation to amass and continue to amass great
riches. It was an invitation to live the orderly and settled life ordained
for one by God, and to perform all the duties pertaining to it.

Robert Crowley was a militant Puritan, and one whose rhymes did
much to further the adoption of the idea of the "calling." His writings
are filled with this conception. Yet nobody could accuse this fearless
champion of the poor, this fervent opponent of the active new social
order, of any bias in favor of capitalism. In 1550 he published his
Voyce of the laste trumpet . . . callyng al estats of men to the ryght
path of theyr vocation. In this he set out to advise the reader as to
the correct pursuit of his "calling." The general advice has been
quoted above, and the particular advice given to the various classes
of men was in the same strain. . . .

It would be easy to multiply instances of the use of the conception of the "calling" as a basis for pronouncements of this sort. Weber very rightly stressed the importance of the vocation or "calling" as a fundamental part of the Puritan ethical system, but he painted a very misleading picture of what it meant. If it encouraged industry, it did so to a much smaller degree than it discouraged covetousness and ambition—the ambition which made men break out of their "calling," which would not let them be content with one "calling" but made them try to engross the livelihoods of many into their hands. It was by the doctrine of the "calling," the doctrine that every one should have *one* settled life-task, that Crowley condemned the enclosing landlords, the graziers, the leasemongers of his day:

> *Of good maisters, what should I cal you? You that have no name, you*
> *that have so many occupations & trades that there is no name mete for*
> *you! You ungentle gentlemen! You churles chikens, I say!*

He had little good to say of those whose enterprise overstepped the bounds of a "calling" in so shameless a way.

The "calling" did not embody a progressive ideal. The demand for an ordered life, for an innerworldly asceticism, which Puritanism made and expressed in the conception of the "calling" had no message of a capitalistic nature to give the world. It placed in the forefront the age-long static ideal of content with the decrees of providence; as the author of a typical seventeenth-century theological treatise put it:

> *Then ye Common-wealth is blessed, and all ye Citizens therof happie;*
> *when every one knoweth his own vocation and diligentlie doth ye Duties*
> *therunto belonginge; and gives others their place, & breake not out of*
> *ye bounds of their owne Callinge.*

Yet Weber has not misconceived the Puritan "calling." His description of the doctrine is exact—but not for all time. A mistake lies in the assumption that the "calling," as a guide to the conduct of life, has meant the same thing throughout its history. He has only studied the later phases of the doctrine. In the latter part of the seventeenth century and in the eighteenth he has found numerous examples of Puritan literature counselling a course of worldy prudence as a religious exercise, as the fulfillment of a "calling." He has projected the prudential character of this doctrine backward as having always been an essential element. Owing to his unhistorical treatment he has not noticed the change in the conception of the "calling" from an antidote against covetous ambition to a comfortable doctrine suitable for a commercial people. He has treated the doctrine as having been the same for all time; and the adherent of the school of "economic determinism" may be excused if he criticizes Weber for neglecting the converse study of the influence of capitalism on the Protestant Ethic.

The development of the new prudential conception of the "calling" (which did not become general until the eighteenth century) may be traced quite easily in the three most influential manuals of Christian conduct of their respective ages—*The Whole Duty of Man* of 1657, Baxter's *Christian Directory* of 1673, and the *New Whole Duty of Man* which appeared first in the reign of George II and retained its popularity for over a century.

The first of these manuals was produced as an antidote against solifidianism. It affirmed strongly, therefore, the necessity for good works and reasserted the need for a strict application of the customary ethical system.

Baxter occupies a much less decided position. His work stands halfway between the wholly traditional morality of the first *Whole Duty of Man* and the freer mode of the second. Weber quotes it largely in support of his thesis; yet the real conservatism of its position is very apparent.

Every one, it is true, was under the necessity of living in a "calling" in which he might redeem his time. But the spirit of gain was not to be allowed as a guide to choosing one's "calling":

> Choose that employment or calling (so far as you have your choice), in which you may be most serviceable to God. Choose not that in which you may be most Rich or Honourable in the world; but that in which you may do most good, and best escape sinning.

One was exhorted to choose the "calling" which most conduced to the public good; only in cases where there were two "callings" equal in this respect might there be any doubts as to which must be chosen, and in this case it was important to choose the one which might be followed with the greater advantage to one's soul, not the more gainful.

Baxter was at pains to point out that:

> If you have a necessity of labouring in your callings, you have no necessity of loving the world or caring inordinately, or of being discontented with your estate.

He also seems to have been very far from the belief that to grow rich in a "calling" was a sign of grace:

> Another thinks he is no worldling because he useth no unlawful means, but the labour of his calling, to grow rich. The same answer serves to this. The love of wealth for the satisfying of the flesh is unlawful whatever the means be.

It must be allowed, then, that even Richard Baxter's conception of the "calling" was not a very wholehearted influence in favor of capitalism. He accepted the purposive philosophy of the social idealist rather than the mechanistic one of the individualist, and so he insisted on giving moral advice as to the conduct of business affairs:

The public welfare, or the good of many is to be valued above our own.

> Regard the public good above your own commodity. It is not lawful to take or keep up an oppressing monopoly or trade; which tendeth to enrich you by the loss of the Common-wealth or of many.

As a result Baxter retained many of the older canons of business dealings. He disapproved of the maxim *Caveat Emptor* and he tended to advise a modified doctrine of *Just Price* being maintained. He said that in buying and selling one should

> . . . have special respect to the common estimate, and to the market price. Though it be not always to be our Rule, yet ordinarily it must be a considerable part of it; and of great regard.

Further, he stood wholeheartedly on the side of the objective determination of the *just* value, quite in the mediaeval manner:

> But if that which you have to sell, be extraordinarily desirable, or worth to some other person, more than to you or another man, you must not take too great an advantage of his convenience or desire.

It is true that in this matter he showed himself ready to make some compromise—he would allow a greater price to be exacted of the rich than of the poor, and he believed that some latitude must be allowed in determining the just price, as "to be alwayes just at a word is not convenient." But the general tenor of his advice was in favor of fixing rules for trade which were inconsistent with a simple search for gain; the contention that his influence lay in promoting the rise of a spirit of capitalism must be accepted with considerable reserve. . . .

It must remain open to dispute whether the most characteristic feature of Baxter's writings was his respect for the traditional morals which the Churches had agreed in applying to the conduct of business, or his practical feeling that the good business man was not necessarily a bad Christian, and his readers are likely to decide the matter according to their own predilections. But of one thing we can be certain—that his favor shown to the business man was not the result of his Puritanism. It was the result of being, through his exceptional relations with his congregation, bound up with the practical life. It is impossible to regard Baxter as lending a wholehearted support, either to the capitalistic or the old traditionalist side. He was not a leader; he was trying to reconcile the Christian and the commercial life, as St. Thomas had tried in the thirteenth century. But he had to make greater concessions to the commercial spirit than Aquinas, and, being a man of his age, he probably made them more easily.

When we come to the book of Christian conduct which succeeded Baxter's in popular esteem, we find that the movement towards looking through business spectacles has made rapid progress. *The New Whole Duty of Man, containing the Faith as well as Practice of a Christian: Made Easy for the Practice of the Present Age . . .* was also undecided in the guidance it offered with regard to some of the economic duties. But on the whole it made greater and more numerous compromises with Mammon. The work bore still evident traces of the old traditional morality—how long it lasted!—such as are exemplified in these "Rules of Traffick":

> . . . *Neither ask far beyond, nor bid much below, what reason must inform you to be the real worth. . . . Do not impose upon any man's unskilfulness or ignorance. So long as you keep within the latitude of lawful gain, you may use your skill against another man in driving a bargain:*

for in an ordinary plenty of commodities there is an ordinary price, which those that deal in them know and understand; and when the contractors equally understand the price, there can be no deception or injustice in the contract, be it made ever so hard. On the contrary, if he whom I contract with be ignorant or unskilful, I must not rate his want of understanding, or set a tax on his ignorance, but use him justly, as one that reposes a trust in me, and casts himself upon my equity; for if I do not do this, I am guilty of injustice. . . .

In spite of this surface conservatism, however, the *New Whole Duty* bears the mark of being, as the title says, "made easy for the practice of the present age." It is recognized that with time's changes new codes of moral guidance were called for, and that the first *Whole Duty of Man* was not "(by any means) suited to the present times; for how can it be? it having been written near one hundred years since."

When the *New Whole Duty* discoursed on honesty, it dealt quite literally with nothing else than the advantages of honest dealing to a nation of shopkeepers. It delivered a long homily on "Honesty is the Best Policy." . . .

By the time of the *New Whole Duty of Man* the doctrine of the "calling" had lost its early character of an antidote against ambition. The author did not see in it any ban on enterprise. In his discussion of the duty of servants he wrote that:

The state of servitude is necessary by the appointment of the wise Creator; the world cannot be governed and maintained without it; and it is their lot to be instrumental to the publick good in that state of life. Yet this is no token of God's displeasure: for, he in no wise forbids them to use honest means to make themselves free as soon as they can. . . .

It was a different outlook from Crowley's "And do not seke thy lotte to chaunge."

The author of the *New Whole Duty* was amongst the first of the English moral writers to consider that worldly success was of great moment, and of paramount importance in deciding in what esteem a man should be held:

. . . As titular dignities intitle men to an outward respect and observance, so also doth wealth and large possessions; for, when God bestows upon one man a larger fortune and possession than on another, he doth thereby prefer and advance him into an higher sphere and condition; and

when God hath set him above us, it is just and fit that we should rise and give that place to him which is of God's appointment. Though, it may be, a wise or virtuous poor man hath more right to our esteem than a fortunate knave or fool; yet, forasmuch as in outward rank or condition God hath preferred the latter, he hath the rights of precedency, and of outward respect and observance; and ought to be treated with greater regard and obeisance.

A very typical and significant illustration of the part which religion had come to play in the mind of the author of the *New Whole Duty* may be found in his attitude to those who leave their "calling" "under a pretence of purer religion":

. . . hereby they are not only rendered useless to the commonwealth, but they do oftentimes a great deal of mischief to it, by unsettling and subverting other men, and filling their heads with abundance of foolish notions and scruples in religion, which are dangerous to government, and the publick peace and happiness . . . the man that serves God by continual application to the duty of his calling and state of life, besides the comfort of a good conscience, which is of all others the greatest happiness, such an honest and industrious labourer may entirely depend upon the goodness of God, that he will always take care of him: God will bless and prosper him in the work of his hands. . . .

It is evident that the influence of this book was in favor of the rise of a spirit of capitalism, and it is on evidence such as this that the assertions have been made that Puritan doctrine had resulted in the growth of the capitalistic spirit. There has been a complete lack of historical method.

It was not till the eighteenth century that the commercial ethics of English Puritanism reached this point. Even then the old conservative views were not entirely lost. They were found still scattered on the pages of the *New Whole Duty.* They were found even more strongly expressed in the writings of Defoe, a Nonconformist as well as an author of books on commercial practice. . . .

It was only in a long progress of time that English Puritanism came to be favorable to the claims of commercial men—that the doctrine of the "calling" ceased to be a Puritan antidote against the temptations of ambition. This fact is insufficiently recognized; and it shows the dangers of trying to explain historical developments without having recourse to historical methods. The shopkeepers' morality of the eighteenth-century *New Whole Duty of Man* is, properly understood, an argument against the thesis which connects the Protestant ethic with the spirit of capitalism; an argument for seeking in social changes the reasons for alterations in religious outlook. In the argument that Calvinist and Puritan Protestantism has provided the religio-sociological background for the rise of the capitalistic spirit too much has been made of those numerous passages in the *Works of the Puritan Divines* and the writings of later Americans which condemn idleness by virtue of the doctrine of the "calling." There are many passages to be found in the same *Works of the Puritan Divines* which condemn covetousness and ambition in accordance with the same doctrine; and many more among the works of these writers' forerunners. The doctrine of the "calling" did not breed a spirit of capitalism. The spirit of capitalism was responsible for a gradual modification and attrition of the Puritan doctrine; and this attrition had barely begun in England before the Restoration.

When one glances at the state of affairs on the continent of Europe, the conviction is deepened, that serious misconceptions of the nature of the relations between religious ethics and the spirit of capitalism have arisen. Generalizations have been too hasty.

One finds amongst the Catholics, both Jesuit and Jansenist, doctrines favorable to the emergence of the steady type of business man who was in favor with the later Puritans. The Catholics employed doctrines cognate with that of the "calling" with the same practical effect. "One must rise, for example," said the Jansenist Nicole, "to obey God, Who only allows us sleep for the body's needs and commands us, when these needs are satisfied, *to busy ourselves with the work which He prescribes for us according to our state.*"

The Jansenist preachers in particular reminded their flocks that the Christian life was "a serious life, a life of toil and not of diversion, play or pleasure" so that one ought never to forget that it "should be filled with some useful and sober occupation suitable for one's state of existence."

The Jesuits stressed almost the same beliefs. Little could have been more favorable to a rational methodizing of life than Father Crasset's panegyric on Order:

> *Order and virtue are two words which mean almost the same thing. It is order which makes Paradise, and disorder, Hell. . . . Everything which God makes, He makes orderly, and everything that is not made in an orderly manner is not of God. Order leads us to God.*

In France the Church went out of its way to welcome the honest bourgeois—the self-made man—on the ground that he was the only type of man who followed God's commands and lived in a "calling." It is true that the phrase was not employed, but the idea was:

> *Do not seek true piety among the great, the noble, the rich, whose life is only amusement and luxury; and do not expect to find purity of behaviour amongst them. Where then may one find it? In the huts of a do-nothing poverty, which has no occupation but begging? No, Christians: they as well as the rich are lost through idleness, and this class of the poor, whom Jesus Christ does not recognize, are also given to disorder. To whom then is purity reduced? I have told you—to these middle states of life who subsist by work, to these less noticeable conditions of men, who are however more assured of salvation, merchants engaged in the cares of lawful business, workmen who measure the days by the labour of their hands, servants who fulfil to the letter this divine command: as ye work so shall ye eat.*

The Catholic Church was forward to reduce all the duties of a Christian to the due performance of his earthly tasks. The Catholics also tried to consecrate the world of labor, even to make it the only world that mattered:

> *All your piety is included in your station[3] and duties. I say: in your tasks faithfully observed. Do not neglect anything that is required by your employment, your bidding, the different relations you enjoy most directly, whether with God, as ministers of altars, or with the public as judges, or with servants in virtue of being masters, or with children as fathers and mothers; it does not matter with whom or how—include everything, accomplish everything, neglect nothing.*

It was easy to serve God in this indirect way by performing all one's worldly responsibilities with a sober sense of duty:

> *One serves God by faithfully serving one's Prince; one serves God by employing one's capital (en faisant valoir son bien) according to all the rules of probity and justice. There are duties to be performed in all conditions of life, and it is in acquitting oneself of these duties that one is sanctified.*

---

[3] If it were not for the risk of being accused of trying to support my argument by inserting in the translation words which are not in the original I should be tempted to translate *condition* here as "calling," not as "station." It would be the only satisfactory translation. It would also suit *charge* a little lower down, which I have translated as "bidding."

The French Jesuits even claimed that there was no incompatibility between self-interest and the service of God:

> God deigns to be grateful to us for what is done on our own behalf, if it is for the love of Him that one does it. So there is no incompatibility of service and business. One is soldier, lawyer, business man, but one is also a Christian. One can serve the same master in all these different states, and one can work fruitfully for God, for men and for oneself.

It might just as easily be claimed for Catholicism as for Puritanism that it made a demand for a worldly asceticism of rational toil. The spirit of Christianity, said the Abbé Réguis, "is a spirit of order and activity, of prudence and precaution, of fear and trepidation, because of the temptations of every sort to which we are exposed, and against which it is impossible to defend oneself if one lives an idle and unproductive life."

And so the ordered life which would be recommended by a Puritan by virtue of the doctrine of the "calling" was also recommended by the Catholics. By them also it was stressed as a religious exercise, and the due performance of its discipline was recognized as a mark of grace:

> When all is ordered, and one does everything in due time, one acts as a Christian, and it is by this means that many become sanctified and perfect. . . . Often they can only be distinguished from others of the same occupation by the application and the nicety with which they perform their tasks; they only do the same as all the others, but do it with an exactitude which takes the place for them of greater and more beautiful actions.

The necessity of worldly labor was incumbent upon the Catholic as well as the Protestant rich, in the days of the eighteenth century:

> Since we are all sinners by birth, we are all included without exception in the decree which condemned Adam to work, sickness and death. As neither rank nor riches, then, discharge anyone from the necessity of death, no one ought to believe himself to be relieved of the obligation to work under pretext of being of distinguished rank or of not requiring to work in order to live.

After a time, also, the belief that labor is a curse fell out of fashion, and it was stated instead that:

The necessity of working is not a penalty; it is the decree of a Father Who makes all creation tributary to our needs.

It was not only recognized by the French Church that it was favorable for business to have these doctrines; it was stressed that this was so, in an attempt to secure the goodwill and support of the commercial classes. "Religion, in making a sacred duty of work and a sin of idleness, is the soul and the nourishment of useful industry," was the actual claim of a Catholic preacher, de Boulogne.

Thus there was nothing exceptional in the Church doctrines of the later seventeenth- and eighteenth-century Puritans. They were shared by the Catholics, and the encouragement given by them to the capitalist spirit was not the contribution solely of the Puritan and Calvinist sects. They did not develop until the end of the seventeenth century, when they spread both amongst Protestants and Catholics. It would appear that this is in itself enough to prove that the problem has been viewed through the wrong end of the telescope—to show that the chief relation between the rise of the capitalistic spirit and the Protestant Ethic is the reverse of what Weber has indicated. The Protestant Ethic changed as the result of the influence of a rising capitalistically minded middle class. The churches of the Calvinists and the Puritans did not always bear the same witness as regards the duties of the man of business. A changing emphasis, reflecting a changing spirit of the age, transformed a doctrine outwardly uniform. From being a hindrance to enterprise it became a spur.

The same change of emphasis took place among the Catholics. Was this due in some obscure way to the influence of the Protestant Ethic? We must think so, if we believe that the Protestant Ethic was the efficient cause of the rise of the spirit of capitalism. Or did both transformations take place under the same influence—the growing strength of an independent spirit of enterprise. The choice of hypothesis can hardly be in doubt.

If it is true that modern capitalism is the product of a new spirit of capitalism introduced with the Reformation, it must necessarily follow that there was no capitalism before that time.

Insofar as we can think of the Middle Ages as a unity, we tend to think of them as a period from which capitalism was largely absent, and if we were to indulge in the habit of dividing history into hard and fast stages, we should be tempted to speak of the Middle Ages as being characterized by a pre-capitalistic stage of economic development. But it is only by concentrating on the static general view that such a conception is possible. If one looks at the changing elements of mediaeval life one receives a different impression.

The typical mediaeval conception of social relations was that the life and activities of the individual should be regulated according to certain preconceptions of a Divine ordering of society—a graded society. The principles of mediaeval life were quite in accordance with this doctrine. In the country there was the authoritarian feudal system, with its clearly marked ranks and well-known customary duties. The general principles of town life (though they were of necessity a little more individualistic) were found chiefly in monopoly —or exclusive rights of buying and selling—and in the regulation of trade by authority. Both in town and country a sort of egalitarianism was mixed with the principle of well-marked class distinctions. Men were regarded as members of functional groups within each of which there was a rough equality of material conditions. All this is saying very little more than that one inevitably thinks of manor and guild when one thinks of mediaeval economic life.

It was opposed completely to the individualism which is the basis of all that is best in capitalism. It is not true, as too many writers nowadays suggest, that the difference between the individualist scheme of life and the typical mediaeval or the typical socialist scheme of life is that the individualist has no social ideals while the others have. What is true is that the individualist has different ideals. Individualism, as a doctrine, sees in the individual and his psychological aptitudes the necessary basis of society's economic organization, believes that the actions of individuals will suffice to provide the principles of society's economic organization, seeks to realize social progress through the individual by allowing him all the scope for his free self-development which is possible. It believes that for this two institutions are necessary: economic freedom (that is, freedom of enterprise) and private property. It believes that different individuals have different aptitudes and that each should be allowed to develop them in competition with others to the best of his ability. Therefore, as a system, individualism is the system of free trade, of competition, of private property. As doctrine and system it is entirely opposed to the typical mediaeval scheme of life. Only the regime of private property is common, and the mediaeval attitude to property was not the same as that of the modern world.

Nevertheless, the Middle Ages were never completely mediaeval in this sense. The mediaeval scene and the mediaeval mind had each of them elements of change, which grew and became more important, until finally they transformed mediaeval life. These are the elements which are of greatest moment to the historian, who is interested more in the physiology than in the anatomy of society. However flat and uniform the Middle Ages may have been, they contained currents flowing straight into modern times. Capitalism, even if not generalized, was not uncommon in the Middle Ages. It will be difficult, then, to look on it as the product of the Reformation.

Sombart, like Weber, believes that modern capitalism is the product of a specific "capitalistic spirit," which found no place in the Middle Ages. He affirms that the principle of economic life in the Middle Ages was the provision for one's needs (the *Bedarfsdeckung-prinzip)* which he contrasts with the pursuit of gain (the *Erwerbsprin-zip*) that is the principle of modern capitalistic life. He defines capitalism as

> . . . *a definite economic system which may be recognized by the following characteristics: it is organized on the basis of exchange, and in it two different classes cooperate; the owners of the means of production, who direct operations, as subjects of the system, and propertyless laborers pure and simple as objects. It is ruled by the principle of gain and economic rationalism.*

The definition seems very just; but it does not show why the whole of the Middle Ages should be considered pre-capitalistic. All these characteristics can be found there.

The *Erwerbsprinzip* is not a modern invention. We have lived in an acquisitive society for some thousands of years. Modern capitalism is not distinguished by exclusive possession of this principle. Aristotle had indeed long ago brought it into light, and traced the ways in which it was satisfied, whether by speculation, labor or usury. That is to say, he had discussed it as a rational pursuit, or rather, as Sombart himself also regards it, as an irrational pursuit rationally pursued. Thus the two criteria of rationality and the striving for gain, which Sombart is prone to suggest are confined to the modern age, were both known in ancient Greece.

Nor were they unknown in the Middle Ages. It may be wrong to follow Brentano in thinking that the exploitation-capitalism of Rome throughout the duration of the Pax Romana, and the fact that the Punic Wars were first and foremost trade wars, have any direct connection with the capitalism of modern times. But it is difficult not to admit that modern capitalism was emerging in Ravenna (which, under Roman Emperors or Gothic Kings was the chief entrepôt for the lucrative trade of the West with Byzantium) as early as the fifth century. Commercial enterprise on a large scale, a wholehearted and rational organization of the pursuit of gain, and the rise to importance of fluid capital capable of being applied wherever the chances of profit were most tempting, were phenomena of very early occurrence in the eastern Mediterranean. The rise of the Saracen power in the Mediterranean acted as a check on this capitalistic development. But it was a check caused by external circumstances, not by a psychological change. There was no loss of the capitalist spirit in Italy; it was not from lack of will but from lack of power that commerce declined in the Mediterranean, just as it was not from love of a self-sufficing economy that the agrarian estates of the greater part of Europe came to adopt the policy of subsistence farming, but because of decline of town life and the dislocation of trade caused by the destructive invasions of the barbarians, and later of the Saracens and Norsemen. As soon as conditions began to be in any way favorable, the commercial spirit emerged in the operations of the merchants of the Italian towns such as Amalfi, Venice, Genoa, Pisa and, later, Florence. It was the same further north, where in Flanders, Artois and Brabant a long-distance trade grew up, at first chiefly in fish and salt and Baltic products, and later in the cloth and metal goods of the Belgian industrial hinterland. Of course, trade between these two centers soon sprang up, raising to prosperity convenient centers along the chief trade routes—in Champagne, at Geneva and Lyons; at Frankfurt, Strassburg, Ulm, Nuremberg, Cologne and Aix-la-Chapelle—and peopling them with capitalistic merchants.

Sombart has been tempted to deny that the activities of these centers were capitalistic. But to do so, he appears to have introduced another criterion of capitalistic development: the amount of trade carried on as compared with the present day. He has collected a great deal of information with the object of proving that no large-scale economic activity was carried on in the Middle Ages, that even commerce was only conducted on a scale comparable with small handicraft industry. He has controverted very strongly Ehrenberg's dictum that commerce must of its very nature be carried on capitalistically. He has based his arguments on these grounds: firstly, on the large number of merchants who were engaged in carrying on a very limited trade; secondly, on the small size of the capital subscribed by merchants going into partnership (of the first fifty partnerships registered in Genoa in 1156 the average capital subscribed was only about 150 lire); thirdly, on the small amounts of property owned by the inhabitants of cities like Basel and Augsburg in the fifteenth century as revealed by their tax returns; and, fourthly, on the small size of the ships generally employed and the small value of their cargoes. He has pointed out, for instance, that seven Spanish ships carrying iron, fruit, and wool, which were captured by English warships in 1470, varied from 40 to 120 tons and were worth, cargo included, from £70 to £180 in sterling money of the time.

He suggests that with regard to commerce, "everywhere the same picture is offered us: apart from a few greater and often not professional merchants, only a swarm of small and insignificant traders." And so the merchant was entirely of a piece with the petty town workman; his whole outlook on life was the same; he was without capitalistic motives, he was content to receive as the reward of his labors what would ensure him the common sort of existence of his social class; he was without the desire to strive after greater and greater gain which distinguishes the modern entrepreneur.

Sombart is right on many points. It does not do to pretend that mediaeval commerce was on a scale comparable with that of the present day. Conditions of transport and the comparative smallness of the population alone would have prevented it. But this means only that technical conditions were not suitable for such a capitalist expansion as we have known in recent times, and on the same grounds one must deny the existence of capitalistic activity before the railway age. The total amount of merchandise carried over the St. Gotthard each year at the end of the Middle Ages would only fill two goods trains passing through the tunnel today, and the tonnage compared with what passes today would be in the proportion of about 1:237. But the rise in the amount of traffic carried over the St. Gotthard by 1831–1833 was only in the proportion of 1:3.2, which is no very enormous growth. And to argue in this manner is, as Pirenne said, like arguing that the Middle Ages knew no urban life, because they knew no large cities like those of the present day. . . .

Should the concept of capitalism, however, be confined to this? Does not capitalism consist in a fusion of a romantic and a rationalist tendency as well as in the purely rational pursuit of gain through industrial organization? Sombart expressed this feeling very well when he wrote in the first edition of his *Der moderne Kapitalismus* that if he were pressed to give a definite birth date for modern capitalism, he would choose A.D. 1202—the year in which Leonardo Pisano's *Liber Abbaci* (the arithmetical treatise which first rendered exact calculation possible) appeared, and in which Venice began the attack on Constantinople which marked the beginning of the exploitation of the East by Western Europeans—especially by the Italian communes—and through which the large-scale accumulation of money began.

Sombart has indicated here what seem to be very valuable considerations. The warfare of the period of the Crusades deserves some prominence in the history of capitalism. It is doubtful if one should dignify much of it with the name of warfare—piracy and brigandage would be more appropriate—but it is important in at least two respects. It was carried on as a commercial undertaking for plunder (Sombart's "one-sided trade"), and the equipment of a warlike band called for a large capital, larger than for any ordinary commercial or industrial undertaking of the time. Also the booty secured was one of the great sources of the early hoards of capital. Thus the pillaging of the Levant was of importance in the early history of capitalism.

The second consideration called forth by Sombart's statement is even more enlightening. The rise of financial science was a necessary condition of the growth of capitalism. It enlarged the institution of private property by mobilizing all forms of capital and removing the obstacles which differences of time and place might set in the way of its profitable employment. It allowed capital to become impersonal and abstract, a mere counter of general purchasing power, of general productive capacity. It enabled one to invest capital in an undertaking and withdraw and dispose of one's holding at will without withdrawing any of the equipment of the undertaking or interfering with the business in any way—the transfer being made in paper which represents a share in the undertaking. It is by attaining to impersonality and so to mobility that capital has gained in strength and security, and it has been the mathematician, the accountant, who has provided the rational basis for giving all forms of capital mobility. The great cause of the rise of rational capitalism was not Christian at all—it was a secular scientific development, taken over by western Europeans from Muslim Arabs and Syrians. . . .

It would take too long to follow out the actual history of these various mediaeval capitalistic developments. It should be noted that the Catholic Church was itself largely responsible for some of them. The industrial and agricultural activities of the Cistercians in the end necessitated complex capitalistic arrangements for the sale of wool. The abbeys used to act as mortgage banks. And the Roman curia was an enormous financial organization collecting taxation from all parts of the Christian world, served by a galaxy of important banks and money-changers. These *campsores Romanam curiam sequentes* must not be forgotten as weighty influences on the history of capitalism.

One other influence on the rise of capitalism already in existence in the Middle Ages deserves some comment. Reference has already been made to the suggestion that the appearance of Pisano's *Liber Abbaci* might be considered a landmark in the history of capitalism. It is to scientific bookkeeping much more than to the ethic of any religious system that we owe the rational methodizing of business life. Systematic organization is one of the most powerful agents of economic progress, and this holds good perhaps more of systematic bookkeeping than of any other form. As Sombart has said:

> *Organization and clearness increases the desire to save and to acquire. A man who manages badly finds himself in a fog; he does not like to correlate the entries to see what he owes. On the other hand, nothing can be more acceptable to a good manager, than to examine every day the amounts of his growing fortune. Even a loss, if it annoys and surprises him, does not perturb him, for he knows at once what profits he has gained to set on the other side.*

Is it not likely that this has had a greater effect than the doctrine of the "calling," which must always remain a little alien to business thoughts?

The organization of business on the basis of double-entry bookkeeping must have had an overwhelming importance in the development of a capitalistic order of society:

> *Capitalism without double-entry bookkeeping is simply inconceivable. They hold together as form and matter. And one may indeed doubt whether capitalism has procured in double-entry bookkeeping a tool which activates its forces, or whether double-entry bookkeeping has first given rise to capitalism out of its own (i.e., rational and systematic) spirit.*

Until the emergence of systematic bookkeeping there naturally remained something of the old "subsistence" ideal of life of the canonists, the ideal of all business activity being carried on primarily to provide subsistence for the merchant and for those with whom he dealt—what might be called a "commodity" conception of business. But the man who devotes himself to transactions on a bookkeeping basis has only one aim—the increase of values comprehended only quantitatively. He does not consider mainly corn or wool or cotton or cloth or the cargoes of ships, or tea or pepper. These (the true realities of commerce) become mere shadows, they become unreal and the apparent reality seems to lie in bookkeeping ciphers. All that the merchant who employs systematic bookkeeping sees are money values which increase or grow less. . . .

It is so difficult to conceive of economic activity today not carried on with a bookkeeping basis that we take its existence for granted, and it is hard to imagine what a revolution the introduction of scientific bookkeeping methods must have caused. Yet nowhere has the rational element entered more strongly into economic activity than through accountancy—it is a necessary condition of the separation of the firm from the individuals of which it consists and therefore of the growth of large joint-stock businesses—and the slow spread of scientific bookkeeping was one of the chief causes of the persistence of traditional and unbusinesslike methods of ordering affairs throughout the Middle Ages. An adequate bookkeeping system is one of the cultural conditions necessary for the emergence of capitalism. It is a purely secular influence, and it was not absent from the Middle Ages. Double-entry was practiced in Italy from the second half of the fourteenth century, though the yearly balance did not come in before the seventeenth century. Its rapid extension throughout Europe after the middle of the sixteenth century—following its introduction into Flanders by Ympym in 1543—was no doubt of great moment in the spread of economic activity and the spirit of capitalism. That the countries in which the science of bookkeeping made the most progress were always those in which most economic progress was being made can no doubt best be explained as a mixture of cause and effect. But working on the same lines as Weber, it would be very easy to substitute systematic books for the Protestant Ethic as the origin of the capitalist spirit. There is no doubt that reliance on good books meant more than reliance on the Good Book. And there is still less doubt that the rise of the capitalist spirit is the same as the rise of economic rationalism—something which took place independently of Church teaching, on the basis of commercial experience. The great cause of the rise of the spirit of capitalism has been capitalism itself; and it has been conditioned by general cultural conditions, more particularly by developments in business technique, and by governmental and legal institutions affecting commerce. . . .

Is there any justification, then, for suggesting that Calvinism introduced a new outlook on the investment of money? The Jesuit doctrine of the direction of the intention, by which one and the same contract might be lawful or usurious according to the intentions of the parties, made it impossible to distinguish unlawful usury, and in that way justified all payments for a loan. The Jesuits accepted the arguments of Calvin against the sterility of money. They went so far as to justify payment of interest on the individualistic grounds that a free contract was in itself just. And the fact that the chief motive for entering a contract was the desire for gain did not make the intention bad. The fact that the Jesuits did not take the step of denouncing or casting aside all usury restrictions does not prove that they were less advanced than the Protestants. It only proves that the Jesuits were satisfied that the contracts which had been evolved to evade the usury prohibition met all reasonable needs. As Pirot said, the rent charge and the triple contract were all that was necessary, for in practice nobody would lend to those who could not offer sufficient security—and if the security offered was a hereditament or property of some sort a rent could be settled on it, while if the security offered was the ownership of some profitable business, a triple contract of partnership and insurance would suffice.

Our studies so far have not shown that the encouragement of the spirit of capitalism has been the exclusive work of any one section of Christians. The development of Protestant thought on usury was certainly no more significant than the development of Catholic thought on rent charges and threefold contracts, and on implicit contracts of which the legitimacy was secured by good intentions. The attempts at strict regulation of the economic life made by the Calvinist churches were definite hindrances to capitalistic development and the spread of capitalistic ideas which formed a strong contrast to the comfortable and accommodating religion of the Jesuits.

These are matters with which the sociological school has not dealt. But a comparative study of Protestant and Catholic thought also disposes of many of the chief arguments which this school does employ. It reduces considerably, for instance, the importance which can be given exclusively to the Puritan doctrine of the "calling"—a doctrine which studied by itself, however, proves to have been by no means always an encouragement to capitalism.

It makes some very favorite arguments drawn from the writings of Benjamin Franklin of small account. Weber had drawn much of his inspiration from reading Franklin. He believed that Franklin's insistence that *Time is Money* and not to be wasted, that *Honesty is the Best Policy,* his love of detail and exact reckoning, were the apotheosis of Puritan doctrines of worldly prudence. He said that Franklin's strict avoidance of time- and money-wasting vanities were typical fruits of his Puritan upbringing. But are they characteristic of any one religious creed? Werner Sombart has suggested that these writings are only an echo of fourteenth- and fifteenth-century Florentines, such as Leon Battista Alberti, Agnolo Pandolfini, Antonio and Lorenzo da Vinci, and that the wealth of the burghers of Florence was built up with parsimony and industry on just such a scheme of life as Franklin's. Nobody could build up a theory to connect Puritanism and capitalism on a basis of studying these Florentine writings, or not dissimilar ones produced by the Roman moralists. Weber had denied the validity of this criticism. He asserts that Sombart has been guilty of mistranslating or misunderstanding the Florentine authors. Whether he has or not—a controversial matter into which there is no present need to enquire—it may be noted that the ordering of one's life for the pursuit of gain, which was not enjoyed, through the exercise of parsimony, was sufficiently established before Luther's doctrine of the "calling" was evolved for Erasmus to lampoon it in his colloquy *Opulentia sordida.* The victim of this attack is supposed to have been one of Erasmus's Italian hosts. It is, moreover, certain that Franklin's advice about the careful ordering of one's daily life and avoidance of unnecessary indulgence were also commonplaces in the writings of seventeenth- and eighteenth-century Catholics. The Christian, said Father Tronson, "does not pluck flowers, or wear any, simply for the pleasure of flaunting them"—"he does not waste his time at a door or window looking at the passers-by."

Father Crasset believed that it was following divine precept to conduct one's everyday life with a rigorous adhesion to plan:

> *Prescribe for yourself an order in the day's routine, which you keep inviolable, unless you are hindered by a higher command which forces you to depart from it. Regulate the time of your resting, your eating, your study and diversion! In Heaven one's whole life is orderly; begin a life which you will continue in eternity; it will be more acceptable to God, more agreeable for your family, if you have one, and more advantageous for your salvation.*

Father Croiset's advice was also not very dissimilar from Franklin's:

> *Have a fixed hour for rising and going to bed; and, as far as you may, fix it so that you may be early to bed and up betimes. Nothing is more opposed to a regular and Christian life than late rising.*

Above all, one had to eschew "laziness," and never forget that "all your devotions should be subordinated to the necessary duties of your estate, of your employment."

Even Franklin's plan for ordering his life was the same as that recommended by French Catholics as a religious exercise. Father Réguis said:

> *One of the greatest advantages which one enjoys in religious houses and in all those where one lives in community, is following a definite rule which accounts for all the hours of the day, prescribing, so to say, the task for every minute. . . . Now, my dear parishioner, why should you not make yourself a rule which sets down in detail what you ought to do from morning till evening?*

*   *   *

Weber has collected a number of Protestant writings which seem to favor capitalism; but he has also mentioned that there was a strong current in Puritan teaching which stressed the dangers of riches, and the Christian's duty of not striving after them. Is he right in saying that this was overshadowed by advice, pro-capitalistic in tendency, to work hard in an orderly way, especially when both elements were also prominent in Catholic teaching? He has not proved that the Puritans introduced a new economic ethic. The Protestants as well as the Catholics spoke with an ambiguous voice. But as a rule the Calvinistic contribution to the capitalist spirit was the same as that of the Jansenists or stricter school of Catholics, consisting of the encouragement of industry, thrift, order and honesty; while the Jesuits went further and favored enterprise, freedom of speculation and the expansion of trade as a social benefit. It would not be difficult to claim that the religion which favored the spirit of capitalism was Jesuitry, not Calvinism.

But there is an explanation of the relations between the churches and the spirit of capitalism which is "more probable" than any other. A historical method of analysis may be introduced into the discussion.

Such a method has here been attempted. It has been shown how English Protestantism underwent a great deal of change between Lever and Richard Baxter, and between Baxter and the second *Whole Duty of Man,* "made easy for this present age." It has been shown how there was a progression from Luther to Gerhard, from Calvin to Saumaise, on the question of interest. It has been shown how there was a gradual relaxation of the economic casuistry of the Jesuits, and a rebuilding on a basis more in favor of capitalistic beliefs. All has gone to prove one point: that the churches, one and all, have had to accommodate themselves to an extraneous development of a busy commercial spirit; that capitalism has created, or found already existent, its own spirit, and set the churches the task of assimilating it.

The Church of the Middle Ages had easily known its duty towards the different classes of men, for there were only two important classes —the rich and great and the poor and miserable. As this simple class division became obsolete the Church was faced with new problems. They were beginning to become urgent when Aquinas wrote his famous half-hearted justification of the merchant's activities. St. Antonino met them more insistent in fourteenth-century Florence. In the sixteenth century they had to be faced for the first time almost throughout Europe. The same problems affected all the churches, and none had any previous experience to call to its aid. . . .

It was a problem which all the churches had to face. A new hard-working, hard-headed type had sprung into prime importance. It was a type predisposed to regard itself as self-sufficient. It basked in the knowledge that it had done no man harm; that it fully deserved the honest portion which it had secured by its trade and industry. Even as sinners the new type sinned less palpably, less full-bloodedly than the other types, and, as we have seen from the reports of some of their confessors in Upper Germany, these "bourgeois" were unwilling to accept a burden of sin thrust upon them by a Church which was unsympathetic because ignorant of their ways, on account of actions in which they could see no wrong.

It was left for the churches to find a place for this newly important class. What we are told to believe is the reformed churches' formation of a capitalistic spirit is in reality only their attempt to find a place for the commercial classes, newly important and freshly aware of their importance. But the Catholics also attempted to fit the middle-classes into the ecclesiastical scheme; in some way to sanctify and find an other-worldly significance in their solidity, diligence and honest respectability—characteristics which were really virtues despite their worldly origin—and to justify the aims and methods of their trade. . . .

It is noteworthy that the writings of the religio-sociological school on the origins of the capitalist spirit are infected with a deep hatred of capitalism. The essay on "Die Protestantische Ethik und der Geist des Kapitalismus" ushered in as heavy an attack on the capitalist position as the materialist writings of Karl Marx. This is not immediately apparent; but even a cursory second glance shows that its general tendency is to undermine the basis of a capitalist society. It attempts to show that modern capitalism is a massive and imposing superstructure on a foundation of shifting and out-of-date religious ideas, a Moloch of Calvinist selfishness. Its great preoccupation has been to show that, as a form of social organization, capitalism was not a natural growth, but a crass construction of the Calvinist mind, and therefore as easily assailed as that which made it in its own image. It tried to demonstrate that capitalism is no mere piece of social mechanism which should be judged only on its own merits, but a creation of evil import and unreasonable origin.

This seems to be the natural corollary of the arguments of all who accept this line of thought. Even Professor Tawney, who, in his *Religion and the Rise of Capitalism,* has admitted that the capitalist spirit was not the offspring of Puritanism, has yet affirmed that it "found in certain aspects of later Puritanism a tonic which braced its energies and fortified its already vigorous temper." He accepted the theory that "Puritanism had its own standards of social conduct, derived partly from the obvious interests of the commercial classes, partly from its conception of the nature of God and the destiny of man," and "became a potent force in preparing the way for the commercial civilization which finally triumphed at the Revolution." He believed that two elements in Calvinism were responsible for this. One was the doctrine of the "calling." The other lay in the fact that though Calvin had given approval to the life of business enterprise whilst subjecting it to an iron discipline, the demand for discipline later dropped into the background, leaving Calvinism as a religion which demanded free play for all forms of enterprise. Mr. Aldous Huxley has stated the position still more clearly:

> The Reformers read their Old Testament and, trying to imitate the Jews, became those detestable Puritans to whom we owe, not merely Grundyism and Podsnappery, but also (as Weber and Tawney have shown) all that was and still is vilest, cruellest, most antihuman in the modern capitalist system.

Yet to follow this modern way of connecting capitalism with the religion founded by Calvin is to follow a mere will-o'-the-wisp. Too much attention has been paid to certain aspects of Puritanism, and too little to what was happening outside the Puritan world. Bunyan's *Pilgrim's Progress* (which is very anti-capitalistic in attitude) has been used to show the singularly antisocial nature of the Calvinist creed which is supposed to have fashioned modern capitalism:

> In the description of Christian's attitude after he had realized that he was living in the City of Destruction and he had received the call to take up his pilgrimage to the celestial city, wife and children cling to him, but stopping his ears with his fingers and crying, 'life, eternal life,' he staggers forth across the fields. No refinement could surpass the naive feeling of the tinker who, writing in his prison cell, earned the applause of a believing world, in expressing the emotions of the faithful Puritan, thinking only of his own salvation. It is expressed in the unctuous conversation which

he holds with fellow-seekers on the way, in a manner somewhat reminiscent of Gottfried Keller's Gerechte Kammacher. *Only when he himself is safe does it occur to him that it would be nice to have his family with him.*

But this fear of earthly ties, even of earthly love, was also strong amongst the Catholics and especially amongst the Jansenists. "Love of God's creatures always diminishing our love of God, deprives us of a part of our true life, which consists entirely in the love of God," said Nicole. "The soul which pauses over His creatures retards the course of the journey by which it reaches to God; and in wishing to enjoy them it deprives itself in proportion of the enjoyment of God." "God having given me a heart to love Him," said Arnauld, "He must be the sole object of our love." As usual, Puritan opinions had their Catholic counterparts.

There were Catholic counterparts for most of the Puritan beliefs which are supposed to demonstrate capitalism's Puritan origins. The special mission of the doctrine of the "calling" in preparing the way for a commercial civilization cannot be determined by reference only to Puritans. The significance of Baxter or Perkins, Steele or Flavell emphasizing the necessity of living an ordered life and serving God by diligence in one's worldly occupation seems much less when one remembers that across the channel priests like Crasset, Croiset, Houdry, Réguis, Bourdaloue were teaching exactly the same thing. The Puritan bourgeois morality of England loses some of its significance when it is considered how similar was the Catholic peasant morality of the Continent. And the relaxation of Calvin's strict discipline of the economic appetites in English nonconformity (on which Professor Tawney lays some stress) seems to be a less important factor in establishing a connection between Puritanism and capitalism when one takes into account the tolerance of the Jesuits.

It was only to be expected that Calvinist discipline should have become less strict. Apart from the fact that a church's practical beliefs in any age are always to some extent unconsciously the product of other influences—the prevailing political, scientific and philosophical temper, material conditions and so on—a church must often be prepared to make concessions to the spirit of an age if it is to retain any influence at all. The concessions which the later Calvinism made to the commercial spirit were in large part the sacrifice of some part of the churches' claims in order to be able to retain others. The English had shown themselves unwilling to tolerate Presbyterian discipline; if the Calvinist churches had refused to temper their claims to control men's everyday actions they would have been rejected as tyrants and reactionaries. Calvinism was not betrayed from within. It lost the power before it lost the will to bind business within the discipline of Christian justice and Christian charity. Catholicism exhibited no greater power over its adherents.

The chief factor in the triumph of bourgeois liberalism was the factor of economic development which made the bourgeoisie important. It came into its own as a secular force. The rise of bourgeois morality in England as a substitute for religion was not the product of Puritanism. In Catholic France one found preachers complaining in the eighteenth century that a "gospel of worldly probity, in which is comprised all the duties of reason and religion" had arisen "on the ruins of the gospel of Jesus Christ"; and that the bourgeois preferred to be known as *honnête homme* rather than as a good Christian. The churches in each country had been unable in the end, in spite of all their efforts, to assimilate the class of self-made men. The decline of the churches in England as witnesses to a Christian code of social ethics was not due to a Puritan belief that "the Lorde was with Joseph, and he was a luckie felowe." It was due to the unwillingness of a rising bourgeoisie to be bound by what it considered to be antiquated rules.

Even so, there is no reason to decry too violently the new bourgeois individualism with its profane, not Puritan, origins. It was not a mere product of greed. It inculcated a belief in honor and justice, it believed firmly in justice, thought that independently of all religion there was implanted in man a love of justice, and on this it built. It did not ask for liberty for men to indulge their antisocial greed. It asked liberty for them to look after themselves in accordance with the rules which life and business both require to be respected and the observance of which was thought to be innate to man's nature; the rules of respecting contracts and of not doing to others what one would not have done to oneself. It did not ask for economic freedom because it believed that man's spirit of emulation raised an antithesis between the common and the private good, but because it disbelieved it.

It believed that man was rational enough to prefer justice to injustice, and that free competition would be more efficacious in promoting just dealing (on the assumption that, in general, men had a preference for justice whilst any who had not would find it bad policy to indulge their love of cheating) than restrictions based on the assumption that all men were rogues.

It was not from greed that the new individualism attacked the restrictions on forestalling and regrating. It was because it believed that free competition would see the market better and more cheaply supplied. It was not greed that silently broke down the restrictions on usury; it was a recognition that the usury restrictions did not work as they were intended. It was not mere greed that protested against the restrictions on foreign trade formed by the existence of the chartered companies. It was a just protest against injurious monopolies. It was a demand that regard should be had for the realities of things, not words; that sentimentalism should not be allowed to mask the grasping selfishness of the corporations which were impairing the well-being of the country they were supposed to serve. Self-interest played a part in promoting the rise of economic individualism, but not the only part—even when it is recognized that much apparently disinterested reasoning may be merely the rationalization of selfish motives. The problem must not be simplified too far. . . .

R. H. Tawney
RELIGION AND THE RISE OF CAPITALISM

One of the best known English economists and economic historians, R. H. Tawney graduated from Balliol College, Oxford; and, after teaching at Glasgow University and Oxford University, moved to the Chair of Economic History at the London School of Economics. Tawney was a leading member of the British Labour Party since its earliest years and could hardly be said to have been friendly to capitalism. No mere propagandist for the Labour Party, however, he wrote an impressive group of scholarly books in addition to Religion and the Rise of Capitalism, *among which are* The Acquisitive Society *and* The Agrarian Problem in the Sixteenth Century.

The most characteristic and influential form of Protestantism in the two centuries following the Reformation is that which descends, by one path or another, from the teaching of Calvin. Unlike the Lutheranism from which it sprang, Calvinism, assuming different shapes in different countries, became an international movement, which brought, not peace, but a sword, and the path of which was strewn with revolutions. Where Lutheranism had been socially conservative, deferential to established political authorities, the exponent of a personal, almost a quietistic, piety, Calvinism was an active and radical force. It was a creed which sought, not merely to purify the individual, but to reconstruct Church and State, and to renew society by penetrating every department of life, public as well as private, with the influence of religion.

Upon the immense political reactions of Calvinism, this is not the place to enlarge. As a way of life and a theory of society, it possessed from the beginning one characteristic which was both novel and important. It assumed an economic organization which was relatively advanced, and expounded its social ethics on the basis of it. In this respect the teaching of the Puritan moralists who derive most directly from Calvin is in marked contrast with that both of mediaeval theologians and of Luther. The difference is not merely one of the conclusions reached, but of the plane on which the discussion is conducted. The background, not only of most mediaeval social theory, but also of Luther and his English contemporaries, is the traditional stratification of rural society. It is a natural, rather than a money, economy, consisting of the petty dealings of peasants and craftsmen in the small market town, where industry is carried on for the subsistence of the household and the consumption of wealth follows hard upon the production of it, and where commerce and finance are occasional incidents, rather than the forces which keep the whole system in motion. When they criticize economic abuses, it is precisely against departures from that natural state of things—against the enterprise, the greed of gain, the restless competition, which disturb the stability of the existing order with clamorous economic appetites—that their criticism is directed. . . .

For Calvin, and still more his later interpreters, began their voyage lower down the stream. Unlike Luther, who saw economic life with the eyes of a peasant and a mystic, they approached it as men of affairs, disposed neither to idealize the patriarchal virtues of the peasant community, nor to regard with suspicion the mere fact of capitalist enterprise in commerce and finance. Like early Christianity and modern socialism, Calvinism was largely an urban movement; like them, in its earlier days, it was carried from country to country partly by emigrant traders and workmen; and its stronghold was precisely in those social groups to which the traditional scheme of social ethics, with its treatment of economic interests as a quite minor aspect of human affairs, must have seemed irrelevant or artificial. As was to be expected in the exponents of a faith which had its headquarters at Geneva, and later its most influential adherents in great business centers, like Antwerp with its industrial hinterland, London, and Amsterdam, its leaders addressed their teaching, not of course exclusively, but nonetheless primarily, to the classes engaged in trade and industry, who formed the most modern and progressive elements in the life of the age.

It is in the light of that change of social perspective that the doctrine of usury associated with the name of Calvin is to be interpreted. Its significance consisted, not in the phase which it marked in the technique of economic analysis, but in its admission to a new position of respectability of a powerful and growing body of social interests, which, however irrepressible in practice, had hitherto been regarded by religious theory as, at best, of dubious propriety, and, at worst, as frankly immoral. Strictly construed, the famous pronouncement strikes the modern reader rather by its rigor than by its indulgence. "Calvin," wrote an English divine a generation after his death, "deals with usurie as the apothecarie doth with poyson." The apologetic was just, for neither his letter to Oecolampadius, nor his sermon on the same subject, reveals any excessive tolerance for the trade of the financier. That interest is lawful, provided that it does not exceed an official maximum, that, even when a maximum is fixed, loans must be made *gratis* to the poor, that the borrower must reap as much advantage as the lender, that excessive security must not be exacted, that what is venial as an occasional expedient is reprehensible when carried on as a regular occupation, that no man may snatch economic gain for himself to the injury of his neighbor—a condonation of usury protected by such embarrassing entanglements can have offered but tepid consolation to the devout moneylender.

Contemporaries interpreted Calvin to mean that the debtor might properly be asked to concede some small part of his profits to the creditor with whose capital they had been earned, but that the exaction of interest was wrong if it meant that "the creditor becomes rich by the sweat of the debtor, and the debtor does not reap the reward of his labour." There have been ages in which such doctrines would have been regarded as an attack on financial enterprise rather than as a defense of it. Nor were Calvin's specific contributions to the theory of usury strikingly original. As a hardheaded lawyer, he was free both from the incoherence and from the idealism of Luther, and his doctrine was probably regarded by himself merely as one additional step in the long series of developments through which ecclesiastical jurisprudence on the subject had already gone. In emphasizing the difference between the interest wrung from the necessities of the poor and the interest which a prosperous merchant could earn with borrowed capital, he had been anticipated by Major; in his sanction of a moderate rate on loans to the rich, his position was the same as that already assumed, though with some hesitation, by Melanchthon. The picture of Calvin, the organizer and disciplinarian, as the parent of laxity in social ethics, is a legend. Like the author of another revolution in economic theory, he might have turned on his popularizers with the protest: "I am not a Calvinist."

Legends are apt, however, to be as right in substance as they are wrong in detail, and both its critics and its defenders were correct in regarding Calvin's treatment of capital as a watershed. What he did was to change the plane on which the discussion was conducted, by treating the ethics of moneylending, not as a matter to be decided by an appeal to a special body of doctrine on the subject of usury, but as a particular case of the general problem of the social relations of a Christian community, which must be solved in the light of existing circumstances. The significant feature in his discussion of the subject is that he assumes credit to be a normal and inevitable incident in the life of society. He therefore dismisses the oft-quoted passages from the Old Testament and the Fathers as irrelevant, because designed for conditions which no longer exist, argues that the payment of interest for capital is as reasonable as the payment of rent for land, and throws on the conscience of the individual the obligation of seeing that it does not exceed the amount dictated by natural justice and the golden rule. . . . But capital and credit are indispensable; the financier is not a pariah, but a useful member of society; and lending at interest, provided that the rate is reasonable and that loans are made freely to the poor, is not per se more extortionate than any other of the economic transactions without which human affairs cannot be carried on. That acceptance of the realities of commercial practice as a starting-point was of momentous importance. It meant that Calvinism and its offshoots took their stand on the side of the activities which were to be most characteristic of the future, and insisted that it was not by renouncing them, but by untiring concentration on the task of using for the glory of God the opportunities which they offered, that the Christian life could and must be lived. . . .

It was that revolution in the traditional scale of ethical values which the Swiss reformers desired to achieve; it was that new type of Christian character that they labored to create. Not as part of any scheme of social reform, but as elements in a plan of moral regeneration, they seized on the aptitudes cultivated by the life of business and affairs, stamped on them a new sanctification, and used them as the warp of a society in which a more than Roman discipline should perpetuate a character the exact antithesis of that fostered by obedience to Rome. The Roman Church, it was held, through the example of its rulers, had encouraged luxury and ostentation: the members of the Reformed Church must be economical and modest. It had sanctioned the spurious charity of indiscriminate alms-giving: the true Christian must repress mendicancy and insist on the virtues of industry and thrift. It had allowed the faithful to believe that they could atone for a life of worldliness by the savorless formality of individual good works reduced to a commercial system, as though man could keep a profit and loss account with his Creator: the true Christian must organize his life as a whole for the service of his Master. It had rebuked the pursuit of gain as lower than the life of religion, even while it took bribes from those who pursued gain with success: the Christian must conduct his business with a high seriousness, as in itself a kind of religion.

Such teaching, whatever its theological merits or defects, was admirably designed to liberate economic energies, and to weld into a disciplined social force the rising *bourgeoisie,* conscious of the contrast between its own standards and those of a laxer world, proud of its vocation as the standard bearer of the economic virtues, and determined to vindicate an open road for its own way of life by the use of every weapon, including political revolution and war, because the issue which was at stake was not merely convenience or self-interest, but the will of God. Calvinism stood, in short, not only for a new doctrine of theology and ecclesiastical government, but for a new scale of moral values and a new ideal of social conduct. Its practical message, it might perhaps be said, was *la carrière ouverte*—not *aux talents,* but *au caractère. . . .*

*   *   *

"The triumph of Puritanism," it has been said, "swept away all traces of any restriction or guidance in the employment of money."[1] That it swept away the restrictions imposed by the existing machinery is true; neither ecclesiastical courts, nor High Commission, nor Star Chamber, could function after 1640. But, if it broke the discipline of the Church of Laud and the State of Strafford, it did so but as a step towards erecting a more rigorous discipline of its own. It would have been scandalized by economic individualism,

[1] Cunningham, *The Moral Witness of the Church on the Investment of Money and the Use of Wealth,* 1909, p. 25.

as much as by religious tolerance, and the broad outlines of its
scheme of organization favored unrestricted liberty in matters of
business as little as in the things of the spirit. To the Puritan of any
period in the century between the accession of Elizabeth and the
Civil War, the suggestion that he was the friend of economic or
social license would have seemed as wildly inappropriate as it would
have appeared to most of his critics, who taunted him, except in
the single matter of usury, with an intolerable meticulousness. . . .

The attempt to crystallize social morality in an objective discipline was possible only in a theocracy; and, still eloquent in speech,
theocracy had abdicated in fact, even before the sons of Belial
returned to cut down its groves and lay waste its holy places. In
an age when the right to dissent from the State Church was still
not fully established, its defeat was fortunate, for it was the victory
of tolerance. It meant, however, that the discipline of the Church
gave place to the attempt to promote reform through the action of
the State, which reached its height in the Barebones Parliament.
Projects for law reform, marriage reform and financial reform, the
reform of prisons and the relief of debtors, jostled each other on
its committees; while outside it there were murmurs among radicals
against social and economic privilege, which were not to be heard
again till the days of the Chartists, and which to the conservative
mind of Cromwell seemed to portend mere anarchy. The transition
from the idea of a moral code enforced by the Church, which had
been characteristic of early Calvinism, to the economic individualism of the later Puritan movement took place, in fact, by way of
the democratic agitation of the Independents. Abhorring the whole
mechanism of ecclesiastical discipline and compulsory conformity,
they endeavored to achieve the same and ethical ends by political
action.

The change was momentous. If the English Social Democratic
movement has any single source, that source is to be found in the
New Model Army. But the conception implied in the attempt to
formulate a scheme of economic ethics—the theory that every department of life falls beneath the same all-encompassing arch of
religion—was too deeply rooted to be exorcised merely by political
changes, or even by the more corroding march of economic development. Expelled from the world of fact, where it had always
been a stranger and a sojourner, it survived in the world of ideas,

and its champions in the last half of the century labored it the more, precisely because they knew that it must be conveyed to their audiences by teaching and preaching or not at all. Of those champions the most learned, the most practical, and the most persuasive was Richard Baxter.

How Baxter endeavored to give practical instruction to his congregation at Kidderminster, he himself has told us. "Every Thursday evening my neighbors that were most desirous and had opportunity met at my house, and there one of them repeated the sermon, and afterwards they proposed what doubts any of them had about the sermon, or any of other case of conscience, and I resolved their doubts." Both in form and in matter, his *Christian Directory, or a Summ of Practical Theologie and Cases of Conscience* is a remarkable book. It is, in essence, a Puritan *Summa Theologica* and *Summa Moralis* in one; its method of treatment descends directly from that of the mediaeval *Summae,* and it is, perhaps, the last important English specimen of a famous *genus.* Its object, as Baxter explains in his introduction, is "the resolving of practical cases of conscience, and the reducing of theoretical knowledge into serious Christian practice." Divided into four parts, Ethics, Economics, Ecclesiastics, and Politics, it has as its purpose to establish the rules of a Christian casuistry, which may be sufficiently detailed and precise to afford practical guidance to the proper conduct of men in the different relations of life, as lawyer, physician, schoolmaster, soldier, master and servant, buyer and seller, landlord and tenant, lender and borrower, ruler and subject. Part of its material is derived from the treatment of similar questions by previous writers, both before and after the Reformation, and Baxter is conscious of continuing a great tradition. But it is, above all things, realistic, and its method lends plausibility to the suggestion that it originated in an attempt to answer practical questions put to its author by members of his congregation. Its aim is not to overwhelm by authority, but to convince by an appeal to the enlightened common sense of the Christian reader. It does not overlook, therefore, the practical facts of a world in which commerce is carried on by the East India Company in distant markets, trade is universally conducted on credit, the iron manufacture is a large-scale industry demanding abundant supplies of capital and offering a profitable opening to the judicious investor, and the relations of landlords and tenants have been thrown into confusion by the fire of London. Nor does it ignore the moral qualities for the cultivation of which an opportunity is offered by the life of business. It takes as its starting-point the commercial environment of the Restoration, and its teaching is designed for "Rome or London, not Fools' Paradise."

Baxter's acceptance of the realities of his age makes the content of his teaching the more impressive. The attempt to formulate a casuistry of economic conduct obviously implies that economic relations are to be regarded merely as one department of human behavior, for which each man is morally responsible, not as the result of an impersonal mechanism, to which ethical judgments are irrelevant. Baxter declines, therefore, to admit the convenient dualism, which exonerates the individual by representing his actions as the outcome of uncontrollable forces. The Christian, he insists, is committed by his faith to the acceptance of certain ethical standards, and these standards are as obligatory in the sphere of economic transactions as in any other province of human activity. To the conventional objection that religion has nothing to do with business—that "every man will get as much as he can have and that *caveat emptor* is the only security"—he answers bluntly that this way of dealing does not hold among Christians. Whatever the laxity of the law, the Christian is bound to consider first the golden rule and the public good. Naturally, therefore, he is debarred from making money at the expense of other persons, and certain profitable avenues of commerce are closed to him at the outset. "It is not lawful to take up or keep up any oppressing monopoly or trade, which tends to enrich you by the loss of the Commonwealth or of many."

But the Christian must not only eschew the obvious extortion practiced by the monopolist, the engrosser, the organizer of a corner or a combine. He must carry on his business in the spirit of one who is conducting a public service; he must order it for the advantage of his neighbor as much as, and, if his neighbor be poor, more than, for his own. He must not desire "to get another's goods or labor for less than it is worth." He must not secure a good price for his own wares "by extortion working upon men's ignorance, error, or necessity." When prices are fixed by law, he must strictly observe the legal maximum; when they are not, he must follow the price fixed by common estimation. If he finds a buyer who is willing to give more, he "must not make too great an advantage of his convenience or desire, but be glad that [he] can pleasure him upon equal, fair, and honest terms," for "it is a false rule of them that think their commodity is worth as much as any one will give." If the seller foresees that in the future prices are likely to fall, he must not make profit out of his neighbor's ignorance, but must tell him so. If he foresees that they will rise, he may hold his wares back, but only—a somewhat embarrassing exception—if it be not "to the hurt of the Commonwealth, as if . . . keeping it in be the cause of the dearth, and . . . bringing it forth would help to prevent it." If he is buying from the poor, "charity must be exercised as well as justice"; the buyer must pay the full price that the goods are worth to himself, and, rather than let the seller suffer because he cannot stand out for his price, should offer him a loan or persuade some one else to do so. In no case may a man doctor his wares in order to get for them a higher price than they are really worth, and in no case may he conceal any defects of quality; if he was so unlucky as to have bought an inferior article, he "may not repair [his] loss by doing as [he] was done by, . . . no more than [he] may cut another's purse because [his] was cut." Rivalry in trade, Baxter thinks, is inevitable. But the Christian must not snatch a good bargain "out of greedy covetousness, nor to the injury of the poor . . . nor . . . so as to disturb that due and civil order which should be among moderate men in trading." On the contrary, if " a covetous oppressor" offer a poor man less than his goods are worth, "it may be a duty to offer the poor man the worth of his commodity and save him from the oppressor."

* * *

The first characteristic to strike the modern reader in all this teaching is its conservatism. In spite of the economic and political revolutions of the past two centuries, how small, after all, the change in the presentation of the social ethics of the Christian faith! A few months after the appearance of the *Christian Directory,* the Stop of the Exchequer tore a hole in the already intricate web of London finance, and sent a shiver through the money markets of Europe. But Baxter, though no mere antiquarian, discourses of equity in bargaining, of just prices, of reasonable rents, of the sin of usury, in the same tone, if not with quite the same conclusions, as a mediaeval Schoolman, and he differs from one of the later Doctors, like St. Antonino, hardly more than St. Antonino himself had differed from Aquinas. Seven years later Bunyan published *The Life and Death of*

Mr. Badman. Among the vices which it pilloried were the sin of extortion, "most commonly committed by men of trade, who without all conscience, when they have an advantage, will make a prey of their neighbour," the covetousness of "hucksters, that buy up the poor man's victual wholesale and sell it to him again for unreasonable gains," the avarice of usurers, who watch till "the poor fall into their mouths," and "of those vile wretches called pawnbrokers, that lend money and goods to poor people, who are by necessity forced to such an inconvenience, and will make by one trick or another the interest of what they so lend amount to thirty and forty, yea sometimes fifty pounds by the year." As Christian and Christiana watched Mr. Badman thus bite and pinch the poor in his shop in Bedford, before they took staff and scrip for their journey to a more distant City, they remembered that the Lord himself will plead the cause of the afflicted against them that oppress them, and reflected, taught by the dealings of Ephron the son of Zohar, and of David with Ormon the Jebusite, that there is a "wickedness, as in selling too dear, so in buying too cheap." Brother Berthold of Regensburg had said the same four centuries before, in his racy sermons in Germany. The emergence of the idea that "business is business," and that the world of commercial transactions is a closed compartment with laws of its own, if more ancient than is often supposed, did not win so painless a triumph as is sometimes suggested. Puritan as well as Catholic accepted without demur the view which set all human interests and activities within the compass of religion. Puritans, as well as Catholics, essayed the formidable task of formulating a Christian casuistry of economic conduct.

*   *   *

"The capitalist spirit" is as old as history, and was not, as has sometimes been said, the offspring of Puritanism. But it found in certain aspects of later Puritanism a tonic which braced its energies and fortified its already vigorous temper. At first sight, no contract could be more violent than that between the iron collectivism, the almost military discipline, the remorseless and violent rigors practiced in Calvin's Geneva, and preached elsewhere, if in a milder form, by his disciples, and the impatient rejection of all traditional restrictions on economic enterprise which was the temper of the English business world after the Civil War. In reality, the same ingredients were present throughout, but they were mixed in changing proportions, and exposed to different temperatures at different times. Like traits of individual character which are suppressed till the approach of maturity releases them, the tendencies in Puritanism, which were to make it later a potent ally of the movement against the control of economic relations in the name either of social morality or of the public interest, did not reveal themselves till political and economic changes had prepared a congenial environment for their growth. Nor, once those conditions were created, was it only England which witnessed the transformation. In all countries alike, in Holland, in America, in Scotland, in Geneva itself, the social theory of Calvinism went through the same process of development. It had begun by being the very soul of authoritarian regimentation. It ended by being the vehicle of an almost Utilitarian individualism. While social reformers in the sixteenth century could praise Calvin for his economic rigor, their successors in Restoration England, if of one persuasion, denounced him as the parent of economic license, if of another, applauded Calvinist communities for their commercial enterprise and for their freedom from antiquated prejudices on the subject of economic morality. So little do those who shoot the arrows of the spirit know where they will light. . . .

The England of Shakespeare and Bacon was still largely mediaeval in its economic organization and social outlook, more interested in maintaining customary standards of consumption than in accumulating capital for future production, with an aristocracy contemptuous of the economic virtues, a peasantry farming for subsistence amid the organized confusion of the open-field village, and a small, if growing, body of jealously conservative craftsmen. In such a society Puritanism worked like the yeast which sets the whole mass fermenting. It went through its slack and loosely knit texture like a troop of Cromwell's Ironsides through the disorderly cavalry of Rupert. Where, as in Ireland, the elements were so alien that assimilation was out of the question, the result was a wound that festered for three centuries. In England the effect was that at once of an irritant and of a tonic. Puritanism had its own standards of social conduct, derived partly from the obvious interests of the commercial classes, partly from its conception of the nature of God and the destiny of man. These standards were in sharp antithesis, both to the considerable surviving elements of feudalism in English society, and to the policy of the authoritarian State, with its ideal of an ordered and graded society, whose different members were to be maintained in their traditional status by the pressure and protection of a paternal monarchy. Sapping the former by its influence, and overthrowing the latter by direct attack, Puritanism became a potent force in preparing the way for the commercial civilization which finally triumphed at the Revolution.

*   *   *

. . . From the very beginning, Calvinism had comprised two elements, which Calvin himself had fused, but which contained the seeds of future discord. It had at once given a wholehearted *imprimatur* to the life of business enterprise, which most earlier moralists had regarded with suspicion, and had laid upon it the restraining hand of an inquisitorial discipline. At Geneva, where Calvinism was the creed of a small and homogeneous city, the second aspect had predominated; in the many-sided life of England, where there were numerous conflicting interests to balance it, and where it was long politically weak, the first. Then, in the late sixteenth and early seventeenth centuries, had come the wave of commercial and financial expansion—companies, colonies, capitalism in textiles, capitalism in mining, capitalism in finance—on the crest of which the English commercial classes, in Calvin's day still held in leading-strings by conservative statesmen, had climbed to a position of dignity and affluence.

Naturally, as the Puritan movement came to its own, these two elements flew apart. The collectivist, half-communistic aspect, which had never been acclimatized in England, quietly dropped out of notice, to crop up once more, and for the last time, to the disgust and terror of merchant and landowner, in the popular agitation under the Commonwealth. The individualism congenial to the world of business became the distinctive characteristic of a Puritanism which had arrived, and which, in becoming a political force, was at once secularized and committed to a career of compromise. Its note was not the attempt to establish on earth a "Kingdom of Christ," but an ideal of personal character and conduct, to be realized by the punctual discharge both of public and private duties. Its theory had been discipline; its practical result was liberty.

Given the social and political conditions of England, the transformation was inevitable. The incompatibility of Presbyterianism with the stratified arrangement of English society had been remarked by Hooker. If the City Fathers of Geneva had thrown off by the beginning of the seventeenth century the religious collectivism of Calvin's régime, it was not to be expected that the landowners and *bourgeoisie* of an aristocratic and increasingly commercial nation, however much Calvinist theology might appeal to them, would view with favor the social doctrines implied in Calvinist discipline. In the reign of the first two Stuarts, both economic interests and political theory pulled them hard in the opposite direction. "Merchant's doings," the man of business in Wilson's *Discourse upon Usury* had observed, "must not thus be overthwarted by preachers and others, that cannot skill of their dealings." Behind the elaborate facade of Tudor State control, which has attracted the attention of historians, an individualist movement had been steadily developing, which found expression in opposition to the traditional policy of stereotyping economic relations by checking enclosure, controlling food supplies and prices, interfering with the money market and regulating the conditions of the wage contract and of apprenticeship. In the first forty years of the seventeenth century, on grounds both of expediency and of principle, the commercial and propertied classes were becoming increasingly restive under the whole system, at once ambitious and inefficient, of economic paternalism. It was in the same sections of the community that both religious and economic dissatisfaction were most acute. Puritanism, with its idealization of the spiritual energies which found expression in the activities of business and industry, drew the isolated rivulets of discontent together, and swept them forward with the dignity and momentum of a religious and a social philosophy.

For it was not merely as the exponent of certain tenets as to theology and church government, but as the champion of interests and opinions embracing every side of the life of society, that the Puritan movement came into collision with the Crown. In reality, as is the case with most heroic ideologies, the social and religious aspects of Puritanism were not disentangled; they presented themselves, both to supporters and opponents, as different facets of a single scheme. "All that crossed the views of the needy courtiers, the proud encroaching priests, the thievish projectors, the lewd nobility and gentry . . . whoever could endure a sermon, modest

habit or conversation, or anything good—all these were Puritans."
The clash was not one of theories—a systematic and theoretical
individualism did not develop till after the Restoration—but of con-
tradictory economic interests and incompatible conceptions of social
expediency.

. . . What in Calvin had been a qualified concession to practical
exigencies, appeared in some of his later followers as a frank
idealization of the life of the trader, as the service of God and the
training ground of the soul. Discarding the suspicion of economic
motives, which had been as characteristic of the reformers as of
mediaeval theologians, Puritanism in its later phases added a halo
of ethical sanctification to the appeal of economic expediency, and
offered a moral creed, in which the duties of religion and the calls of
business ended their long estrangement in an unanticipated reconciliation. Its spokesmen pointed out, it is true, the peril to the soul
involved in a single-minded concentration on economic interests. The
enemy, however, was not riches, but the bad habits sometimes associated with them, and its warnings against an excessive preoccupation with the pursuit of gain wore more and more the air of afterthoughts, appended to teaching the main tendency and emphasis of
which were little affected by these incidental qualifications. It insisted, in short, that money-making, if not free from spiritual dangers,
was not a danger and nothing else, but that it could be, and ought to
be, carried on for the greater glory of God.

The conception to which it appealed to bridge the gulf sprang
from the very heart of Puritan theology. It was that expressed in the
characteristic and oft-used phrase, "a Calling." The rational order
of the universe is the work of God, and its plan requires that the
individual should labor for God's glory. There is a spiritual calling,
and a temporal calling. It is the first duty of the Christian to know
and believe in God; it is by faith that he will be saved. But faith is not
a mere profession, such as that of Talkative of Prating Row, whose
"religion is to make a noise." The only genuine faith is the faith
which produces works. "At the day of Doom men shall be judged
according to their fruits. It will not be said then, Did you believe? but,
Were you doers, or talkers only"? The second duty of the Christian
is to labor in the affairs of practical life, and this second duty is
subordinate only to the first. "God," wrote a Puritan divine, "doth
call every man and woman . . . to serve him in some peculiar employ-

ment in this world, both for their own and the common good. . . . The Great Governour of the world hath appointed to every man his proper post and province, and let him be never so active out of his sphere, he will be at a great loss, if he do not keep his own vineyard and mind his own business."

From this reiterated insistence on secular obligations as imposed by the divine will, it follows that, not withdrawal from the world, but the conscientious discharge of the duties of business, is among the loftiest of religious and moral virtues. "The begging friars and such monks as live only to themselves in no one thing to further their own subsistence or the good of mankind . . . yet have the confidence to boast of this their course as a state of perfection; which in very deed, as to the worthiness of it, falls short of the poorest cobbler, for his is a calling of God, and theirs is none." The idea was not a new one. Luther had advanced it as a weapon against monasticism. But for Luther, with his patriarchal outlook on economic affairs, the calling means normally that state of life in which the individual has been set by Heaven, and against which it is impiety to rebel. On the lips of Puritan divines, it is not an invitation to resignation, but the bugle-call which summons the elect to the long battle which will end only with their death. "The world is all before them." They are to hammer out their salvation, not merely *in vocatione,* but *per vocationem.* The calling is not a condition in which the individual is born, but a stren-uous and exacting enterprise, to be undertaken, indeed, under the guidance of Providence, but to be chosen by each man for himself, with a deep sense of his solemn responsibilities. "God hath given to man reason for this use, that he should first consider, then choose, then put in execution; and it is a preposterous and brutish thing to fix or fall upon any weighty business, such as a calling or condition of life, without a careful pondering it in the balance of sound reason."

Laborare est orare. By the Puritan moralist the ancient maxim is repeated with a new and intenser significance. The labor which he idealizes is not simply a requirement imposed by nature, or a punish-ment for the sin of Adam. It is itself a kind of ascetic discipline, more rigorous than that demanded of any order of mendicants—a disci-pline imposed by the will of God, and to be undergone, not in soli-tude, but in the punctual discharge of secular duties. It is not merely an economic means, to be laid aside when physical needs have been satisfied. It is a spiritual end, for in it alone can the soul find health, and it must be continued as an ethical duty long after it has ceased to be a material necessity. Work thus conceived stands at the very opposite pole from "good works," as they were understood, or misunderstood, by Protestants. They, it was thought, had been a series of single transactions, performed as compensation for particular sins, or out of anxiety to acquire merit. What is required of the Puritan is not individual meritorious acts, but a holy life—a system in which every element is grouped round a central idea, the service of God, from which all disturbing irrelevances have been pruned, and to which all minor interests are subordinated.

*   *   *

The springs of economic conduct lie in regions rarely penetrated by moralists, and to suggest a direct reaction of theory on practice would be paradoxical. But if the circumstances which determine that certain kinds of conduct shall be profitable are economic, those which decide that they shall be the object of general approval are primarily moral and intellectual. For conventions to be adopted with wholehearted enthusiasm, to be not merely tolerated, but applauded, to become the habit of a nation and the admiration of its philosophers, the second condition must be present as well as the first. The insistence among men of pecuniary motives, the strength of economic egotism, the appetite for gain—these are the commonplaces of every age and need no emphasis. What is significant is the change of standards which converted a natural frailty into a resounding virtue. After all, it appears, a man can serve two masters, for—so happily is the world disposed—he may be paid by one, while he works for the other. Between the old fashioned denunciation of uncharitable covetousness and the new-fashioned applause of economic enterprise, a bridge is thrown by the argument which urges that enterprise itself is the discharge of a duty imposed by God. . . .

The transition from the anabaptist to the company promoter was less abrupt than might at first sight be supposed. It had been prepared, however unintentionally, by Puritan moralists. In their emphasis on the moral duty of untiring activity, on work as an end in itself, on the evils of luxury and extravagance, on foresight and thrift, on moderation and self-discipline and rational calculation, they had created an ideal of Christian conduct, which canonized as an ethical principle the efficiency which economic theorists were preaching as a specific for social disorders. It was as captivating as it was novel. To countless generations of religious thinkers, the fundamental maxim of Christian social ethics had seemed to be expressed in the words of St. Paul to Timothy: "Having food and raiment, let us be therewith content. For the love of money is the root of all evil." Now, while, as always, the world battered at the gate, a new standard was raised within the citadel by its own defenders. The garrison had discovered that the invading host of economic appetites was, not an enemy, but an ally. Not sufficiency to the needs of daily life, but limitless increase and expansion, became the goal of the Christian's efforts. Not consumption, on which the eyes of earlier sages had been turned, but production, became the pivot of his argument. Not an easy-going and open-handed charity, but a systematic and methodical accumulation, won the need of praise that belongs to the good and faithful servant. The shrewd, calculating commercialism which tries all human relations by pecuniary standards, the acquisitiveness which cannot rest while there are competitors to be conquered or profits to be won, the love of social power and hunger for economic gain—these irrepressible appetites had evoked from time immemorial the warnings and denunciations of saints and sages. Plunged in the cleansing waters of later Puritanism, the qualities which less enlightened ages had denounced as social vices emerged as economic virtues. They emerged as moral virtues as well. For the world exists not to be enjoyed, but to be conquered. Only its conqueror deserves the name of Christian. For such a philosophy, the question, "What shall it profit a man?" carries no sting. In winning the world, he wins the salvation of his own soul as well.

Kurt Samuelsson

RELIGION AND ECONOMIC ACTION

While preparing a study on Max Weber for a collection of essays on economic history, Professor Kurt Samuelsson of the University of Stockholm was urged to write a separate book on Weber's ideas on Protestantism and capitalism. Ekonomie och religion *was the result. First published in 1957, it was translated into English as* Religion and Economic Action, *from which the following selection is taken. Dr. Samuelsson's many publications in economic history include studies of the great trading companies of Stockholm in the eighteenth century; and another of his works which has earned wide acclaim in translation as well as in the original Swedish is* From Great Power to Welfare State: Three Hundred Years of Swedish Social Development (London, 1968). *His activities as an economic historian, however, were possibly secondary to his work as an editor of* Dagens Nyheter, *considered Sweden's largest and most influential liberal newspaper, and to his editorial position on the Social Democratic newspaper* Aftonbladet *from 1961 to 1965. During the next three years he served as Director of the School of Social Studies in Stockholm where he still resides, now an established free-lance writer and radio and television commentator.* Ekonomie och religion *is the first major contribution in Swedish to the Weber thesis debate, and its translation into French in 1972 is a measure of its continuing impact on the controversy.*

One of the most widely read religious writers was Bunyan; enormous editions of his *Pilgrim's Progress* and *Life and Death of Mr. Badman* were printed. How does he deal with economic activity and the day-to-day observance of duty in general? Christian forsakes his family and his trade to seek the Kingdom of Heaven. In the course of his pilgrimage he meets a succession of persons representing the most common vices. They seek to entice him back into ordinary life. But he withstands the test. Years later, his wife and children follow his example. One of the vices that must be forsworn is avarice, the lust for riches. Christian walks proudly past the alluring silver mine, and those of his companions who succumb to the temptations of illusory wealth are buried in the mine and forfeit their celestial bliss. The businessmen whom Christian and his companion Faithful meet in Vanity Fair are wicked men, striving to become rich by satisfying men's desire for beautiful but vain objects. To renounce the world, not to serve it by fulfilling the daily call, is the way to salvation.

The idea of bringing God into worldly affairs, of regarding success and riches as a sign of piety and godliness is most emphatically rejected by Bunyan. The allegorical figure which represents the love of gold asks why a priest or a merchant should not, through displaying godliness, secure advancement and a larger income. The former thereby becomes a more able preacher and thus pursues his calling. The latter may perhaps get a rich wife and better customers by displaying this virtue; and godliness *is* a virtue irrespective of why it is practiced. Bunyan makes Christian repudiate such ideas. If it is unseemly to follow Christ for the sake of one's daily bread, then how infamous it is to make of religion and Christ the Lord a cloak under which to seek riches and worldly esteem. He who puts on piety and godliness for the sake of the world may just as well cast them off in favor of worldly success. This is the piety of Judas Iscariot, a piety tainted by lucre. The true piety is not of this world, and only by renunciation of this world can it be achieved.

> *Love not the world, neither the things that are in the world. If any man love the world, the love of the Father is not in him. For all that is in the world, the lust of the flesh, and the lust of the eyes, and the pride of life, is not of the Father, but is of the world. And the world passeth away, and the lust thereof: but he that doeth the will of God abideth for ever.*

These words from the First Epistle of John (2, xv–xvii) are *not* cited by Bunyan, but if there is any passage of the Bible that could be taken as a maxim for the pilgrimages of Christian and his wife, it would be difficult to find one that better epitomized the basic idea of both books. Estrangement from this world, and the avoidance of sin by means of wholly spiritual exertions, two of the strongest themes of Puritanism—and perhaps especially of Pietism—come very much into their own in Bunyan. There is nothing of that "worldly asceticism" which, according to Weber, so sharply differentiated the Puritan movements from Catholicism.

In Mr. Badman it is usury, unjust prices, covetousness and avarice, all of them "mostly commonly committed by men of trade" that are chiefly castigated. Mr. Badman is the shopkeeper who "bites and pinches the poor." Trade and traders represent evil.

In general, then, if there emerges from the most important writers and preachers of the various Puritan sects a single common factor in their approach to business life and economic activity, it is the exhortation to subordinate them to the requirements of Christian morality; and to moderate what are regarded as excesses, in the form not only of unjust prices and morally reprehensible transactions but also of rising turnover and expanding business. It is the picture of the small trader or craftsman, conducting his enterprise after the fashion of a good Christian, thinking of the general good, being kind to the poor, honorable in all transactions, free of the aspiration to enlarge his business and gain riches, that is portrayed as the ideal. The inculcation of habits of diligence and thrift was sought, but so too of contentment and restraint. It was made quite clear that special exertions were demanded of the wealthy and sucessful if they were to win salvation.

Tawney's observations about Baxter are much the same as those put forward here. Nevertheless he reaches the conclusion that "the capitalist spirit," though "as old as history found in certain aspects of Puritanism a tonic which braced its energies and fortified its already vigorous temper." How is this possible? It is made possible by means of a somersault in the best Weberian style. The Puritans tried to foster Christian morals and virtuous habits in their followers amongst the trading and industrial communities; they strove to evolve "a Christian casuistry of economic conduct." Unquestionably, this ought to have impeded rather than promoted a capitalistic trend. But, says Tawney, it did not succeed; and the roots of this failure are to be found not merely in the obstacles created by an economic environment that became ever more hostile as that capitalistic trend progressed, but primarily in "the soul of Puritanism itself." The Puritans did not range themselves against the admonitions of the traditional Christian ethic concerning the "numberless disguises assumed by the sin which sticketh fast between buying and selling," writes Tawney. Instead, the Puritan character offered "a polished surface on which these ghostly admonitions could find no enduring foot-hold. The rules of Christian morality elaborated by Baxter were subtle and sincere. But they were like seeds carried by birds from a distant and fertile plain and dropped upon a glacier. They were at once embalmed and sterilized in a river of ice. In Tawney's view, this icy soil was the true and genuine Puritan spirit which the Puritan fathers sought in vain to cultivate. Puritanism in some other and more capitalistic sense, by virtue of its superior strength over the doctrines proclaimed by its founders and greatest preachers, becomes the capitalistic spirit's principal source of power, even if not its creator as Weber alleged.

Could anything offer a better demonstration that this concoction, coming as it does from so brilliant a writer as Tawney, of how the whole concept of the contribution of Puritan teachings to the rise of capitalism has led to a hopeless morass of loose thinking, generalizations and reinterpretations. If we accept Tawney's view that no success was achieved by the efforts to induce entrepreneurs and merchants to make it their first duty to satisfy the demands of Christian morality and the common good, indeed deliberately to limit the scope of their operations and to shun riches (and there is good reason to agree with Tawney on this point), then the obvious conclusion is quite different from his: the economic views of the Puritans neither encouraged nor obstructed the spirit of capitalism. This spirit existed and throve quite independently of religious belief. Insofar as successful businessmen were also members of Puritan sects, they were not impelled to economic transactions by their religion. But sometimes they tried to construe these transactions, both to themselves and to others, in as favorable a religious light as possible; they thereby provided, to the confusion of posterity, an impression of a link that did not exist.

What was this true and genuine Puritanism, evidently so different from that preached by the foremost Puritan teachers? On what religious concepts was it based?

Neither Weber nor Tawney leaves us entirely without guidance on these important questions. The starting-point is the special Calvinist idea of vocation, the concept of the "calling." This idea, say Weber and Tawney, rested on Calvin's doctrine of election and predestination. Energy in daily work and success in his trade or vocation were signs that the individual was of the company chosen for salvation. And so in the long run, no matter how the Puritan fathers preached of the perils and the curse of riches, it was religion that inspired adherents of the Reformed church to unremitting diligence and the relentless accumulation of riches.

Is this view correct?

We can begin by noticing that Weber has difficulty in making up his mind on an extremely important point. Was success in his chosen work only a *sign* that the diligent person was of the elect, or was the practice of this virtue also a *means* of winning salvation? The former hypothesis is entirely consistent with the doctrine of predestination, although far from indispensable to it. The latter is logically incompatible with the doctrine of predetermined election: in His infinite knowledge and wisdom, God must have foreseen the attempt to influence His decision. Weber vacillates between the two ideas. The Calvinist, he says, "himself creates his own salvation," but adds for safety's sake "or, as would be more correct, the conviction of it." A fundamental distinction is thus neatly reduced to a mere matter of relative precision in phraseology. "However useless good works might be as a means of attaining salvation . . . they are indispensable as a sign of election. They are the technical means, not of purchasing salvation, but of getting rid of the fear of damnation." There follows a characteristic *non sequitur:* "in practice this means that God helps those who help themselves."

Weber admits that the idea of predestination did not always give birth to diligence and "worldly asceticism." Another and quite contrary contingency is open, and this second solution comes close to Lutheranism. Here, religious experience is expressed by a *Gefühlskultur,* colored by mysticism, rather than in the trade and worldly activity of Calvinism. He makes no attempt, however, to explain why this latter outcome should be found simply amongst the Calvinists, referring to it instead as a matter of common knowledge, undisputed and indisputable.

His whole exposition of the concept of predestination and the ethos of vocation, of the "sanctity of labor" in Calvinism, is, to put it mildly, of dubious validity. The concept of predestination was already fully evolved in St. Paul, and it was urged with much vigor by Augustine, in whose theology the doctrine of election, of the few chosen for salvation, was a central principle. Why it should be only in Calvin and Calvinism, not in St. Paul, Augustine or Luther, that the idea of the "sanctity of labor" came to be used, Weber is unable to explain. In fact, Calvin reveals not the faintest trace of any conception of the "sanctity of labor," of the prospect of changing God's decision, once made, or of obtaining knowledge of that decision through the medium of worldly success. For Calvin predestination was an inevitable consequence of the omniscience and infinite wisdom of God. To seek to influence or discover God's decision by means of work and worldly deeds was improper. Inner spiritual intuition was for Calvin as much as for Paul the only means of learning God's decision. To influence the decision in any way was unthinkable: God, who had foreseen and foreordained all, would also have foreseen this attempt to influence Him. Furthermore, predestination, both in Augustine and Calvin, had nothing to do with the goodness or wickedness of the individual or with good or wicked deeds. All men are wicked, born in original sin; all are doomed to perdition. But in His inscrutable mercy and to the glory of His holy name, God has chosen certain people for salvation.

Weber suggests that the concept of the "calling," the idea that God's decision can be influenced, appears in later Calvinist theologians. As late as 1647, at all events, the Confession of Westminister—which Weber himself quotes—clings to the same conception of predestination as Calvin held:

> Those of mankind that are predestinated unto life, God before the foundation of the world was laid, according to His eternal and immutable purpose, and the secret counsel and good pleasure of His will, hath chosen in Christ unto everlasting glory, out of His mere free grace and love, without any foresight of faith or good works, or perseverance in either of them, or any other thing in the creature as conditions, or causes moving Him thereunto, and all to the praise of His glorious grace.

The others, those doomed to perdition, nave been chosen in the same manner, without reference to deeds or faith, "for the glory of His sovereign power over His creatures." The same idea, expressed with varying degrees of clarity, can be found amongst the great Free Church preachers, in Wesley, Fox, Baxter, and Bunyan.

Unable to find in Calvin any support for his theory of the importance for the "sanctity of labor" of the concept of predestination, Weber turns instead to the ordinary Calvinist believer. Here is the same arbitrary method as can be seen in later writers: in van Gunsteren, when he deals with the same topic; in Tawney, both in his treatment of the doctrine of predestination and on the question of that true, genuine Puritan spirit, so utterly opposed to what the Puritan fathers sought to inculcate. The world was to be sanctified by toil and struggle. And the proof that Calvin's doctrine of predestination, so alien to this conception, could lead to this conclusion? Why,

Calvinism, with all its renunciation of personal gain, is so tremendously practical. The proposition that was to be proved must itself serve as proof.

Let us for a moment ignore the question of whether the ordinary Calvinist believer, despite Calvin and the later Calvinist preachers, regarded his industriousness as the sign that he was chosen, and indeed as a means of becoming chosen. Let us suppose that Weber, Tawney and van Gunsteren are right on this point. Their proof still does not hold. If, contrary to the essential tenets of Calvinist doctrine, the adherents of that doctrine adopt the belief suggested and then turn it into a vital component of their religious faith, does this not indicate a relationship directly the reverse of that suggested by Weber, Tawney and van Gunsteren? Does it not indicate that hardworking, economically successful men have elevated their industry and prosperity into religious virtue; that the ordinary civic virtues such as diligence, thrift and honesty in business have come to form an element of the faith of the believer? If, of course, a connection needs to be assumed at all.

In the earlier references to Brentano and Robertson it was shown how Weber wrongly assumes that the double connotation in the word "calling" (*Beruf*) is the sole property of Calvinism; the same double meaning is to be found, long before the Reformation, in the corresponding words of several languages. Something similar occurs in his account of predestination and industry, where the expression *gute Werke* is used. Tawney speaks of "good works" in the same way. These two expressions may signify both good deeds in the ordinary religious and ethical sense of "doing good," or they may alternatively denote a "good job of work." In the one connotation, only the industrious and persevering can boast of good works, *gute Werke*. In the other—surely far more customary and appropriate in religion—even the laziest and most incompetent can pride himself on his good deeds.

It is obviously this latter meaning that Calvin, Wesley, Fox, Penn and Baxter generally intend when they use the expression. In this they are following St. Paul. It is precisely this meaning that is apparent in the First Epistle to Timothy (6, xvii–xviii) and which guided the Free Church fathers in the sixteenth, seventeenth and eighteenth centuries. Aftter denouncing the pursuit of riches—for we brought nothing into this world, and it is certain we can carry nothing out—

and asserting the importance of contentment, St. Paul exhorts those who are already rich "that they do good, that they be rich in good works"; by this means they shall avoid entrusting their hopes to the vain riches of this world and escape the dangers that riches involve. At times St. Paul and the Calvinist writers are guilty, as we saw Baxter to be, of slipping into the connotation of "a good job of work" as suggested by Weber. But there is no hint of "unrelenting zeal" or of struggle to acquire riches as a sign of election or Divine love. The counsel of Baxter, Wesley, Fox and Penn—as well as St. Paul—in this kind of context includes no admonition to seek advancement and "fight one's way forward," but to remain in the station to which one has been called, industrious, faithful and content with one's lot. Perform your daily tasks without striving for advancement and riches, and devote your free time to serving God and doing good— this was the precept that circumscribed the business activities of so many Quakers. The mystically tinged *Gefühlskultur* which Weber alleged to be the property of Catholicism and Lutheran evangelism was by no means absent among the Puritans.

But we certainly do not find it in Benjamin Franklin, or in the great American captains of industry a hunded years later. The "capitalistic spirit" which they exhibit is not a culmination of the Puritanism encountered in the great fathers of the free sects. On the contrary, the feature that stands out is the utter dissimilarity of the one from the other.

Before dealing with this topic, however, a few words need to be said about the general trends of economic thought embraced in the overall evolution of ideas both before and after the Reformation. Naturally, they can only be discussed briefly. To omit them from the argument entirely, however, would be unduly to isolate our problems from their general context.

*   *   *

. . . The doctrine of diligence and thrift that was preached to mankind for three centuries—roughly the sixteenth, seventeenth and eighteenth—was not unique to Protestantism, Calvinism and the free religious sects. It constituted a most important feature of the moral outlook of mercantilism, which everywhere reigned supreme. It was preached in Catholic France with the same zeal as in Switzerland and the Netherlands.

Idleness and luxury were the great vices. Scarcely a single mercantilist writer or politician failed to emphasize the point. In England, some time before the Reformation, the abominableness of "idle and unprofitable" persons was vigorously proclaimed, and a number of sixteenth and seventeenth century writings free of all religious bias single out idleness as the "root of all evil," or the "foundation of all those vices which prevail amongst us," or are concerned lest it should "suck the breasts of industry." The abhorrence of idleness was even stronger in France, where this iniquitous phenomenon was most energically scourged. Idleness was "the grave of living men." In the matter of urging his subjects to diligence and thrift, Colbert was more ardent even than Calvin himself. Child labor—often starting at the age of six—was decreed because "experience has always certainly shown that idleness in the first years of a child's life is the real source of all the disorders in later life." This corresponds practically word for word with the view expressed by Wesley, and everywhere in vogue. It was, too, such universally held opinions that Cunningham, when he found them in Scotland, viewed as peculiarly Puritanical. In fact, the child labor in Scotland that Cunningham regarded as proof of Presbyterianism's ethos of toil was practiced with the same severity and on exactly the same grounds in Catholic France. In 1668, Colbert prescribed that in certain of the textile districts children should begin manufacturing work at the age of six so as to escape the perils of youthful idleness.

Luxury also was pilloried everywhere, at any rate when it manifested itself in circles other than the court and higher nobility or when not of direct importance as a sales outlet for native industries. When luxury produced utility in this latter way, it was unhesitatingly applauded, by Franklin for example. But otherwise, luxury and extravagance were harmful. Everywhere, merchants and manufacturers were sharply criticized on the ground that they neither worked nor saved hard enough, and that they perpetually resorted to credit instead of creating the capital they needed out of their own resources.

These attacks can, of course, be variously interpreted. The very zeal of the preachers may be seen as a sign that the virtues of diligence and thrift were more praised than practiced. Why emphasize so assiduously qualities universally present among the people? Or, leaving aside Weber's erroneous interpretation of the meaning of the doctrine of predestination, it may be suggested that there was a difference between, on the one hand, the effect produced by mercantilism's "utility doctrine," with its stress on the secular, and on the other, a religious conception that spiritual welfare was involved as well as temporal, indeed that temporal welfare was an index of the spiritual eternity awaiting the diligent and thrifty. There may be some truth in such hypotheses. Perhaps Colbert thundered so loudly because his rules were not being followed. Perhaps Calvin, aided by the power of religious faith and fanaticism, penetrated the roots of the soul more deeply and secured the translation of these injunctions into action.

But how far were they translated into action? To what extent were diligence and thrift virtues that were practiced in one place more than in another? And to what extent did they contribute to economic progress? No clear and unequivocal answer can be given. This absence of an answer is sufficient in itself. For as long as these questions cannot be answered, then at all events Weber's theory remains uncorroborated. Not only the influence of diligence and thrift upon economic progress but the very existence of these qualities must be substantiated if the Weberian correlation between them and Protestant doctrine is to bear any kind of meaning.

Even though a clear answer remains out of the question, there are, nevertheless, two relevant points which can be established.

Firstly, it is quite evident that, with few exceptions, those persons and classes in the most economically advanced countries who were the main representatives of the kind of economic activity relevant to the present purpose were not characterized by thrift in its strict Puritan or ascetic sense. It is true that contemporary complaints about the extravagant way of life of big merchants, manufacturers or ironmasters were exaggerated in the sense that such complaints overlooked the element of "competitive consumption," the essential business entertainment, the improvement of creditworthiness and enhancement of social standing that were contained in a high style of life. It is also true that the ratio of these costs to the total was greatly overestimated. This does not prevent the details recorded often being correct in themselves. Practical reality was as far removed from the frugality enjoined by Calvinism and Puritanism as it was possible to be. The palatial old residences of businessmen in one mercantile city after another—Berne, Geneva, Zürich, Amsterdam, Antwerp, London, Lübeck, Danzig, Stockholm—are testimony enough. Summer residences, country estates and pleasure yachts, records of servants, vehicles, clothes, funerals, weddings and other festivals complete the picture. A way of life verging on the lavish was far more typical than the pathological niggardliness that Calvin, Colbert and the Free Church fathers all exalted as the ideal.

Rockefeller and Carnegie are often instanced as examples of an almost morbid thriftiness. Yet the effective role of this trait—when it existed at all—was surely negligible. The great palaces, the princely courts with which such seigneurs surrounded themselves must not be obscured by the vision of the frugal meals or turned suits they may have affected. Many great capitalists have taken pleasure or snobbish pride in a certain personal simplicity, in economy over trivialities; and this has often duped both contemporaries and posterity. People note and magnify the image of a Rockefeller or a Morgan holding a glass of milk. In the popular image, should not such men drink champagne every morning? Or of a Carnegie in a turned suit. Surely a legendary figure in sables, his fingers glittering with precious stones?

Secondly, the whole concept of an intimate association between thrift and the large-scale accumulation of capital is doubtful. Obviously thrift and diligence were often a prerequisite of a successful start in life: the capital saved by parents or relatives, hard years of self-denial to secure sufficient education, to perfect an invention, to get an idea successfully launched, or to scrape up a little capital to branch out independently. Swedish industrial entrepreneurs, for example, seem usually to have followed moderate, if not exactly frugal, habits of life during the early years when they were establishing themselves. But standards rose as incomes rose, and among the fairly prosperous the standard of living seems generally to have been at a level appropriate to the upper class of the period. And thrift as a virtue of necessity rather than a virtue in itself is *not* what Weber meant, but the very antithesis of this.

Nor can thrift have been the principal means of amassing such concentrations of capital as the enormous fortunes of the great manufacturers and merchants in England and the Netherlands. The possession of great wealth and the command of really important capital assets—and this is what we must consider, not the painfully hoarded coppers of small traders and craftsmen—can scarcely have derived, even exceptionally, from "saving up" in the connotation usually implied by this expression, a connotation which Weber must also have intended if his argument is to make any sense at all. Although hard work has certainly and often made its contribution, great fortunes are, and for the most part always have been, the product of "fortunate speculations," of vast profits from vast risks and vast luck—in short, of speculation and capital gains usually in association with extensive structural changes and innovations in economic life.

Except in one or two instances during the modest early days, it was certainly not thrift that, in Sweden, brought riches to the Arfwedsons, Grills, Lefebures and Jennings, or later on to Wingquist, the Wallenbergs, the Johnsons and Wenner-Gren; nor was it thrift that made millionaires and multi-millionaires of the De Neufvilles, Hopes, Cliffords and Hogguers in eighteenth-century Holland, or of Morgan, Carnegie, Rockefeller, Vanderbilt and Harriman in nineteenth-century America. The determining factors were the volume and fortune of business, enormous capital gains on unexploited, or previously ill-exploited, natural assets, and the monopolization of markets or credit.

With few exceptions, all great fortunes, far-flung economic empires and individual concentrations of economic power have been built up at tremendous speed, in the course of a single generation, not of two or three (although time may have increased wealth still further), in a single decade or even a single year. As W. W. Jennings points out when discussing the great American fortunes, it needs no very advanced mathematics to demonstrate that thrift cannot have been the explanation of the wealth of such as Carnegie or Rockefeller. If Carnegie had saved 10,000 dollars a year he would have needed 4,500 years to reach 45 million dollars, i.e., he would have had to start at about the time that the pyramid of Cheops was built. It would not be proper to assume compound interest on the capital sums over this long period, because of course Carnegie only had a few decades at his disposal. When he retired, it was with a personal fortune of 375 million dollars. If John D. Rockefeller, who was estimated in 1921 to possess three thousand million dollars, had saved 100,000 dollars a year, he would have needed 30,000 years. At this time (1921) fifty American families had fortunes of over 100 million dollars each and a hundred families over 50 million dollars each. Let us take another example. Anyone who bought 20,000 dollars' worth of shares in General Motors in 1913 would have been worth about 15 million dollars in 1957. At 5 percent compound interest, it would need an annual saving of 200,000 dollars for at least 30 years to reach a like amount. "No man," Jennings sums up, "can legitimately save millions in a lifetime." Genius, sheer luck, a clear eye for market opportunities, a flair for publicity, hard work, low cunning, vast capital gains on natural assets—all these are possible and plausible factors. But to speak of thrift as a decisive or even substantial factor where large fortunes are concerned is utter nonsense.

For a purpose quite different from that of this book Frederick Lewis Allen analyzed a series of Horatio Alger's stories to see how the hero won his riches. Alger is one of the group of writers, religiously inclined and preaching thrift and diligence, cited by Wyllie and others; he is generally considered to have exerted a tremendous influence on the American sense of values. The hero of Alger's books was always a poor boy who finished up rich. His first steps on the road to success were invariably marked by the twin virtues of diligence and thrift. This much is in harmony with the Weber theory. But at the crucial point, this harmony vanishes. To have the little lad reach the higher realms of wealth simply through diligence and thrift was straining credulity much too far even in moralistic stories for young people. In the end, Alger always resorted to a gigantic inheritance, left to his hero by some previously unknown relative, or as a gift from a multi-millionaire who felt the virtuous boy to be worthy of a reward. Thrift and diligence were adequate instruments for winning the favor of rich relatives or bosses or millionaires' daughters, but not for achieving wealth single-handed. Alger understood, and appreciated that his young readers would also understand, something that had evidently never occurred to Weber: in the real world, capital formation by individuals, the accumulation of large fortunes, and the concentration of economic power all occur through a variety of different media, and virtuous work and assiduous saving are clearly among the less usual and less effective of these.

*   *   *

. . . The industrialization of England and Belgium is particularly interesting. To explain why these countries were the first to industrialize is an undertaking upon which we shall not embark. There are certainly many factors worthy of notice. But we cannot measure their internal significance. We cannot even determine whether the absence of one or another of them would have retarded or precluded industrialization.

To make a comparison with a country which became a powerful industrial nation much later, England differed from Germany at the end of the eighteenth and beginning of the nineteenth century primarily in its national unity, which had been maintained unbroken for centuries. In England there was a fairly integrated market within a comparatively small area with well-developed communications. Add to this the empire, which formed an additional source of raw materials and a partial outlet for finished products, and the contrast of markets with Germany, split as it was into a host of principalities, becomes very striking. Furthermore, England experienced relatively early the emergence of a fairly broad "middle class," i.e., of groups with purchasing power adequate to support industrial "mass production."

England differed from France and other mercantilist countries by virtue of the gradual disintegration of the system of economic regulation and corporate enterprise during the internal dissensions of the seventeenth and eighteenth centuries. Central authority never lost its grip on the body politic for very long. The market was not dismembered. But the mercantilist apparatus of control, sustained and exploited by guilds, corporations or chartered companies, broke down. Although still very much alive on paper, it signified little or nothing in practice. This apparatus of control had been contrived largely in order to protect the old-established economic organizations in trade, handicrafts and manufacturing from the competition of new types of enterprise. We know what difficulty new manufacturers must once have had to force an entry into the traditional, monopolistic system, and how difficult it must invariably have been for new forms of enterprise to prevail against the old wherever the latter were bolstered by organizations enjoying the support of the state. It is therefore easy to understand how greatly the decay of *dirigisme* and the system of monopolies facilitated the industrialization of England. Furthermore, a social revolution was working in the same direction. On the one hand there was the comparatively early rise of a fairly broad "middle class," in the sense defined above, and on the other, the early disruption of older social forms through the growth of population, the transformation of agricultural operations by the enclosure movement, and the emergence of a large landless class from which the new industrial districts could quickly recruit their supplies of labor.

The unity of the market and the wider freedom of movement for new enterprise were supplemented by an abundance of capital, low interest rates and a raw material, coal, that was vital to the new technology. If to this is added the fact that some of the most important inventions happened to be either made in or carried to England, then a large number of the most vital prerequisites of the industrial revolution in that country have been listed.

But was no influence exerted on all this by religion, by the strong Puritan element present in English society—and in particular precisely amongst those groups who, according to many observers, were chiefly responsible in their primary capacity as inventors and entrepreneurs for the industrialization of England? Perhaps an answer to this question can be supplied by a comparison with trends in Belgium. Belgium, of course, was the next country to industrialize and it therefore affords a particularly interesting contrast. A number of factors may be considered that seem to merit inclusion in any explanation of the rapid industrialization of Belgium.

Belgium had long been one of the foremost centers of manufacturing, especially of textiles. The Napoleonic Wars and the Continental System had forced industrial growth, as in a hothouse. The old system of regulation and the former ascendancy of guilds and companies had perished. Access to ore and coal; copious influx of capital which had long been flowing from Dutch mercantile houses; a geographical location propitious for the development of communications: to these important elements in stimulating Belgian industrialization must be added the pool of occupational skills, which had been a feature of the iron industry in the Walloon areas of the country for generations and which the new industrial districts could now exploit.

With the best will in the world, this country, for hundreds of years in the vanguard of economic advance and now pressing close upon the heels of England in the race to industrialize, cannot be fitted into the Weber framework. Belgium is and always has been quite overwhelmingly Catholic. (For a long time it had been anti-Jesuit Catholic too, and so does not fit the Robertson hypothesis either.) Only 2 or 3 percent of the inhabitants belong to non-Catholic denominations. Of these, something like half have been Jews in the last few centuries. The most important business and industrial districts have always been Catholic. The Protestant element, formerly as now, is so insignificant as not to be worth mentioning in the present context.

Thus, for both England and Belgium we can trace a number of factors, similar in kind, that may be seen as vital preconditions of the early arrival of the industrial revolution in these two countries. In the light of this knowledge, there is nothing puzzling in the fact that Belgium very quickly followed along the trail blazed by England— except from one angle of approach: if we start from the assumption that Weber was right. The great contrast between England and Belgium lay in the domain of religion. According to Weber's theory, Belgium ought to have lacked the most vital prerequisite of an industrialization that was very nearly as rapid as that of Protestant, Puritan-influenced England. But this difference brought no corresponding difference in economic expansion.

Of course, the association in Belgium of Catholicism and vigorous economic growth does not in itself exclude the possibility that Protestantism in general and the Puritan sects in particular made a substantial contribution to the economic development of England. But Belgium does at least supply a strong indication that Protestantism and Puritanism were not ingredients wholly indispensable to an economically progressive environment. At all events, food for thought is provided by the reflection that the one factor alleged by Weber to form a common characteristic of the successful should also be the principal factor differentiating the two most successful.

It seems, then, that even before the Reformation strong tendencies towards economic expansion were making themselves felt in the Netherlands and England; and that no correlation or "covariation" between economic and religious trends in these countries can be established. In Scotland and Switzerland, the sequence of events differs. Here, despite the fact that both countries were Protestant from the sixteenth century onwards, economic expansion does not begin until well into the eighteenth century, and it is then evident that its impetus derives from quite other factors than the religious. In New England too, despite a correlation that certainly appears superficially strong, we have been unable to find anything suggesting the existence of a connection, in the deeper meaning of the word, between Puritanism and capitalism; the Puritan South—for it has long been much more Puritan than the states of the North—is economically "under-developed." Portugal, an entirely Catholic country, was long in the van of the great expansion of the fifteenth and sixteenth centuries, and its chief mercantile city is still an important maritime and commercial center. Catholic Belgium was the first country in the world to industrialize after England; and it retains its status in the comity of industrial nations despite the ravages of two world wars.

*   *   *

. . . This is an appropriate point at which to reexamine the observation, fundamental to Weber's thesis, that in regions of Germany where religious faiths were mixed, Protestant children were sent more usually than Catholic children to schools where the mode of instruction was particularly suitable for future merchants and industrialists; and that Protestant journeymen were more ready than Catholic to abandon handicraft work and become artisans rather than masters. In this Weber saw one of the mystic effects of religious belief.

The first thing to be said about the influence upon journeymen of membership of a particular religious faith is that, insofar as any generally significant and statistically verifiable variation in the volume of movement into industry can be revealed, factors quite other than *die geistige eigenart** could clearly have been responsible; for instance, the industrial demand for artisans may have chanced to be particularly brisk or the opportunities for making a living out of handicraft work particularly few in some of the Protestant districts. But aside from the fact that a variety of explanations is possible, to construe the movement into industrial wage-labor as a sign of the economically progressive spirit of the individual is surely a most curious hypothesis. Save for a few particularly unremunerative handicraft trades outside industry and a few well-placed groups of artisans within it, it was more desirable to become a master tradesman than

---

* Mental and spiritual peculiarities derived from environment—Ed.

a factory worker. The economic, social, and perhaps also the cultural, standard of the former was, or was believed to be, far superior to that of the latter. And it is still much the same today; that it was so in Weber's time and during the *Gründerperiod* that was nearest to him is beyond question. The skilled factory workers of that era were nowhere particularly numerous, particularly well educated or particularly well paid.

Furthermore, quite apart from considerations of social and economic status, the master tradesman as a rule certainly carried a heavier economic responsibility than the wage-earning artisan and had a great need of the "spirit of enterprise." The master tradesman was not infrequently the very man who developed into the industrial entrepreneur. And in that case, Weber's own information shows that the Catholics, not the Protestants, should be regarded as being the better endowed with the "spirit of capitalism."

Weber clearly attached much more importance, however, to the data extracted from Offenbacher's paper, classifying pupils at nonobligatory secondary schools by religious faith. Weber reproduces one of Offenbacher's tables, showing that in 1895, while 37 percent of the inhabitants of Baden were Protestants, 61 percent Catholics and between 1 and 2 percent Jews, 48 percent of secondary school pupils were Protestants, 42 percent Catholics and 10 percent Jews. Both Offenbacher and Weber were at pains to stress the extreme importance of the fact that this relative Protestant preponderance was particularly noticeable in the *Realgymnasien* and *Oberrealschulen.* (We may for the moment ignore the fact that a typographical or arithmetical error—see below—led them to overvalue the proportion of Protestants by ten units, equivalent to a good 15 percent.)

Weber offers no figures other than those above. But Offenbacher also gives figures for the population of Baden as a whole, classified by religious faith: Protestants 638,000, Catholics 1,057,000, Jews 26,000, making a total of rather more than 1.7 million. Neither author tells us how many pupils there were in the schools investigated. However, the *Statistisches Jahrbuch für das Grossherzogthum Baden* for 1895–1896 discloses that the total numbers for that academic year amounted to 14,587 pupils, of whom 12,138 were male. All the girls attended special *Mittelschulen für die weibliche Jugend* and are of no interest in the present context. The table which follows classifies the 12,138 boys by religious faith and types of school:

	Protestants	Catholics	Jews	Others	Totals
Gymnasien	2,073	2,095	329	26	4,523
Realgymnasien	787	577	137	3	1,504
Oberrealschulen	789	648	89	12	1,538
Realschulen	1,537	1,317	337	16	3,207
Höhere Bürgerschulen	655	551	160	0	1,366
Totals	5,841	5,188	1,052	57	12,138

In his table of percentages, Offenbacher used average figures for the years 1885–1895. The percentages he obtained therefore differ from those which can be derived from the table for the academic year 1895–1896. The comparison is very interesting:

	1895–1896			
	Protestants	Catholics	Jews	Total
Gymnasien	46	47	7	100
Realgymnasien	52	39	9	100
Oberrealschulen	52	43	5	100
Realschulen	48	41	11	100
Höhere Bürgerschulen	47	40	13	100
Totals	48	43	9	100

	1885–1895			
	Protestants	Catholics	Jews	Total
Gymnasien	43	46	9.5	98.5
Realgymnasien	59	31	9	99
Oberrealschulen	52	41	7	100
Realschulen	49	40	11	100
Höhere Bürgerschulen	51	37	12	100
Totals	48	43	12	100

The aggregate average for the academic year 1895–1896 corresponds fairly closely with that derived from an average calculation for the decade 1885–1895. But the disparities as between the various categories of school taken separately are notably less marked in the academic year 1895–1896. Protestants are about as numerous as Catholics in the *Gymnasien;* in the *Realgymnasien* and *Oberrealschulen* their preponderance is much less considerable; and in the

Realschulen too the proportions are rather more even. (Through a typographical or arithmetical error, Offenbacher also made the proportion of Protestants in the *Realgymnasien* 69 percent *instead* of 59 percent; Weber later took over and used this incorrect figure.)

It would certainly be wrong to view these differences as indicating a trend; such deviations arise from fluctuations in particular years. If we refer back to 1884, the year before Offenbacher's averages start, the proportions are more similar to those of 1895 than to the averages for the intervening period: the Catholic aggregate is 43 percent, with 47 percent in the *Gymnasien,* 36 percent in the *Realgymnasien,* 42 percent in the *Realschulen* and 40 percent in the *Oberrealschulen.*

At this stage it is imperative to evaluate these figures and their fluctuations; a matter which Offenbacher and Weber evade by giving only relative figures. Of the 12,000 persons concerned in 1895—and the proportions were similar in 1884—4,500, which is to say nearly 40 percent, went to the *Gymnasien,* the division between Protestants and Catholics being generally about even. Only 1,500 went to *Realgymnasien,* i.e., only 12 percent of the total. No reliable evidence can emerge from a comparison between the percentage proportions of Catholics and Protestants comprised in the whole population of 1.7 million and the corresponding proportions in a total of 1,500 school children. For only relatively small absolute movements of the latter figures are needed to change the percentage figures appreciably, as the discrepancies between Offenbacher's average values and the values for 1895 also demonstrate. One newly established school in a district with a preponderance of Catholic or Protestant inhabitants is sufficient to distort the statistics.

This brings us to a particularly serious point. Neither Offenbacher nor Weber tried to ascertain in what proportions the various denominations were represented among the inhabitants of those school districts where Protestants predominated in the schools. Let us take the *Realgymnasien,* in which, according to Offenbacher, 59 percent of the pupils were Protestant and according to the figures for the academic year 1895–1896, 52 percent. These schools turn out to have been situated in the following districts: Karlsruhe, Mannheim, Ettenheim, Mosbach, Billingen and Weinheim. If we count only the two Christian denominations, in 1895 almost exactly 55 percent of the inhabitants of these districts were Protestant. Even in detail, the conformity is so close that in Ettenheim and Billingen, where Protestants accounted for only 13 and 32 percent respectively of the Christian population, they accounted for 13 and 23 percent respectively of the Christians in the *Realgymnasien.* In Buchen, Schweitzingen, Wiesloch and Ettlingen there was a group of *Höhere Bürgerschulen,* separately recorded in the statistics, to which Catholics contributed 59 percent of the Christian children. In these districts Catholics constituted 58 percent of the population. In Schweitzingen Protestants were rather more numerous both in the category of school in question and in the population as a whole. In the city of Baden there were twice as many Catholics as Protestants; the Catholic enrollment in the Baden *Realschulen* was almost exactly twice the Protestant. In Ueberlingen and Waldshut, with over 70 percent Catholics, the *Realschulen* were over 70 percent Catholic.

Thus, school by school and district by district it appears that the proportions of school children classified by religious faith are almost exactly the same as the corresponding proportion of the total populations of the appropriate district. That the Protestants in Baden as a whole display a "school frequency" higher than their share in the aggregate population is thus due entirely to the fact that more Protestants than Catholics lived in districts where *Realgymnasien, Höhere Bürgerschulen* and *Realschulen* were available. If one reckons not in terms of total population but of inhabitants of districts containing the respective categories of schools, there remain no differences worth mentioning.

How trivial the business was, even on Offenbacher's own accounting principles, is disclosed by certain data that he regards as specially significant. In the years 1891–1894, he declares, 35 Protestants but only 14 Catholics chose the career of an officer. In what way the officer corps could be considered more "capitalistic" than the priesthood, which was a more usual career amongst Catholics, is not specified. Eleven Protestants and 9 Catholics went in for accountancy, 142 Protestants and 111 Catholics chose the law, and 54 Protestants and 51 Catholics entered medicine. In civil and mechanical engineering and chemistry there were 54 Protestants as against 22 Catholics. At the same time, however, Catholics preponderated in the two economic fields of public finance and financial legislation—in both cases 71 percent of the total. Veterinary surgeons were almost wholly

Catholics; the larger landed estates in Baden were almost all owned by Catholic families.

To draw conclusions about *die geistige Eigenart* of Protestants and Catholics respectively, from such figures as these is surely absurd. The whole Weberian correlation, based on school conditions in Baden, turns out to hinge upon the simple fact that in certain towns with a particularly large Protestant majority in a country otherwise predominantly Catholic there were more Protestants than Catholics at the secondary schools. If the religious denominations of the children are compared with demographic conditions in each individual school district, Catholics and Protestants exhibit precisely the same "propensity for schooling." In brief, Weber's alleged difference is a myth.

In addition to the schools, first Offenbacher and then Weber refer to the distribution of wealth. Protestants are said to be richer than Catholics. It is evident that the material produced as evidence is, to say the least, unreliable, consisting as it does of taxation figures. Methodologically worse than this, however, is the fact that the material is dragooned into yielding conclusions that would be inadmissible even if the sources were unexceptionable.

In 1897, taxable wealth in Baden amounted to 4.7 billion marks. Of this 1.6 billion belonged to Protestants, 0.3 billion to Jews and 2.8 billion to Catholics. Thus Catholics held about 60 percent of the total wealth known to the tax inspectorate; in other words, their share of statistically recorded wealth corresponded almost exactly with their representation in the total population. But, says Offenbacher, the situation is different where interest on capital is concerned. There it is the Jews who come first, followed by the Protestants. Here is his table, using the original nomenclature of the Grand Duchy of Baden, so as to avoid all confusion of meaning:

Capital attributable to: (percentages)	Protestants	Jews	Catholics
1. Grund-, Häuser- und Gewerbesteuer	28.1	4.4	67.5
2. Spezielle Einkommensteuer	37.2	7.5	55.3
3. Kapitalrentensteuer	45.5	8.3	46.2

Offenbacher is only interested in item 3, where Protestants were "over-represented." At the 1895 census, he adds, the capital assets comprised in this item worked out at 4.1 million marks per 1,000 Jews, 0.95 million marks per 1,000 Protestants and only 0.59 million marks per 1,000 Catholics. This, he claims, reveals the intimate connection between the superior education of Protestants and their higher incomes.

In fact, on Offenbacher's own mode of calculation it is the Jews whose average wealth in terms of this form of capital asset stands revealed as noteworthy. The difference between Protestants and Catholics is moderate by comparison. So, *die geistige Eigenart* must have been particularly well developed among the Jews, whom we have already seen to have been "over-represented" in the schools. The true explanation is quite different and more credible. In Baden there happened to be a relatively large number of rich Jews and not very many poor ones, and since it was only exceptionally that landed property entered into the composition of Jewish fortunes, the fortunes of rich Jews were channelled into forms of investment that weighed particularly heavily under the heading *Kapitalrentensteur*. A study of Russia, Poland or the United States, for example, where there were large numbers of poor Jews at this time, would have produced low average values. Thus, the same Judaism that promoted business aptitude in certain states engendered business ineptitude in others. Very odd.

Yet the situation of the Protestants is in principle the same. As we have seen from the foregoing, they tended to live in towns to a far greater extent than the Catholics; obviously this would cause them to invest their money differently. Offenbacher has this situation clearly in mind when discussing real assets; he cites figures which disclose that 61.5 percent of the Catholics but only 46.5 percent of the Protestants lived in communities with less than 2,000 inhabitants, while 24.3 percent of the Protestants but only 13 percent of the Catholics lived in communities with over 20,000 inhabitants. A comparison of urban with rural Catholics reveals the same differences in the form of capital investment as Offenbacher postulates for Protestants as compared with Catholics. Regional distribution, not religion, is the primary factor.

This raises a further question. May there not have been religious causes leading to this Protestant preponderance in towns, especially the larger ones? Does not a correlation exist after all, even though Offenbacher and Weber discovered it by the roundabout route of "school frequency" and distribution of wealth instead of by exploring residential distribution direct? The possibility obviously cannot be dismissed out of hand. But in the first place, it is clear that the whole line of reasoning becomes much more complex than it would be if it could be shown that, *under otherwise similar circumstances,* Protestants displayed a greater "propensity for schooling" than Catholics. It is a priori arguable that *die geistige Eigenart* might affect this propensity, the form taken by capital accumulation, and similar direct patterns of conduct. That it should also promote human migration on any appreciable scale is a notion that carries little plausibility—it should be observed that this is not a question of migration occasioned by religious persecution but by *die geistige Eigenart,* in other words, it was voluntary, or as one might say, generated solely by "inner compulsion." In the second place, quite a large measure of correlation could exist between Protestantism and residence in large towns without the explanation necessarily being that people were impelled by their religious faith to congregate in towns. Protestantism was the new religion. It is not inconceivable that in certain parts of Germany the towns were the easiest places for disseminating propaganda; more people were reached, perhaps less conservative resistance was encountered than in the country—and, moreover, the ideology of the French Revolution made its strongest appeal to urban dwellers. It is not impossible that townspeople may have become Protestants because they were townspeople, thus luring Offenbacher and Weber into making false correlations from such unremarkable facts as that urban dwellers tended to hold their capital in forms other than land, that schools tended to be located in towns, and that landless citizens tended to become engineers rather than veterinary surgeons.

There is worse to come. The fact that Protestants tended to live in large towns, and conversely that the inhabitants of large towns tended to be Protestants, is a proposition that held good in Baden and certain other parts of Germany but which is by no means universally applicable. A multitude of historical accidents enter into the equation. At least 90 percent of the rural population of the United States are Protestants of one sort or another—insofar as they belong to any church at all. The Catholics live in urban areas, especially the large cities of the eastern states. The "Puritanism" that is practiced in these quarters, particularly by the Irish Catholics, may even be more rigid than Weber's idea of "real" Puritanism. And as for the conversion to Protestantism of various groups in Germany—a quotation from Offenbacher himself is to the point:

> *In accordance with the principle* cuius regio, eius religio *the determining influence was not as a rule the social and religious convictions of the masses but the religious posture adopted by the secular ruler, which was conditioned by a combination of political and strictly spiritual factors and was usually unaffected by economic considerations.*

This should already have been a clear warning signal to Weber.

The crucial factor determining which school course was chosen in Baden was—let it be repeated—quite simply the educational facilities available in the particular district. But this fact is obscured by the average figures for the country as a whole, and a false correlation between religious faith and school attendance creeps in. With the help of this observation the scope of our criticism of Weber can be enlarged. Weber fell into error by starting from the assumption that Protestants, especially Puritans, and Catholics were the real "primary groups." The economic divergences which he thought he had discovered—and we have seen in the case of Fugger and Alberti how artificial these often were—are interpreted in terms of religion as the "primary factor."

In just the same way and using exactly the same material as a base, Weber and his successors could have "proved" that geographical or climatic conditions were responsible for the great economic contrasts. Thus, in recent years northern Europe has been more prosperous than southern Europe (and incidentally Belgium can be accounted for by this theory), while on the other side of the Atlantic, North America as a whole has been more prosperous than South America, and the northern part of North America itself far more prosperous than the south. Or equally, Weber could have worked on the hypothesis of the "Teutonic" and "Latin" races—generalizations would be based on degrees of "contamination" or "improvement" by blood of other racial stocks: it is all a question of "ideal types"— and he could thus have "proved" the Teutons to be cleverer than other races and to have a more "capitalistic" approach to life.

In fact, in all such "proofs" we can never escape the absurdities of circular reasoning. In the last analysis, all we can establish is that merchants and manufacturers were more interested in commerce and industry than were landowners and farmers; that many schools in large mecantile cities taught commercial subjects; that a state, province or city where industrialization was in progress quite soon developed an interest in technical education for children and young persons; that diligent people worked harder, saved more and no doubt went to church more often than the careless and lazy.

Wherever a state turned from Catholicism to Protestantism (whether by royal decree as in England, Scandinavia and many states of Germany, or after a national struggle for liberation as in the Netherlands) we have magnificent raw material for constructing specious correlations and causal connections between Protestantism on the one hand and educational systems and occupational preferences on the other. Sometimes, perhaps, it may even have been that a sovereign's success in shaking off the fetters of Rome proceeded from his country's economic strength, and therewith—in that era of money-hungry mercenary armies—its military strength. In such a case as this—here of course much simplified—the nation in question could be regarded as having become Protestant because it was rich, even though the connection was indirect. But the manner of the transition, it should be noted, is quite different from Robertson's concept of the propagation of religion through economic channels.

In other words, we can produce pretty well whatever correlation or causal connection we like, according as we start from this feature or that as the "primary" or "differentiating" factor. The number of possible variations is so large that only one conclusion seems possible: we must refrain, in the interests of truth and common sense, from *all* such generalizations.

Weber's hypothesis of a direct correlation between Puritanism and economic progress represents a generalization which, quite apart from the question of its factual basis, is methodologically inadmissible. The two phenomena are so vague and universal as to be incapable of evaluation by the technique of correlation. Moreover, Weber's own definitions are exceedingly imprecise. "Protestantism" is used in a variety of different connotations. Sometimes it means Protestantism in general. Even here we run into the difficulty of drawing the boundary with Reformist-flavored Catholicism. Usually, however, Weber includes in it "only" Calvinism and the Free Church sects—it is apparent that the strong links between Puritanism and the Lutheran school of thought, through such creeds as Moravianism and Pietism, are to be excluded. Sometimes he speaks of "original" and sometimes of "later" Calvinism—but how are these two stages of Calvinism to be distinguished from one another in the context of Weber's theory? Sometimes, like Tawney later, he postulates a Puritanism that is "true and genuine," "Puritan" in a deeper sense and specifically distinct from that of the great Puritan fathers. The fallacy of this gyration has already been demonstrated. Finally, Weber hits on the idea that what he really means is what he calls the secularized Puritanism of Benjamin Franklin. He serenely ignores the fact that the strong influence of Puritanism upon economic development over a span of nearly three hundred years before Franklin, which he himself postulated, thereby becomes difficult to explain.

It is even more impossible, if that were conceivable, to devise any precise definition of the second factor, "capitalism" and the "spirit of capitalism." The very fact that numerous authors have labored assiduously to make capitalism pedagogically manageable by fabricating such concepts as "pre-capitalism" and "mercantile capitalism," not to mention "pre-capitalistic capitalism" and "high capitalism," reveals how hazy it all is. There are no clear definitions nor even any reasonably distinct periods to work with. The very fact that, even where the final economic outcome seems to have amounted to the same thing, development did not however pass through the same stages in every country, makes it impossible to define capitalism and its various periods closely. England, Germany, the United States, Russia—the mere mention of these countries proclaims that any sufficiently unambiguous definitions of "economic growth," "capitalism" and "industrialization" are impossible. To quote Marc Bloch, capitalism has as many birth certificates as there are historians studying the subject.

Weber himself appears to have sensed this. At all events, it seems probable that it was a feeling of uncertainty in formulating his concepts that caused him to shift from "capitalism" to "capitalistic spirit." He could define the latter pretty much as he liked—using the circular arguments described [earlier].

Weber worked in terms of what he called "ideal types." The very term itself shows that these are theoretical constructions conjured up for the purpose of making simple models, unambiguous in conception, that will elucidate vital themes of social evolution. In principle there is nothing objectionable in this approach. The error lay in the fact that Weber's "ideal types" were anything but unambiguous in conception. In attempting to make his "ideal types" faithful to reality and historical truth, he rendered them much too complex to be "ideal types," thus contravening the principles of the "model method" and losing sight of the need for firm definition. A model constructed on these eccentric lines was then employed, not as a theoretical structure, but as an interpretation of reality. The resulting explanation could scarcely fail to be pure nonsense.

In the guise of "ideal types" the Reformation, the later Puritanism and the Free Church sects appeared much more clearly divorced from another "ideal type," Catholicism, than they were in reality. All transitional forms, everything they had in common, were lost. Differences were grossly exaggerated. The same sort of treatment was given to "capitalism" and the "capitalistic spirit" in Puritan countries on the one hand, and to economic life and thought in Catholic countries on the other. Rationalism was depicted as a unique and vital characteristic of Quaker manufacturers in England and Methodist millionaires in the United States. But the highly developed rationalism, in Weber's own meaning, to be found in the Catholic families of Fugger and Brentano was explained away. It was simply declared to be a quite different rationalism from that of the Puritans and Franklin.

The complete arbitrariness of the technique of coupling, of "correlating," such vaguely defined and in fact indefinable phenomena should be obvious to anyone. It is strange that so many authors after Weber have been able to study his theories without pausing before his basic weakness: the fogginess of the concepts he employs. Perhaps the explanation is that Weber's theories have been universally viewed as a rebuttal of the materialist interpretation of history.

Even aside from the extreme vagueness of his concepts, Weber's method is unwarrantable. There is no justification for isolating, as he did, a single factor in a prolonged and intricate pattern of development—no matter how clearly definable or capable of isolation from other factors—and correlating it with a vast aspect of the whole history of Western civilization. It is in general a hopeless undertaking to try to isolate one particular factor even from a relatively limited sequence of events, in one particular country and over a very short period of time, with the object of determining the extent to which the factor in question evolved in harmony with the general process under consideration, i.e., the degree of "correlation" and "covariation." But Weber does not hesitate to embark on such an undertaking for so complex a phenomenon as Puritanism and for so wide a concept as economic development, not over a short period but over about four hundred years, not in a limited geographical region but over the Western world as a whole!

> *Lay not up for yourselves treasures upon earth, where moth and rust doth corrupt, and where thieves break through and steal: But lay up for yourselves treasures in heaven, where neither moth nor rust doth corrupt, and where thieves do not break through nor steal: For where your treasure is, there will your heart be also.*

These verses from the Sermon on the Mount are fundamental to the Christian outlook. No matter what the church or sect, the guiding principle is the renunciation of the world and the quest for a secure place in the Kingdom of Heaven. The doctrine of predestination, which permeates the whole of Pauline Christianity and was not invented by Calvin or the Puritans, does not alter this fact. On the contrary, it may rather have intensified the sense of estrangement from things temporal and the resolve to lay up treasures in heaven and not on earth. Insofar as worldly affairs claimed any interest, they were measured in terms of eternity and the Kingdom of Heaven. Insofar as economic problems were considered, the aim was to subordinate business and enterprise to a rigorous Christian code of morality that obstructed and confined them. Calvin, Wesley and Baxter did not differ from Paul, Augustine or Thomas Aquinas in this matter.

Mercantilism, the Enlightenment, Darwinism, economic liberalism —all these systems of thought, in which a central role was played by economic expansion and the belief in a better future for nations or men through the increase of capital and the raising of standard of welfare—cut across all religious creeds, or went over or around them. The elements of these philosophies that were fundamental from the economic point of view were not borrowed from Protestantism and Puritanism but were entirely separate from and unrelated to these religious faiths: rationalism, faith in capitalism and the blessings of capitalism, the demand for untrammelled liberty for—to quote the spokesman of the American mineowners in the coal strike of 1902, George F. Baer—"the Christian men to whom our God in His infinite wisdom has given control of the property interest of the country."

Although the rationalism of the Enlightenment, the "survival-of-the-fittest" notions of social Darwinism, and laissez-faire liberalism were all able to exhibit themselves to advantage in both the ideological and the practical worlds, this did not always or even usually imply the emancipation of the individual from religious faith, from belief in God the Redeemer. God and Mammon were unconcernedly worshipped at one and the same time, and God was equated with Mammon. Under the environmental influence of wealth, enterprise and speculation—from which the churches too received economic benefits—priests and preachers began to hail capitalists, entrepreneurs and speculators as the elect of God. But it is over-hasty to infer from this that Protestantism and Puritanism created capitalism and capitalists, or were a necessary prerequisite of their rise to a position of dominance. In all religious faiths, the servants of God have invoked Him as a guarantee of the righteousness and prosperity of their own social class, their own nation, their own race—in short their own interests. But we cannot assert that Christianity was therefore the cause of all the oppression of one social class by another that has been committed in God's name, or of all the wars in which the weapons have been blessed by Christian priests, or of all the aggressions perpetrated by representatives of the white races upon other peoples in the alleged service of God and the Holy Trinity.

Thus, our scrutiny of Puritan doctrine and capitalist ideology, of the capitalistic spirit that Weber saw personified in Benjamin Franklin and the American captains of industry, has rendered untenable the hypothesis of a connection between Puritanism and capitalism in which religion motivated economics.

Nor have we found Weber's theories tenable in the matter of the special Puritan virtues of diligence and thrift that he postulated. In the first place it is uncertain what role they played in economic expansion at all; secondly, the Puritans were undoubtedly not alone in their endeavor to inculcate diligence and thrift. These virtues were preached as zealously in Catholic France as in Puritan Scotland.

Similar considerations have been found to apply to the problem of usury. The approach of Calvin and his successors was not intrinsically different from that of Catholicism; emancipation was achieved independently, as it were, of the religious code. For hundreds of years after the Reformation, in Protestant countries as well as Catholic, the attempt to keep interest rates down and enforce low legal maxima largely continued to find expression in the secular, commercial law dictated by mercantilism. Furthermore, it cannot be determined whether high and freely moving interest rates promoted economic expansion or whether it was not the contrary phenomenon of low rates of interest that was a more effective force encouraging expansion.

The correlation from which Weber started we have also found dubious, aside from the impossibility, in the last resort, of correlating concepts as broad and vague as those in question. Even if, speaking in quite general terms, Protestant countries did in fact achieve greater economic prosperity than Catholic, it is evident in the first place that the range of variations within the Protestant group, just as in the Catholic group, is very wide, and secondly that the Protestant states have no position of preeminence over the Catholic, nor the Puritan states over the rest of the Protestant group.

Persons of Free Church and Puritan persuasion have sometimes made outstanding contributions to economic life. But this fact constitutes no justification for linking economic success with religious faith. In many instances there are more plausible explanations, such as special education, family relationships and alien status; or that within the groups subjected to religious persecution it was the merchants who migrated and were received by other countries with particular eagerness and especially good prospects of success; or that the practice of religion and a certain degree of prosperity were associated with a generally industrious personality—and that industriousness was the primary factor. It is plain, however, that in many respects the contribution of Free Church denominations has been violently exaggerated. The formed a quite small element in a broad and general phenomenon, as is shown by an analysis of such factors as the influence of family relationships and the "role of foreigners" in trade. It is simply that this tiny element is the one that has been particularly noticed.

Thus our conclusion is that, whether we start from the doctrines of Puritanism and "capitalism" or from the actual concept of a correlation between religion and economic action, we can find no support for Weber's theories. Almost all the evidence contradicts them.

Niles M. Hansen
SOURCES OF ECONOMIC RATIONALITY

A Professor of Economics and a member of the graduate faculty at the Austin campus of the University of Texas, Dr. Hansen is particularly interested in the fields of regional and urban economics, statistics, and comparative economic systems. He completed his undergraduate work at Centre College, Kentucky and earned his advanced degrees at the University of Indiana. He has written extensively on the economic aspects of both European and American planned regional growth and teaches advanced courses on comparative economic systems, quantitative economics, economic statistics, and prices and economic organization. While several of Professor Hansen's publications deal with the Weber thesis, the following selection was chosen because it is intended specifically as an evaluation of Professor Samuelsson's view of the Weber thesis.

Professor Kurt Samuelsson's recent critique of Max Weber has been widely acknowledged as a definitive rebuttal of Weber's thesis concerning the role of ascetic Protestantism in the development of modern rational capitalism. Samuelsson's study expands on nearly all prior arguments against Weber's position and adds several new points as well. The present paper analyzes these criticisms in the light of the aims and analytic and historical context of Weber's own thought. Specifically, it is argued here that Samuelsson's analysis is based on a faulty appreciation of Weber's intentions and, further, that it wrongly diverts attention from some of the principal factors in contemporary, as well as past, problems of economic development.

From Niles M. Hansen, "On the Sources of Economic Rationality," *Zeitschrift für Nationalökonomie* XXIV, 4 (1964). Used by permission of *Zeitschrift für Nationalökonomie*. Footnotes omitted.

I

In the first place, Samuelsson is not clear on what relationship should be established between the Protestant ethic and rational capitalism in Weber's thought. The link is defined variously by Samuelsson as a mystic effect, a causal connection and a correlation or covariation. While these concepts are not wholly inconsistent one with another, none adequately indicates Weber's position, which involves the concept of "elective affinity." As Bendix has pointed out, this concept was used frequently by Weber "to express the dual aspect of ideas, i.e., that they were created or chosen by the individual ('elective') and that they fit in with his material interests ('affinity')." Thus Weber believed that an already emergent capitalism was strongly reinforced and conditioned by certain aspects of Protestantism, but he postulated no simple causal or mechanical relationship between these variables. He had "no intention whatever of maintaining such a foolish and doctrinaire thesis as that the spirit of capitalism . . . could only have arisen as the result of certain effects of the Reformation." Numerous passages in the works of Weber and Weber scholars refute the contention that Weber attributed the birth of capitalism to Protestantism and the interested reader is referred to them.

Much of the difficulty with Samuelsson's approach is his failure to consider the essay on the Protestant ethic within the larger context of Weber's thought. As Frank Knight recognized, Weber's greatest contribution was in calling attention to the importance of quantitative rationality in the modern development of Western culture. Moreover, Weber was particularly concerned with the conditions favoring or precluding the emergence of economic rationality. His monumental studies of the world religions were concerned to a large extent with this problem. Knight also recognized that "there is surely one respect in which Max Weber towers above all the other writers noticed, he is the only one who really deals with the problem of causes or approaches the material from that angle which alone can yield an answer to such questions, that is, the angle of comparative history in the broad sense. It seems to the writer that the question of the origin of capitalism would gain by being stated in negative form: Why did capitalism *not* develop (in the sense in which it did not) in other times and places than modern Western Europe? . . . Weber discusses these questions."

II

Throughout his critique, Samuelsson never discusses Weber's thought in its broad comparative context. Thus while he acknowledges that many of the American industrialists of the late nineteenth and early twentieth centuries belonged to Calvinist and Puritan sects, he attributes their successes to their having experienced the beneficial effects of industry and commerce in their youth. This "general influence of the environment" was, according to Samuelsson, the important factor, not their religious values. As discussed below, Weber in fact completely agrees with this argument. But he also raises the question of *how* "the environment" comes to be favorable to the development of economic rationality, an issue where Samuelsson never quite gets beyond circular reasoning. For example, the prosperity of New England is held to have had nothing to do with Puritanism, but rather, "a particularly marked propensity to accumulate capital and take risks must have been prevalent in New England —because these qualities were necessary there for success and well-being." Where Weber finds the value orientation fostered by the Reformed church a vital element in the promotion of trade, industry and capital formation, Samuelsson finds other factors "far more obviously" of importance: "England, the Netherlands, Scotland, the North Sea and Baltic districts of Germany, Switzerland—they all furnish examples: their location on ocean shores of transcontinental routes that were in use hundreds of years before the Reformation; the definitive shift of the center of gravity of European trade to the North Sea and Atlantic as a result of the great discoveries and the throttling of the Mediterranean routes by Arab countries; the frequent inability of agriculture and stock-raising alone to provide adequate sustenance."

Ignoring the reference to Pirenne's doubtful thesis concerning the importance of Moslem expansion, it is nowhere clear in Samuelsson's account why the economic growth that characterized the West did not take place before and why it has been absent in most of the world right down to the present. At various points in his text Samuelsson points out numerous factors other than value orientation which contributed to Europe's economic development, but one may be sure that Weber would not have denied their importance. He himself stated that the emergence of economically rational behavior required, among other things, a free market for labor and commodities, rational capital accounting, calculable law, rational technology, a legally free labor force and commercialization of economic life. However, such preconditions are not in themselves sufficient to provide the motivation necessary for an ordering of life which leads to explicit economic rationality. In addition, Weber clearly saw that the acquisitive impulse has always existed but that it should not be confused with economic rationality or modern capitalism:

> *Traditional obstructions are not overcome by the economic impulse alone. The notion that our rationalistic and capitalistic age is characterized by a stronger economic interest than other periods is childish; the moving spirits of modern capitalism are not possessed of a stronger economic impulse than, for example, an oriental trader. The unchaining of the economic interest merely as such has produced only irrational results; such men as Cortez and Pizzaro, who were perhaps its strongest embodiment, were far from having an idea of a rationalistic economic life.*

The important question is under what conditions the economic impulse becomes tempered in such a fashion as to produce rational economic institutions. Although the emergence of an economically rational system of resource allocation is partly dependent on the various factors mentioned above, it is also dependent on the ability and disposition of men to adopt certain types of practical rational conduct. When such conduct has been obstructed by traditional or magical constraints the development of rational economic conduct has also encountered significant resistance. To Weber, the "extent and direction of 'rationalization' is . . . measured in terms of the degree to which magical elements of thought are displaced, or positively by the extent to which ideas gain in systematic coherence and naturalistic consistency." In general, a religion or any other system of value orientation is obtrusive to economic development if it is of a contemplative nature or if it relies on magical or sacramental means of grace which devalue action in this world. The dominant religions of the underdeveloped countries are of this nature. They are, as Professor Hunt has written, "far removed from any stress on the Puritan virtues. The tradition-bound rigidity of Islam, the otherworldly emphasis of Buddhism, the asceticism of Hinduism and the fiesta-laden Catholicism of countries with a Spanish tradition may embody important teachings, but their emphasis is not calculated to produce industrious workers, thrifty capitalists or daring promoters."

Samuelsson argues that the teachings of Calvin and other Puritan divines also were not calculated to encourage capitalist economic behavior. For example, he states that "Baxter's conception of the 'calling' has no connection with the notion that success in worldly affairs and the increase of business and fortune are a mark of God's favor. . . . It is no incitement to unrestricted economic individualism that Baxter intends, but an exhortation to labour, under strict moral laws, for the general good." But Weber was concerned with the effects on economic behavior of certain beliefs and not with religious teachings per se. He was quite clear about the distinction between the teachings of clergymen such as Calvin and Baxter, and the practical implications of these teachings, which might, paradoxically, have a very different effect from that which was intended. "The author has always underscored those features in the total picture of a religion which have been decisive for the fashioning of the *practical* [Weber's emphasis] way of life, as well as those which distinguish one religion from another." Weber notes that "examples of the condemnation of the pursuit of money and goods may be gathered without end from Puritan writings and may be contrasted with the late mediaeval ethical literature, which was more open-minded on this point." The element in ascetic Protestantism which was unique in its economic implications is not found in theological compendia but rather in the effects on economic behavior of the elimination of belief in the efficacy of the sacraments, which Weber held to be magical means of attaining the grace of God. Without intermediaries tremendous emphasis is placed on the individual. The source of the utilitarian character of the Protestant ethic lies in the fact that the individual becomes an instrument rather than a vessel or repository. Without sacramental means of absolution the ascetic Protestant is compelled to plan his life in a systematic, rational order. The discipline characteristic of Catholic monasticism is thus transferred to the secular life. Of course, it must be recognized that "no economic ethic has ever been determined solely by religion," for "the religiously determined way of life is itself profoundly influenced by economic and political factors operating within given geographical, political, social and national boundaries." For instance, Weber held that Puritanism was in many respects a relatively late phenomenon which reinforced tendencies which had been developing for a considerable time, especially in the mediaeval cities of Northern Europe. This context is important in considering some further criticisms by Samuelsson.

III

Samuelsson quotes Tawney with approval to the effect that capitalism had existed on a grand scale in mediaeval Flanders well before the Reformation. "With the best will in the world," writes Samuelsson, Belgium, "for hundreds of years in the vanguard of economic advance and . . . pressing close upon the heels of England in the race to industrialize, cannot be fitted into the Weber framework." Again Samuelsson errs by failing to consider the place of *The Protestant Ethic* in the general context of Weber's thought.

Weber showed that the ancient city was generally organized as a military or ecclesiastical fortress or seat of government and that military and political lords prevented a community organization of city residents. Even during the Renaissance, Italian cities were ranked according to the grade of their resident nobility and officials. City residents generally were still members of their original rural communities or, as in the Greek city, individual rights were dependent on belonging to kinship groups organized on military and political bases. In the mediaeval city of Northern Europe, on the other hand, the urban community developed as an oath-bound fraternal organization which eventually assumed the form of a corporation. In contrast to previous cities, where differing degrees of social, legal and kinship status entailed correspondingly different rights, the citizen of the mediaeval town swore his oath of citizenship as an individual whose qualification was based on communal religious equality. Moreover, the mediaeval city required military service of all citizens, though its army was solely defensive. The ancient city, on the other hand, had subordinated the development of industry to a system of distribution of tribute and booty by a political-military monopoly. In general, then, the urban population of late mediaeval Northern Europe had already been well prepared for the doctrines of the Reformation by virtue of institutions which provided a single ethical standard in business and community controls on legal procedure and personal conduct, an oath-bound confederation similar to congregational church government, a destruction of kinship group connections in favor of free association of individuals, and a weakening of traditional sanctions by the separation of the family from commerce and industry.

There can be little doubt that the economic activity of mediaeval Flanders was unique in its importance. "Throughout the history of mediaeval Europe no other region presented this character of an industrial country which distinguished the basin of the Scheldt. It offers, in this respect, a contrast to the rest of Europe which brings to mind England in the eighteenth and nineteenth centuries." The intensity and scope of this early development certainly laid the groundwork for and gave the impetus to Belgium's relatively long history of economic importance. Moreover, much of the explanation for this important breakthrough lies, as Weber saw, in the unique institutions of the mediaeval towns, institutions which closely paralleled in their nature and practical consequences those of the Reformed church. "The city of the Occident, unique among all other cities of the world, has been a major theater for . . . the [Protestant] sects of the Reformation up to pietism and methodism." It is here too "that elective affinities for special types of religion stand out" and where "the tendency towards a *practical* rationalism in conduct is common to all civic strata." In Belgium, the chief centers of the spread of Calvinism "were to be found just where the great industries were supreme. It made the most rapid progress at Tournai, Valenciennes, Lille, Hondschoote, and Armentiéres, around Oudenaarde, in the ports of Holland and Zealand, finally at Antwerp, the very center of the economic life of the Low Countries." Moreover, when Philip II succeeded Charles V in 1555, "the emigration for the Netherlands of thousands of Calvinists fleeing from religious persecution brought about an industrial crisis."

Accordingly, not only can the Belgian case be fitted into the general framework of Weber's treatment of the emergence of economic rationality—it is an integral part of a full appreciation of his contribution.

IV

One of the principal themes of Samuelsson's critique is derived from the allegation that "According to Weber, it was in Franklin that the capitalist ethic reached full maturity and by the captains of industry that it was practiced in full measure." But the capitalist outlook that they exhibit, argues Samuelsson, "is not a culmination of the Puritanism encountered in the great fathers of the free sects. On the contrary, the feature that stands out is the utter dissimilarity of the one from the other." Therefore, the argument continues, it is to the secularizing forces of the Enlightenment that one must look in explaining the behavior of Franklin and his contemporaries, just as in seeking explanations for the conduct of the captains of industry of the late nineteenth century one must look to movements such as Social Darwinism.

Weber's position on these matters is quite clear and in no way jeopardizes his basic thesis. In the first place, he was well aware of the thoroughly utilitarian character of the economic actions of Franklin and the captains of industry. Although Franklin's father was a strict Calvinist, he himself was, as Weber put it, "a colorless deist." Franklin's moral attitudes toward virtues such as honesty, punctuality, industry and frugality are "only in so far virtues as they are actually useful to the individual, and the surrogate of mere appearance is always sufficient when it accomplishes the end in view." However, it would be wrong to attribute this outlook to pure hypocrisy, for Franklin's sense of duty in these matters represents a part of the social ethic of capitalist culture. The important point to note is that by the time of the Enlightenment the economic ethic of capitalist culture is a *social* rather than a religious ethic. By this time the religious roots of the devotion to the calling of making money or laboring with diligence is dead. Already in Mandeville's Fable of the Bees "Ascetic religiosity has been displaced by a pessimistic though by no means ascetic view of the world . . . which teaches that private vices may under certain conditions be for the good of the public." With the Enlightenment a belief in a harmony of interests "appeared as the heir of Protestant asceticism in the field of economic ideas."

Samuelsson is aware that Weber regarded the economic ethic of Franklin as a largely secularized phenomenon, and from this he argues that "This admission is in itself so damaging that Weber's thesis really falls to the ground," for "if purely religious conceptions are claimed to be the decisive factor, then it is clearly preposterous to declare that this spirit reaches full maturity . . . in someone who in certain vital respects is far removed from these conceptions."

Therefore, in the centuries before Franklin, Protestantism "cannot of itself possibly have possessed to any appreciable extent the power ascribed to it by Weber, i.e., that it imparted a forward impetus to economic trends and thus constituted a source of the 'spirit of capitalism'." Furthermore, Samuelsson holds that "this secularized capitalism, endeavoring to equate the expedients of good business with true virtue, was not unique to Franklin; he was not the only one or even the first. Long before Franklin, there were many writings, both in Catholic and Protestant countries, in which these same or similar ideals had been preached—as an element, not of religious education, but of the training of capable businessmen."

There are several fundamental problems with this line of criticism. First, as we have seen, there is no such thing in Weber's thought as a "purely religious" force influencing the direction of capitalist development, although it is true that he believed that the elective affinity of unique elements in ascetic Protestantism did impart a unique stimulus to the development of economic rationality. Secondly, there is no reason why those forces which generate social and economic change should be necessary to a dynamic system once such change has reached a certain point. In other words, there is no logical reason why the forces which generate the momentum for self-sustained economic growth should be necessary to a system once such development becomes self-sustained. Thirdly, Samuelsson's account is misleading when it asserts that Weber held that the economic ethic of capitalism reached maturity only in the era of Franklin and should therefore be divorced from the religious conceptions of a prior epoch. Weber explicitly pointed out that in New England the economic ethic of capitalism was fully present as early as 1632, well before the development of an actual capitalist economic order. In the same context Weber noted that while the southern states were founded by wealthy capitalists for business motives, the more economically developed New England colonies were founded by preachers, craftsmen and yeomen for what were in significant degree religious reasons. In fact, the principal reason why Weber dwells on Franklin is not because a rational economic ethic was more fully developed at this period, but because he wished to examine the nature of rational capitalism at a time when it still existed in a relatively pure form and, more importantly, because he deliberately wished to examine its nature at a time when it "has the advantage of being free from all direct relationship to religion, being thus, for our purposes, free of preconceptions."

Finally, no one would deny that in both Protestant and Catholic countries, and even in other cultures, there were writers prior to Franklin who propounded similar ideals in "endeavoring to equate the expedients of good business with true virtue." However, Weber was not interested in the writings of scattered individuals as such— one generally can "prove" anything using this approach; he was concerned with individual thought insofar as it reflected the nature of an entire economic system: "In order that a manner of life so well adapted to the peculiarities of capitalism could be selected at all, i.e., should come to dominate others, it had to originate somewhere, and not in isolated individuals alone, but as a way of life common to whole groups of men. This origin is what really needs explanation."

Alberti and other individuals quoted by Samuelsson may indeed individually have had ideas with economic implications similar to those of more specifically Protestant writers, and they may well have entertained such ideas with a greater consciousness of their implications. Nevertheless, it does not follow that "the essential difference in conduct and outlook between the Italian merchant classes of 'pre-capitalism' and the capitalists of Protestantism was slight." It is a matter of fact that the type of rationalized entrepreneurship and labor which emerged in Northern Europe failed to develop in Italy. Bert Hoselitz has pointed out that an important factor in this regard was the failure of the Italian financial aristocracy to allow the Reformation to take roots in Italy. Pirenne also noted that Renaissance liberalism was an aristocratic liberalism which tended to produce only disdain for the crafts and industry. Thus if a mere acquisitive impulse were a determining factor in producing an economic rationality conducive to economic development it is probable that Italy would have been in the vanguard of Europe's modern economic development. That it was not can be explained in Weber's terms.

Finally, there is the widely held but confused notion concerning the Protestant ethic and the activities of the late nineteenth- and early twentieth-century captains of industry. Weber would wholeheartedly agree with Samuelsson that despite the fact that many of the industrialists and financiers of this period were Protestants, religion as such probably had little to do with their behavior. In the first place, if Weber found the religious roots of a rational economic ethic dead by the latter part of the eighteenth century it would follow directly that a similar condition should hold a century later. But he was more explicit than this:

> In the history of any economic area on earth there is no epoch, except those quite rigid in feudalism or patrimonialism, in which capitalist figures of the kind of Pierpont Morgan, Rockefeller, Jay Gould, et al. were absent. Only the technical means which they used for the acquisition of wealth have changed . . . they have never been decisive in determining what economic mentality was to dominate a given epoch and a given area.

There can be no doubt that in spite of the attention given by Samuelsson and others to such charismatic capitalists, they should have little place in any serious consideration of Weber's thought on religion and economic behavior.

V

The various aspects of Samuelsson's critique would be in themselves of little more than purely historic interest were it not for the broader conclusion which they imply, namely, that the noneconomic value orientation of an individual or a society has little relevance to economic behavior. It is the contention of the present paper that such a conclusion is not only false, but that it distracts attention from one of the central problems of economic development: the nature of the process by which self-sustained economic growth is attained.

As indicated above, Weber believed that purely economic and technical factors were indispensable to the growth of modern capitalism, but that in addition a subjective factor is needed to provide a causally sufficient explanation. The principal such factor Weber found in the generally unintended effects of certain Protestant ideas which encouraged economic rationality and worked against tradition dominated modes of conduct not conducive to economic development.

At the time of Weber's death (1920), Western capitalism was the only economic system to have ever achieved large-scale industrialization. It is not surprising, therefore, that Weber himself apparently attributed only historic significance to his study of the Protestant ethic. Nevertheless, his work on the relationship between noneconomic values and economic rationality, of which *The Protestant Ethic* is only a fragment, still provides relevant insights into problems associated with the world-wide economic development effort which has characterized recent decades.

Soviet Russia is the first case of a nation which has industrialized under a noncapitalist system. The religious ethos prevalent in Tsarist Russia was strongly antithetical to economic rationality, and Soviet attitudes toward the Orthodox Church (and Catholicism in Eastern Europe) must be viewed in this light. In achieving self-sustained economic growth the Soviet Union has, by the application of Marxist ideology, consciously tried to develop a rational economic ethic of the type that ascetic Protestantism fostered more or less without intention. In spite of its own magical and ritualistic overtones, Marxism's effects have been similar in essential respects to those of Calvinism. "The resemblance is more than incidental: the two ethics meet on the common ground of historical 'contemporaneousness'—they reflect the need for the incorporation of large masses of 'backward' people into a new social system, the need for the creation of a well-trained, disciplined labor force, capable of vesting the perpetual routine of the working day with ethical sanction, producing ever more rationally ever increasing amounts of goods, while the rational use of these goods is ever more delayed by the 'circumstances'. In this sense, Soviet ethics testifies to the similarity between Soviet society and capitalist society. The basis for the similarity was established in the Stalinist period."

Furthermore, the Soviet pattern of development has tended to follow that of the West in that the intensity of the motivating ideology has tended to decline as the rational economic ethic of the initial phase of development has been superseded by the stable patterns of a rationalized bureaucracy. As in the West, "Sanction may indeed come from the *res publica* instead of being vested in a transcendental agency or in the moral autonomy of the individual conscience." Marcuse points out that such sanction would be effective "only if the *res publica,* in its institutions, were to protect and promote a truly human existence for all individuals." Recent Soviet decisions to allocate larger proportions of total output to the consumer sector will certainly work in this direction. In contrast to the abatement of the militant nature of the noneconomic values which have fostered economic rationality in the Soviet Union is the fervor of Chinese insistence on economic, as well as political, doctrinal correctness. However, even though China's economic problems may be greater than those faced by the Soviet Union during the initial period of her development, there are historical grounds for supposing that China's noneconomic values will change if her economic progress can be sustained.

In the presently underdeveloped countries there are numerous indications of the general validity of the propositions we have been making. In Indonesia, for example, Geertz has found that "In the light of the theories of Max Weber . . . it is perhaps not surprising that the leaders in the creation of . . . a [business] community in Modjokuto are for the most part intensely Reformist Moslems, for the intellectual role of Reform in Islam has, at least in some ways, approached that of Protestantism in Christianity." Likewise, in India the most successful persons in business have been members of the more ascetic religious sects, such as the Jains and the Parsees. "In neither the East nor the West has it been the secular-minded materialists, primarily interested in money and what it will buy for them personally who have been successful in business."

In general, Weber's inquiry into the nature of the noneconomic element in the development of rational capitalism provides important insights concerning the development of economic rationality within the framework of other economic systems. Conversely, the generality of a noneconomic value basis for economic rationality in systems which have appeared and evolved in the present century tends to confirm the essential credibility of Weber's propositions concerning the development of capitalism.

H. Stuart Hughes

WEBER'S SEARCH FOR RATIONALITY IN WESTERN SOCIETY

One of America's most distinguished authorities on the intellectual history of nineteenth- and twentieth-century continental Europe, Dr. Hughes earned his degrees at Amherst and Harvard. He has taught at Brown, Stanford, and Harvard universities as well as at the University of Paris. A member of the Institute for Advanced Studies at Princeton and a Guggenheim Fellow, Professor Hughes has also served as a director of research for the United States Department of State and is a professor of history at Harvard. In his work Consciousness and Society *Dr. Hughes' concern with the changing orientation of European thought from the 1890s to the beginning of the great depression of the 1930s led to his interest in Max Weber who sought a rational explanation and arrangement of the powerful, mutually antagonistic social forces he observed around him.*

Intellectual Origins and Early Production

Durkheim and Weber are conventionally held in honor as the two most important founders of the discipline of sociology as we know it today. And it has on occasion proved possible to find in their leading concepts a wide area of agreement. This reconciliation, however, has been a kind of *tour de force*—a dramatic illustration of the extent to which early twentieth-century social thought was heading in a single direction, despite the most extraordinary personal and intellectual divergences among its creators.[1] From the more general standpoint of intellectual history, the dissimilarities between the two have remained unresolved.

To recall that Durkheim was French and Weber German, that the former was Jewish and the latter the offspring of the Prussian upper middle class—and that both were more than usually patriotic—is only to begin to sketch their differences. Obviously it is relevant to add that while one came out of the positivist tradition, the other was by origin a German idealist. And this idealist pedigree suggests the whole intellectual atmosphere that has differentiated French soci-

From H. Stuart Hughes, *Consciousness and Society: the Reorientation of European Social Thought 1890–1930* (New York, 1958). Used by permission of Alfred A. Knopf, Inc., and Macgibbon & Kee, Ltd.

[1] Parsons: *Structure of Social Action*, pp. 13–14.

ology from German—Durkheim's tradition from Weber's. In France, as we have repeatedly observed, the dominant temper was rationalist, science-minded, anticlerical—in short, inspired by a sober confidence in modern society and the works of man. In Germany there had lingered on from the early nineteenth century a nondogmatic religiosity, an emphasis on the spiritual and a distrust of the material world. German social thinkers characteristically came from conservative, religiously oriented families: clergymen's sons were not infrequent. In this tradition it seemed natural to set emotion against reason, community sentiment against technological change, and to protest, either directly or by implication, against capitalism and the rationalized society.[2]

To put the difference in personal terms, Durkheim does not strike one as a particularly troubled individual. Indeed, his chief intellectual weakness was a tendency to dogmatism. Weber, for all the intemperance of his polemical style, was hesitant, self-divided, and enormously troubled. For that very reason he is the key figure of our study. He stands at more decisive meeting points than any other thinker. To begin to list these confrontations is to suggest his range and the ambiguous nature of his achievement: idealism and scientific method; economics and religion; Marxism and nationalism; political commitment and an insistence on "objectivity" in social science. He was both a democrat in his personal convictions and a contributor to that radical critique of democracy which Pareto and Mosca had launched. He was skeptical about the viability of the Enlightenment under twentieth-century conditions, yet his temperamental reaction to events was more often than not of an "enlightened" character. Even in his contributions to the terminology of social science his contradictions and ambivalences are mirrored.

As we associate Durkheim with the concept of *anomie,* so we think of Weber in connection with the linked notions of bureaucracy and *charisma.* These concepts contradict and balance each other, and Weber's attitude toward them is in turn one of attraction and repulsion. On the one hand he was convinced that the deepest tendency of the contemporary Western world was toward a bureaucratization of all phases of public activity: this was the tangible mani-

[2] Raymond Aron: *La Sociologie allemande contemporaine* (Paris, 1936), translated from the second edition (1950) by Mary and Thomas Bottomore as *German Sociology* (Glencoe, Ill., 1957), pp. 114–15.

festation of that more general process of rationalization which had distinguished the West from all other known civilizations. As a rationalist himself, as an heir to "the Protestant ethic," Weber with one part of himself applauded this tendency. At the same time he fully appreciated the dangers that bureaucracy presented for personal and intellectual freedom—which was another of his deeply cherished values.

In this situation, he surmised, "charismatic" leadership might offer a way out. With one side of his nature, Weber always responded to the notion of a "chief": he himself, had he chosen to exert his talents in this direction, could have been an incomparable leader of men. But here also the danger to liberty was acute. In his very definition of his new term, Weber suggested all that was primitive and threatening about it:

> *"Charisma" shall be understood to refer to an* extraordinary *quality of a person, regardless of whether this quality is actual, alleged, or presumed. "Charismatic authority," hence, shall refer to a rule over men . . . to which the governed submit because of their belief in the extraordinary quality of the specific* person. *The magical sorcerer, the prophet, the leader of hunting and booty expeditions, the warrior chieftain, the . . . "Caesarist" ruler . . . are such types. . . . The legitimacy of charismatic rule thus rests upon the belief in magical powers, revelations and hero worship. . . . Charismatic rule is not managed according to general norms, either traditional or rational, . . . and in this sense . . . is "irrational." It is "revolutionary" in the sense of not being bound to the existing order.*[3]

Partly because he possessed so much charisma himself—because he himself was so profoundly shaken by the "demonic"—Weber distrusted it and held it at arm's length. In the same fashion he was aware of the lurking danger within his own thinking: he saw how dissolving and destructive were its implications, and he refused the role of an intellectual guide. In Weber's thought, the whole vast ambiguity of our century was held for one brief moment in a desperate synthesis. As his widow put it, he took it upon himself "to bear" without flinching "the *antinomies* of existence"—to live without illusions and at the same time in accordance with his personal ideals. When he

---

[3] *"Die Wirtschaftsethik der Weltreligionen. Einleitung"* (1915), *Gesammelte Aufsätze zur Religionssoziologie,* I (Tübingen 1922), pp. 237–75; translated by H. H. Gerth and C. Wright Mills as "The Social Psychology of the World Religions," *From Max Weber: Essays in Sociology* (New York, 1946), pp. 295–6.

was once asked what his learning meant to him, he answered quite simply: "I want to see how much I can endure."[4]

In facing his intellectual problems, Weber enjoyed the dubious advantage of having the contradictions of his world built right into his family inheritance and personality. His mother's family were Rhineland liberals, to whom intellectual and spiritual concerns were second nature. His father came of a line of merchant patricians, orderly, disciplined, hard-working men, on whose image Weber was to draw when he began to analyze the "spirit of capitalism." The elder Weber had become a lawyer: during Max's boyhood he sat in the Reichstag as a National Liberal deputy—one of those "realists" who had followed when Bismarck called the turn. Between father and mother, there was an ever-widening spiritual gulf: she was religious, high-minded, devoted to the poor, generous in projects of social welfare; he was shrewd, good-humoredly authoritarian, conventional and superficial in his interests, and self-indulgent in his personal habits. The son was to suffer greatly from this temperamental misunderstanding as its full import gradually dawned upon him.

He himself eventually sided with his mother. But throughout his life, traces of the paternal influence remained. Although he grew to be ashamed of his student beer-drinking and dueling days, even as a mature man he would challenge his antagonists to a duel when he thought that honor was involved, and he took a strictly conventional pride in his rank as a Prussian reserve officer. His father's politics he never adopted: he started to the right of him, as still more conservative and nationalist, and ended far to the left as a most eccentric sort of democrat. But he betrayed what he owed his father by the imperious—indeed, brutal—quality of his political utterances, and by the uncompromising fashion in which he insisted on Germany's national greatness right down to the day of his death.

Similarly, on the eve of his death he was still not sure what was the true purpose of his life. As a young man he was attracted to politics. In the early part of his scholarly career he maintained this interest as an avocation parallel to his professional labors; it was only when he had become crippled by psychic illness that he abandoned the thought of public life and devoted his full energies to

---

[4] Marianne Weber: *Max Weber: Ein Lebensbild,* new edition (Heidelberg, 1950), p. 731.

scholarship. With the war, however, Weber—like so many others—was drawn into active political partisanship, and for a brief period in 1919 it looked as though he would play a leading role in the new German republic. This expectation came to nothing—but the vague hope lingered on. Weber never thought of himself as a "true scholar" in the usual sense.[5] It was perhaps for this reason that he insisted so strongly on a radical separation between the vocation of science and the vocation of politics: he feared the dual allegiance in his own soul.[6]

Today we think of Weber primarily as a sociologist. But this was only the last of a succession of disciplines with which he was professionally associated. He began his scholarly life as a student of the law, and it was in this field that he received his first teaching appointment in 1892, when he was just turning twenty-eight. His legal researches, however, were already directed toward economic and social history, and when he was called to a university chair, at Freiburg in 1894, it was as professor of economics. And it was in the same field that he received the invitation to Heidelberg three years later. It was only at the end of his life, when he taught as a visiting professor in Vienna and subsequently accepted a chair at the University of Munich, that he began to lecture specifically on sociology.

Similarly, in terms of an intellectual progression, we may trace Weber's course from law through economic history to the general methodology of the social sciences, and then, after a series of preparatory labors in the sociology of religion, to systematic sociology itself. From one standpoint, we might adduce this series of shifts as further evidence of Weber's intellectual contradictions. At the same time—and more profoundly—it suggests his heroic efforts to bring his diverse interests into some sort of synthesis. For when we look at them more closely, we discover that all these concerns are dominated by one overriding problem—the problem of rationality in Western society.[7]

---

[5] Ibid., pp. 192, 723.

[6] See the parallel lectures, delivered before student audiences in Munich in 1918: *"Wissenschaft als Beruf," Gesammelte Aufsätze zur Wissenschaftslehre,* second edition (Tübingen, 1951), pp. 566–97 ("Science as a Vocation," *From Max Weber,* pp. 129–56), and *"Politik als Beruf," Gesammelte Politische Schriften* (Munich, 1921), pp. 396–450 ("Politics as a Vocation," *From Max Weber,* pp. 77–128).

[7] Introduction by Talcott Parsons to Weber's *The Theory of Social and Economic Organization* (translation of Part I of *Wirtschaft und Gesellschaft,* published originally

In his efforts to reach a synthesis, Weber held on to a number of the characteristic presuppositions of the intellectual tradition that had produced him. Although he was eventually to subject his masters to the most searching sort of criticism, he retained throughout his life the traces of their beneficent influence. The weaknesses of the German social science tradition are already familiar to us—its penchant toward metaphysical speculation and its infatuation with "the spirit." We might add the German practice of teaching economics in terms of history alone and of disparaging the claims of theory—an attitude that infuriated Pareto, himself a convert, like Weber, from economics to sociology, but from a very different economic school: Pareto, as a rigorously classical and mathematical theorist, was outraged by what he regarded as the slipshod quality of German economic thinking.

Yet when all this has been said, the enormous merit of German social thought was that it dwelt *in the historical world.* History was one subject that Weber never specifically studied or taught. But his whole intellectual life was suffused with historical thinking. Law, like economics, was taught in Germany as a historical discipline. Sociology was being cast in a similar mold. And philosophy, as we have seen, had posed as one of its central problems the elaboration of the categories of historical thought. It was from the philosopher Rickert, who was his colleague and friend at the University of Freiburg, that Weber first learned to formulate the question of value-judgments in the methodology of social science.

More directly, the professors whom Weber had respected in his university days had been the economic historians Wilhelm Roscher— Ranke's former pupil—at Berlin, and Karl Knies, whom he was eventually to succeed at Heidelberg. From them he learned a brand of economics that embraced virtually the whole field of social science and that was energetically committed to ethical judgments and practical applications. For in Germany the study of economics was intimately involved in social reform, and the professors who were facetiously called "socialists of the academic chair" devoted their talents to the problems of the relations between capital and labor in their newly industrialized nation. In 1873 they had founded the *Verein für Sozialpolitik,* of which Weber became an active and enterprising

as Volume 3 of the collaborative *Grundriss für Sozialökonomik* [Tübingen, 1921]), p. 12.

member. Thus at the very start of his academic career he was prepared for the inevitable confrontation with Marx: to achieve by more conservative means the social justice at which the Marxists aimed had become the major purpose of the *Verein*. In its very effort to counterbalance the influence of Marx, it betrayed how much it owed him.

As a self-conscious younger generation of economic historians, Weber and his friends tried to free themselves from those parts of their intellectual preparation they they felt to be old-fashioned and confining. In particular, they wanted to formulate in more specific terms than their elders had proposed the pervading "spirit" of economic institutions. The young Werner Sombart's approach was boldly impressionistic: Weber was more careful and more concerned with conceptual rigor. Almost alone of the German historical school, he was ready to grant a limited validity to the theoretical schema of classical economics.

Yet Weber's early writings showed few signs of exceptional intellectual independence. They were detailed, learned, immensely competent—quite conventional in their characteristically German combination of historical erudition, nationalism, and concern for the welfare of the laboring classes. Already, however, these youthful studies were beginning to point toward the interests that occupied their author's mature years. This was particularly the case with the survey of the situation of agrarian labor in eastern Germany which Weber undertook on behalf of the *Verein für Sozialpolitik* in 1891. Here for the first time he found himself face to face with a major conflict between national values and economic rationality. For he soon discovered that the central point in question—the replacement of German workers by Poles in the great estates east of the Elbe—could not be approached in purely economic terms. From the economic standpoint, the issue was simple: Polish labor was cheaper than German. But from the standpoint of national interest, this was proving to be a dangerous solution, since it increasingly exposed Germany's vital eastern frontier to Slavic penetration. And Weber finally felt that he had understood the crux of his problem when he came to the realization that it was the same East Elbian aristocrats who in their political and military capacity were irreproachably loyal to national values, who in their economic role were pursuing a thoroughly antinational course.

The ambiguities of value-judgments—the conflicts of allegiances and of planes of understanding—all these riddles that were to torment Weber's maturity were implicit in this first major study. More immediately, it produced in his mind a vast disillusionment with his country's governing classes. Now that he had understood that they were incapable of living up to their national professions, he was ready to look for a new and more broadly based élite—hence his interest in Naumann's Christian-social aims. But Weber's reasons for passing over into the opposition were quite different from those that usually inspired such apostasies: his originality consisted in "directing against the Wilhelminian monarchy not the customary attacks based on principle, but rather those very arguments of which it—the monarchy—made itself the guardian and proponent: the interest and power of the state, and the vigor and authority of its political direction." To Weber, the more usual arguments about "state forms"—monarchy, democracy, and the like—seemed merely secondary issues of "techniques" and "mechanisms."[8] It was the strength of the nation alone that really counted.

Thus his early professional studies had already shaken Weber out of his original political allegiance. They had only begun, however, to disrupt the categories of his abstract thought. This latter reorientation was to be the indirect product of an unexpected disaster that very nearly ended his intellectual life altogether.

The Methodological Phase

In early 1898, when Weber had been only a year in Heidelberg, "an evil something out of the subterranean unconscious . . . grasped him by its claws" and deprived him of all power to teach or study.[9] For the next four years he was sunk in a depression of extraordinary severity. He felt unable to read, to interest himself in living—he barely existed. It was only during the winter of 1901–1902, which he and his wife passed in Rome, that he gradually began to recover his intellectual powers.

To search out the origins of Weber's ailment is a task for the psychiatrist rather than the historian. Even the psychiatric amateur, however, may speculate on the elements in Weber's earlier life that

8 Carlo Antoni: *Dallo storicismo alla sociologia* (Florence, 1940), p. 135.
9 Marianne Weber: *Max Weber*, p. 269.

contributed to it. Most obviously there was the enormous burden of work involved in the shift-over from law to economics and in the combination of academic pursuits with semi-public activity. There was also the spiritual cleavage between his mother and father: it is significant that Weber's collapse followed shortly upon a violent scene with his father, in which the son's pent-up animosity had for the first time burst forth—and which was in turn succeeded by the father's death a few weeks later. So far as we can tell, the vulnerable point in Weber's psychology was his doubt of his own ability to play the role of husband and father. Concomitantly, he had a strong attachment to his mother, whose pride in and ambition for Max, her first-born, revealed the familiar search for compensation of a strong-willed woman disappointed in her own marriage.

Weber's wife, Marianne, resembled her mother-in-law in the loftiness of her ethical goals and the strength of her will. Reading between the lines of the former's vastly informative and sensitive biography of her husband, we may surmise that the two women early struck up a tacit alliance directed toward the goal of making a great man out of the individual whom they cherished in common. Before his marriage Weber had had a five-year relationship with a distant female cousin, a gentle, vaguely ailing neurotic: this sad, unexpressed, unfulfilled love left him with a deep sense of remorse and the "enigmatic feeling that he did not have it in him . . . to make a woman happy." He entered marriage "encrusted" with "guilt feeling, renunciation, and repressions of all kinds"; the marriage remained childless; yet between husband and wife there seems to have been established the sort of spiritual communion that had been so notably lacking in the case of Weber's parents.[10]

In brief, "one may certainly infer an inordinately strong Oedipus situation."[11] There is a grim appropriateness in the fact that the only rival of Freud for the title of the leading social thinker of our century should have been a classic example of the latter's most famous theory—that he should have lain crippled by mental suffering at the very moment when *The Interpretation of Dreams* was appearing in print—and that he should have undergone the ministrations of a series of psychiatrists, none of whom helped him at all, while remain-

[10] Ibid., pp. 186, 208.
[11] Introduction by Gerth and Mills to *From Max Weber,* p. 29.

ing in total ignorance of the work of the one physician who might have cured him.

Weber did not come into contact with Freud's theories until about 1907, when a self-styled disciple of the Viennese physician appeared in Heidelberg and—so far as we can tell from Frau Weber's account —began to preach the doctrine of free love. Thus it was in this highly partial and sensationalized form that Weber first encountered the teachings of psychoanalysis. His first reaction was repugnance: he and his wife held to a concept of the relationship between the sexes that was "pure" in the extreme. But as he came to devote closer attention to the problems of personal morality in modern society, Weber reached a more tolerant conclusion. Even a breach of the principle of monogamous marriage might be understandable, he reasoned, if the new tie were based on "responsibility." In this formula, we encounter one of Weber's most characteristic ways of thinking. And we find another of them in his eventual verdict on Freud's work: it was unquestionably of scientific importance, but from it, no more than from any other scientific doctrine, could one derive a *Weltanschauung*—as Freud himself was to try to do in the speculative writings of his later years.

Weber's widow tells us that her husband "plunged into Freud's teachings."[12] Presumably this means that he read widely in the latter's works. But we know very little of the result. Weber did not comment on nor analyze the theory of psychoanalysis in his own sociological writings. Nor did he and Freud ever meet in person. In all the essentials the two followed separate paths: the intellectual confrontation that held the greatest possibilities for our era never occurred. We are left with the paradoxical suspicion that the most probing social theory of our time was the indirect sequel of an *unresolved* neurosis of a classic Freudian type.

To the extent that Weber ever was cured, he cured himself without medical help. In early 1902, for the first time in nearly four years, he found himself able to read a book—a book of art history. This choice reflected the basic necessity of his intellectual restoration. It was the mental overload, the pressure of *professional* labor, he felt, that had undone him, and during the first part of his recovery,

[12] Marianne Weber: *Max Weber*, pp. 413–21, 429–31.

he refused to read any books in his own field. It was only gradually that he worked his way back to them. And even then he felt permanently unable to carry out any intellectual assignment to which a deadline was attached. Hence, on his return to Heidelberg in 1902, after a few unsuccessful efforts to resume teaching, he gave up the attempt entirely: for the next fifteen years he was simply an honorary professor without teaching responsibility.

During the decade from 1903 to the outbreak of the war—the most productive period of his life—Weber lived on the careful regime of a semi-invalid. He always feared a recurrence of his malady, and on at least two occasions he went into a moderately severe relapse. But in general he found that frequent trips—preferably again into the Italian sun—restored him sufficiently to permit him to resume his work. At home in Heidelberg he followed a strict schedule: a working-day limited to six hours, a carefully regulated amount of contact with his friends and a minimum of general social life, no public speaking—above all, no evening activity that might disturb his precarious sleep.[13] He suffered and grumbled mightily over his intellectual production; it seemed to progress with appalling slowness; but as the years passed it began to mount to a most impressive total.

In all this I think we may properly discern the egocentric, infinitely painstaking labor of the neurotic of genius—we are reminded of Proust—to provide the external circumstances that will alone make his work of creation possible. Like Proust, Weber was setting up artificial walls, apparently senseless barriers and taboos against the intrusion of the irrelevant. Unconsciously exploiting his illness for his own intellectual purposes, he used it ruthlessly to strip down to the essentials all the meaningless paraphernalia of existence.

Similarly, at the level of the intellectual life itself, Weber was able to make a virtue out of his misfortune—to find the spur to creativity in his neurosis itself. His four years of intellectual paralysis were only apparently wasted. Actually Weber seems to have been thinking—and thinking hard—a good deal of the time. Indeed, one subsidiary reason why he may have felt unable to read and write was that he was digging into a new sort of problem for which the conventional methods of his youth were proving quite inadequate. Obviously, Weber's four-year absence from scholarly labor provided

13 Ibid., pp. 287–94, 298–300, 514–16.

the intellectual advantage of a clean break (and we may note that the years he lost were the very years of the great critique of Marxism in the Western European world: Weber thus missed the main phase of criticism—but only to resume the work of Pareto and Croce and Sorel a few years later and in a still more rigorous form). Above and beyond that, Weber's impatience with the literature of his own discipline turned him to broader concerns. From now on, he was to be satisfied only with what was most troubling and difficult in the profession of social science—the philosophy and methodology of that science itself: the net result of Weber's psychic collapse was that he decided to worry in a systematic fashion about the really worrying issues of social theory.

This new phase started in 1903, when Weber was just under forty, with the desperately slow composition of a long and inordinately difficult critique of the work of his economic masters Roscher and Knies.[14] It proved to be the first of the series of essays on methodology to which, more than to any other of his writings, Weber owes his great contemporary influence. These essays make extremely heavy reading. In composing them Weber quite frankly paid no attention to style: it was sufficient for him if his thought had been expressed with rigor and precision. One suspects that it was only by making some such self-limitation that he succeeded in completing them at all. It is part of the irony of Weber's career that he, who was one of the most forceful speakers of his time, should have been condemned to sixteen years of silence and to the torment of a wretched literary style.

*　　*　　*

The Studies of Religion

Weber's own chief application of his ideal-type method was to the study of religion—which also constituted the main focus of his empirical labors in the decade and a half following his psychic col-

---

[14] *"Roscher und Knies und die logischen Probleme der historischen Nationalökonomie,"* after having been published in three installments between 1903 and 1906 in *Schmollers Jahrbuch,* XXVII, XXIX, XXX, was republished as pp. 1–145 of the *Gesammelte Aufsätze zur Wissenschaftslehre.* It is one of two important methodological essays that have not been translated into English. On this whole phase of Weber's writing the standard work is Alexander von Schelting's *Max Webers Wissenschaftslehre* (Tübingen, 1934).

lapse. This series of studies he first undertook in 1904, and he continued to work on it nearly up to the time of his death in 1920. Thus the religious phase overlapped the phase of methodological analysis—but it was the latter that necessarily offered the presuppositions for this new variety of empirical study.

Besides being the first *conscious* application of the ideal-type procedure, Weber's studies of religion are significant for his intellectual development in two other important respects. First—as with Pareto or Durkheim—they offer the crucial test case in his confrontation with the nonlogical world. Second—and again as with his great contemporaries in Italy and France—they document his encounter with Marx. But in Weber's case, as opposed to that of Pareto or Durkheim, the reckoning with religion did not come *after* the settling of accounts with Marx, as the consequence of a further maturation of thought. The two went on simultaneously: their effect was interacting. As a result, Weber was able to see farther and more clearly in both respects than was possible for his contemporaries from the Latin world.

Weber's widow has suggested that his lasting interest in the sociology of religion represented the transmuted "form in which the genuine religious sentiment in his mother's family lived on in him." He himself had no defined religious belief. "I am . . . absolutely unmusical in religious matters," he wrote in 1909, "and I feel neither the need nor the capacity to raise up in myself any sort of spiritual edifices of a religious character. Yet after careful self-examination I find myself neither antireligious *nor irreligious*." This quality of suspended judgment in spiritual matters constituted one of Weber's great assets. As opposed to the militantly antireligious Freud and Pareto, the skeptical and rationalist Durkheim, or the avowedly mystical Bergson, Weber was almost alone among the major social thinkers of his time in remaining open to religious impressions while succumbing to no specific dogmatic teaching. Like Sorel—but more systematically and analytically than Sorel—Weber gave to religion his full respect without letting it catch him in its toils.

Moreover, under the intentionally dry and "scientific" style of his religious studies, we can catch glimpses of Weber's own spiritual commitment to his subject matter. We may detect the surging of deeply experienced emotion at the enigmas and paradoxes of human destiny that the study of religion disclosed. And we may also surmise that in the "sublime figures of heroic Puritanism" which he presented in his work on the Protestant ethic, "certain of his own traits" stand revealed. In this earliest of his religious studies, Weber seems to have felt himself into the role of a Calvinist leader of iron resolve—a man who had conquered the demon in his own soul and chained himself to the wheel of duty. Subsequently—like Freud—he was to see himself in the image of a Hebrew prophet. During the war years, he was to warn his people in the tones of a Jeremiah of their political irresponsibility and of the dangers to the nation that lay ahead.[15]

In Weber's view, all social theories or ideologies could be classified as ideal types. And of these, Marx's had obviously been a particularly suggestive and influential specimen. Like Croce, Weber granted a "relative legitimacy to the materialist conception of history," that is, if it were understood "not as a general interpretation of history but as a *heuristic principle*"—a path to understanding— whose "unilateral character" was "inherent in any point of view that tries to delimit its own field of investigation."[16] In common with Croce, Weber saw that the very partiality of the Marxian analysis gave it a sharper edge: it cut cleanly into an area of life in society that earlier theories had neglected. But, unlike Croce, Weber did not stop when he had incorporated what he had found valid in Marxism into the canon of his own thinking; he went on to relate the one-sidedness of historical materialism to the unilateral character of all social theory, and to give to Marxism a new dimension by running another unilateral sequence of his own.

Of all the critiques of Marxism that came out of the generation of the 1890s, Weber's was the most subtle and the widest in range. This last critique, as we have seen, partly for accidental reasons followed the others by half a decade, and the fact that it was presented in the context of the sociology of religion gave it a special point and relevance. Furthermore, as opposed to Pareto or Croce, to whom Marx's way of thinking was basically distasteful, Weber had much in common with the founder of dialectical materialism. Once more he recalls Sorel in his intuitive understanding for the way in which Marx's mind had worked.

15 Marianne Weber: *Max Weber,* pp. 370, 382–3, 385, 639.
16 Rossi: *Storicismo tedesco,* p. 345.

The two had in common the *radical* character of their analysis of society—radical, that is, not in the ordinary political sense of being "on the left," but in the original philological meaning of a concern with the roots of social difficulties. Both were impatient men—and more particularly impatient with the verbal superficialities and euphemisms that customarily concealed harsh reality. And both attempted a kind of philosophical sociology of contemporary man: what Marx called the "alienation" of the workers from the means of production, Weber broadened into the more inclusive category of the rationalization of modern life. Weber "relativized" Marx's theory by fitting it into a wider hypothesis as a "special case" that the latter had "dramatized" with telling effect.[17]

But in following—or better, paralleling—Marx in these respects, Weber made a basic alteration in emphasis. In Weber's hands, "capitalism" was enlarged into an even more ramifying conception than it had been for Marx; indeed, it became questionable whether such an economic term was adequate to cover at all what Weber was talking about. Viewed in the context of the rationalization or bureaucratization of living, the distinction between capitalism and socialism ceased to be of major importance; in effect, Weber emphasized their continuity. Still more important, and in line with his inheritance from the neo-idealists, Weber held that an "indispensable . . . element in the explanation" of a phenomenon like capitalism "lay in a system of ultimate values and value attitudes."[18] Thus he refined on Marx's notion of a class by adding to it a new category in which the value aspect of group relationships would stand out in sharper fashion: a class, he asserted, was an economic category of people united by material interests; a status group *(Stand)* could be defined as one in which considerations of prestige and honor were paramount.

Already in his early agrarian studies, Weber had come to the conclusion that in the large-scale flight from the land of German rural workers east of the Elbe, ideal and spiritual motives had at least as great an influence as material considerations. And his sub-

---

17 Karl Löwith: *"Max Weber und Karl Marx,"* Archiv für Sozialwissenschaft und Sozialpolitik, LXVII (1932), 54, 60–2, 80; Introduction by Gerth and Mills to *From Max Weber*, p. 50.
18 Parsons: Introduction to *Theory of Social and Economic Organization*, p. 79, *Structure of Social Action*, pp. 509–10.

sequent reflections had simply deepened this conviction. A decade after his agrarian survey, when he undertook his studies of religion, it was with the express intention of documenting through systematic empirical findings the interlocking action of economic and spiritual factors in producing the great social transformations of the past.

The first of these studies, *The Protestant Ethic and the Spirit of Capitalism,* early became the most widely read of Weber's writings.[19] And this popularity was unquestionably justified. Despite all the criticism to which it has been subjected, and the corrections of detail that it has undergone,[20] *The Protestant Ethic* remains one of the great works of the social thought of our time—an almost unique combination of imaginative boldness in its central hypothesis and meticulous scholarship in its documentation. In its careful balancing of the material and spiritual, it pursues an argument of a subtlety that has frequently thrown the overhasty reader off the track.

Weber's critics could have been spared most of their pains if they had pondered more carefully two of the author's guiding pronouncements. In the first place, he carefully specified that he was not arguing that Protestantism had "caused" the rise of capitalism. "We have no intention whatever," he wrote,

> *of maintaining such a foolish and doctrinaire thesis as that the spirit of capitalism . . . could only have arisen as the result of certain effects of the Reformation or even that capitalism as an economic system is a creation of the Reformation. . . . On the contrary, we only wish to ascertain whether and to what extent religious forces have taken part in the qualitative formation and the quantitative expansion of that spirit over the world, and what concrete aspects of our capitalistic culture can be traced to them. In view of the tremendous confusion of interdependent influences among the material basis, the forms of social and political organization, and the ideas current in the time of the Reformation, we can only proceed by investigating whether and at what points certain correlations between forms of religious belief and practical ethics can be worked out. At the*

[19] Translation by Talcott Parsons (New York and London, 1930). After having originally been published as articles in volumes XX (1904) and XXI (1905) of the *Archiv für Sozialwissenschaft und Sozialpolitik,* "*Die protestantische Ethik und der Geist des Kapitalismus*" was reprinted in the *Gesammelte Aufsätze zur Religionssoziologie,* I, 17–206.

[20] Notably by R. H. Tawney in his *Religion and the Rise of Capitalism* (London, 1926).

same time we shall as far as possible clarify the manner and the general direction in which, by virtue of those relationships, the religious movements have influenced the development of material culture.[21]

Or, as Weber put it in another place, "the 'world images' that have been created by 'ideas' have, like switchmen, determined the tracks along which action has been pushed by the dynamic of interest": at certain decisive points in history, a spiritual program and the pressure of a material-interest group have converged. Obviously, Weber was not trying to chart a simple causal sequence. He was attempting the infinitely more complex task of delineating the "elective affinity" between capitalism and Protestantism—the largely unconscious similarities of outlook that led the second and third generations of Calvinists to put their stern, self-denying, ascetic capacities into the service of God's purposes on earth and, in the process, to give a new rationality and dynamism to the techniques of expanding capitalism.[22] He was trying to show how an ethic originally devised for otherworldly purposes became transmuted into a marvelously efficient stimulus to material gain.

In the second place—and this was simply another way of phrasing the first pronouncement—Weber denied any intention of "refuting" Marxism or the materialist interpretation of history. It was not his aim, he wrote, "to substitute for a one-sided materialistic [interpretation] an equally one-sided spiritualistic causal interpretation of culture and of history." He was simply trying to show what would happen when one treated "only one side of the causal chain." Marx had run the causal sequence in one direction, i.e., from economic to spiritual factors. Weber wanted to run it in the reverse order as a complement to what Marx had done. Each method, he argued, was "equally possible." Both of them—and others besides—were perfectly permissible. But neither was exhaustive: each could serve only "as the preparation," not "as the conclusion of an investigation."[23] Actually, according to Weber's own methodology, such a conclusion could never be achieved. But it could be approached more closely through combining a number of *alternative causal sequences* of the sort that he himself and Marx had run.

[21] *Protestant Ethic*, pp. 91–2. I have altered the translation slightly.
[22] "Social Psychology of World Religions," *From Max Weber*, p. 280; Introduction by Gerth and Mills, *Ibid.*, p. 62–3.
[23] *Protestant Ethic*, pp. 27, 183; Löwith: *"Weber und Marx,"* pp. 210–11.

In his study of Protestantism Weber drew, as so many of his contemporaries had done, on the scholarship and example of William James. On his trip to the United States—which in fact interrupted the composition of this work—Weber not only met James but also derived some of the first-hand impressions that enliven his discussion of the more eccentric of the Protestant sects.[24] The sects offered a curiosity-shop of extravagant and apparently irrational religious behavior. Yet, as Weber soon discovered, the same individuals who in their religious capacity endorsed these practices, in their role as American businessmen were the epitomes of rational and ordered living. Here lay another of the paradoxes in the relationship between Protestantism and capitalism. In most respects, however, Weber found that the United States offered an extreme case of the rationalization of existence. It seemed to mark the farthest point yet reached on the path along which the Western world as a whole was apparently heading. It was in America that the fusion of the Protestant and the capitalist ethic had been most complete, and that society came closest to that uniform, soulless efficiency that loomed up as the model of the future.

Throughout the foregoing discussion it has doubtless become apparent that Weber thought of capitalism as a complex of rational procedures. In this respect he differed sharply from Marx's insistence on its contradictions. For Weber, capitalism—like bureaucracy—was simply another of the major manifestations of that all-embracing process of rationalization that concerned him most profoundly in the history of the Western world. Why, he asked himself, had this process occurred to its full extent in the West alone? Why had it stopped short in India, in China, in all the other parts of the world that were the equals of the West in religious and humanistic culture? In these civilizations also there existed a kind of capitalism; but it had not pursued the same course as in the West. Why did "the capitalistic interests" of China and India not find their way to the full rationalization of life? "Why did not the scientific, the artistic, the political, or the economic development there enter upon that path

---

[24] See the shorter essay, dating from 1906, that supplements the main study of the Protestant ethic: *"Die protestantischen Sekten und der Geist des Kapitalismus,"* *Gesammelte Aufsätze zur Religionssoziologie,* I, 207–36 ("The Protestant Sects and the Spirit of Capitalism," *From Max Weber,* pp. 302–22); also Marianne Weber: *Max Weber,* pp. 316–45.

. . . which is peculiar to the Occident?"[25] This was the deepest of the riddles that had inspired Weber to undertake his studies of religion. Beyond the confrontation with Marx, beyond the reckoning with the spiritual world, Weber was interested above all in seeking out the reasons for the historical uniqueness of his own civilization.

In *The Protestant Ethic* he had reached an initial solution. He had come to the conclusion that it was the dynamic force of Protestantism, and more particularly of Calvinism, that had made the decisive difference. In the studies of the great Asian religions that succeeded it, he tried to work the proof in reverse. He attempted to show what was lacking in Buddhism or Hinduism—namely, an ethic that endorsed and encouraged the life of rationally oriented business activity. Thus these subsequent studies had a broader range than the original work on Protestantism. In his effort to establish the economic mentality of the Asian cultures, Weber found it necessary to run more than one causal sequence: he not only traced the influence of religion on economic life; he searched out the geographic and material conditions that had helped to direct religious thought itself into certain well-defined channels.

As the publication of these studies proceeded, Weber clearly revealed his personal commitment to the rational values of his own society. His profound concern for reason—his distress at the paradox that made it both the highest achievement of the West and the source of the "soullessness" of contemporary life—inspired him to subject the culture of rationality itself to searching examination. This concern for the status of reason in contemporary society emerges with particular clarity in the last phase of Weber's life and work.

*   *   *

Unquestionably Weber's chief intellectual weakness lies in the field of psychology. His "isolation of rationality" and his "treatment of affect as *only* a factor of deviation from rational norms is clearly incompatible with the findings of modern psychology, which rather point definitely to the integration of affective and rationally cognitive elements in the same action."[26] Weber, like Croce or Pareto, was *directly* interested only in what was rationally understandable. The

---

[25] *Protestant Ethic,* p. 25.
[26] Parsons: Introduction to *Theory of Social and Economic Organization,* p. 27.

illogical, the affective, remained for him no more than a residual category.

A second weakness—and perhaps the one instance of intellectual faltering in his whole theoretical production—was his refusal to recognize the implicit relativism of his own thought. We have seen that none of Weber's predecessors or contemporaries consented to call himself a relativist. And Weber was no exception. He rejected relativism as the "crudest misunderstanding" of his point of view.[27] In the sense of a radical skepticism—in the sense of a philosophy which questions the whole notion of responsible choice—Weber was certainly not a relativist.[28] But in the sense of a point of view that denies any metaphysical certainty—whether of ethics or of historical truth—Weber can properly be characterized by this term. He frankly recognized the personal, affective origin of his own convictions: he found no ultimate grounding for them. But he grew dizzy at the abysses that this line of reasoning seemed to open. We of the generation of his grandchildren, who have grown up in an atmosphere of intellectual and moral relativism, may find ourselves less frightened.

[27] "Meaning of 'Ethical Neutrality,' " *Methodology*, p. 18.
[28] The contrary, however, has been persuasively argued by Lee Strauss in his *Natural Right and History* (Chicago, 1953), Chapter 2.

Bruce Mazlish

ARTHUR MITZMAN'S PSYCHO-HISTORICAL STUDY OF MAX WEBER

A specialist in intellectual history at the Massachusetts Institute of Technology, Professor Mazlish received his undergraduate and advanced degrees from Columbia University. He has taught at the University of Maine and Columbia University and serves as an editor of the journal History and Theory. *In addition to European intellectual and social history, Dr. Mazlish has particularly concerned himself with the development of historical methodology and its relation to other methods of investigation, such as psychoanalysis. As the editor of* Psychoanalysis and History *(Englewood Cliffs, N.J., 1963), for example, Professor Mazlish brings an uncommon expertise to the task of evaluating Arthur Mitzman's* The Iron Cage: An Historical Interpretation of Max Weber *(New York, 1969). Mitzman's work is probably the most outstanding psycho-historical study of Max Weber to appear in recent years, and it is subjected to careful review by Professor Mazlish in the following selection.*

By now, we are all familiar with the effort to use a man's writings to illuminate his personal, psychological development. Erik Erikson's brilliant *Young Man Luther* and more lately *Gandhi's Truth* are in this genre, although they go beyond it by also relating their subjects to larger historical events. In each case, an historically important man is analyzed, in terms of psycho-biography or psycho-history, and his words, so to speak, are used against him. Less frequently is the direction followed by Arthur Mitzman, in which a great thinker's personal, psychological development—in this case, Max Weber's—is used to illuminate the meaning of his theoretical writings. (The movement from the writer's personality to his creations is, of course, more common in literary studies.)

Since Marx, the sociology of knowledge has been recognized as an accepted discipline. We are all alerted to the need to search for the material and social basis of a man's thought. But the "psychology of knowledge," if I may coin the phrase, is only now coming into its own. Under this rubric, we look for the psychological, especially psychoanalytic, basis of a man's conscious thoughts. How do his personal defenses and adaptations affect the way he views the world? What transferences does he bring to his perception of men and events? As usual, Erikson has pioneered in analyzing some of these problems. Moreover, he has also concentrated on the role of the psycho-historical investigator himself, as illustrated by his article, "On the Nature of Psycho-Historical Evidence: In Search of Gandhi" (*Daedalus,* Summer 1968).

Unlike Erikson, Mitzman does not attempt a theoretical and typological treatment of the methodological problems of this psychology of knowledge, but offers us, instead, a formal case study of the method in operation.

Mitzman's choice of Max Weber is unusually apt. For Weber not only is identified with the thesis of Western civilization's increasing rationality, but is intimately related to the concept of value-free research. If Weber can be shown as a man of subterranean passions flawing his rationality, and, even more importantly, undermining his putative value-free work, then the "psychology of knowledge" will indeed have made a telling point. It is largely to this task that Mitzman has addressed himself. He has done it with subtlety and judgment, and, as I shall try to show, with possible conclusions different from the ones to which he comes in the end.

In 1964, the hundredth anniversary of Weber's birth was celebrated. It coincided with the publication of various documents from the *Nachlass* in Eduard Baumgarten's *Max Weber, Werk und Person* (Tübingen, 1964), as well as the appearance of personal memoirs by a number of Weber's close friends. These publications, along with two fundamental earlier works—Marianne Weber's *Max Weber, ein Lebensbild* (Tübingen, 1926) and Weber's early letters, *Jugendbriefe* (Tübingen, 1936)—have made possible the sort of analysis undertaken by Mitzman. The Baumgarten family was especially important to Weber's development; and Hermann Baumgarten, married to the sister of Weber's mother, appeared to have become a model, a substitute father, for young Max. Max's first love was his cousin Emmy, the Baumgarten's daughter. Mitzman has been very fortunate, therefore, in being able to draw on Eduard Baumgarten, who is the son of Max's cousin, Fritz, not only through his book, but in person, even to the extent of having him scrutinize the present work in detail. Without Eduard Baumgarten, for example, we would not know many intimate details of Weber's life, such as the fact that "he never consummated his marriage" (276) and that between 1911–1914 he had a deep personal relationship, perhaps an affair, with a young woman in Heidelberg (277). Indeed, there are still many unpublished letters— including over a hundred from Weber's correspondence with the young woman—in Baumgarten's possession. What Mitzman makes of these personal details—the sort of details which are beneath the concern and often the contempt of traditional intellectual historians —remains to be seen.

Mitzman uses Friedrich Meinecke's review of the *Lebensbild* in 1927 as a point of departure. According to Meinecke, "in Max Weber himself, we can see an Orestes [to his mother's Iphigenia], when we learn how, out of love for mother, he intervened ruthlessly against his father and then shortly afterward was shattered by his sudden death." Moreover, according to Meinecke, Weber's opposition to his father mirrored "the historical opposition of two generations" (307). But Meinecke's line of thought remained unfollowed in the following decades, for good reasons as Mitzman points out: involved family members were still alive, the necessary *Nachlass* was unavailable, and the application of psychoanalytic categories to intellectual biographies was less acceptable than it is now. As a result, instead of Oedipus, or Orestes, Weber was portrayed as a stately German liberal, pursuing his magisterial social science without values, emotions, or the intrusion of his own personality. It was not until Wolfgang Mommsen's penetrating study, *Max Weber und die deutsche Politik* (Tübingen, 1959), that the placid picture of Weber the value-free scientist was shattered and he was shown to be "a prime mover in German liberalism's embracement of imperialism in the mid-90s and a ruthless advocate for most of his career of nationalist *Realpolitik*" (311). With Mommsen having deepened our understanding of Weber as a public figure Mitzman now sets out, in Meinecke's footsteps, to do the same for the private person, and to show how the two figures coalesce as one personality.

Mitzman's major theses are: 1. "Weber's view of the world in the years before 1897 was shaped by his struggle to escape from and finally challenge the dominance in the Weber household of his father, a dominance which he identified subconsciously with the political hegemony of the Junkers over the landworkers in particular and the German people in general" (6); 2. in 1897, aged 33, Weber finally stood up to his father, and ordered him out of his house; seven weeks later the father died and Weber gradually succumbed to feelings of guilt which left him psychically incapacitated until around 1902, and intermittently thereafter; 3. thus, Weber's "view of the world in the years after 1902 was structured by the lessons he drew, consciously or otherwise, from the agonizing collapse which resulted from this struggle" (6–7); 4. Weber's Oedipal struggle was representative of that of his generation, who could no longer discharge their aggressive feelings against the aristocracy, because bourgeois politicians, i.e., their fathers, now ruled alongside or in the former's place; thus, "revolt against the generation in power no longer permitted the easy transference of patricidal aggressions to enemies condemned by Reason and History" (9).

As Lewis Coser judiciously remarks in his Preface, Mitzman's account is "suggestive—even though it may not be fully convincing in all its details" (vii). Let me take my stand openly. I find Mitzman's book a major contribution—always heuristic, even in its faults—to the comprehension of Weber's work and to the newly emerging field of psycho-history. It supports the view, convincingly, I believe, that intellectual history ungrounded in psychoanalytic understanding tends to be incomplete. One can no longer treat Freud as merely a figure in intellectual history; one must now also apply Freudian insight to intellectual history.

I am, therefore, on Mitzman's side. With this firmly said, I must admit that I find more convincing his relating of Weber's psyche to his writings than I do the larger thesis relating Weber's struggle to the generational conflict of the time. Mitzman may very well be right; but the evidence he offers is too gross, more assertive than demonstrative. (He promises us another book, on the roots of twentieth-century German social theory in general, and I suspect he will make a more convincing case there.) For the moment, a book such as *The Wish To Be Free* (Berkeley, 1969), by Fred Weinstein and Gerald Platt, takes us farther along the road of understanding the movement toward increased autonomy of the sons from the fathers.

In any event, Mitzman's overall conclusion is reflected in his title,

The Iron Cage. The phrase comes from Weber's *The Protestant Ethic and the Spirit of Capitalism,* which he ends with a warning that the ascetic ethos, freely adopted by the early Puritans and which played such an important role in the development of Western capitalism, may be becoming a deterministic and mechanistic cloak suffocating modern man. As Mitzman reminds us, Weber's phrase is *"ein stahlhartes Gehäuse"*—literally, a housing hard as steel, or, in Talcott Parsons' translation, an "iron cage."

Now, Weber's writings are filled with references to the "secure homes" that German fathers had built for their sons, and it is clear that Weber had a difficult, even traumatic, time breaking free from control by his father's "house." Part of Weber's inheritance—a combined inheritance from his capitalist father and his Calvinist-inclined mother—was undoubtedly the "iron cage," the Protestant Ethic as elaborated by Weber himself. On the basis of this background, Mitzman claims that Weber's "discovery that his inherited ethic led to collapse coincided with a similar discovery by his generation and the one following. With the prospects of the political sublimation of repressed instinct brought to an end by the victories of European liberalism between 1860 and 1870, the mortal hostility of the bourgeois superego for libidinal impulse—the psychological underpinning of the Victorian ethic of transcendence—would have to cease or all Europe would become a madhouse" (304).

This claim, as I have suggested, while partly right, is too large. Weber, at the end, did see a danger in Western civilization's becoming an "iron cage," and Mitzman offers us a healthy corrective to the prevailing view of Weber as a sort of chamber-of-commerce proponent of modernity and "rationality." There was ambivalence, and an enormous creative tension between passion and reason, in Weber's life and thought; and it is this that makes him so relevant—increasingly so in the portrait so well painted by Mitzman—for our time. Yet I would claim that Weber's "house" was not Mitzman's "madhouse," and that in the greatest part of his work Weber reaffirmed rationality—which he equated with modernity—more strongly than he might have otherwise, because, in fact, he had tested his convictions in the traumas of his own soul. Was it not, rather, the very cessation of the hostility of the "bourgeois superego for libidinal impulse"—and, like Freud, I make no claim here for maintenance of the excessive aspects of Victorian morality—that led to the madhouse of Nazism? It was Weber, we must remember, not Stefan George, who opposed the impulsive elements that eventually went into Hitler's National Socialism.

With this friendly disagreement aside, let me now return to Mitzman's analysis of Weber and his writings. We are all accustomed to a "Life and Works" treatment of distinguished thinkers. Mitzman's book is in this tradition—but with a difference: his Life is an inward life, which is then related intimately to the outward works. Weber's ancestors on both sides were Protestants, originally of strong evangelical convictions. His paternal ancestors, however, became capitalists in the linen trade (one thinks of Engels, and his similar textile background), although Weber's own father studied law and became a magistrate and eventually a member of the Reichstag. Weber's maternal ancestors included French Calvinists, who, emigrating to Geneva and then Frankfurt, accumulated a great deal of wealth while retaining their religiosity. Weber's own father was a typical authoritarian Victorian in his own household, with robust tastes and little inner religion. The mother was a deeply pietistic woman, who, although she bore her husband numerous children out of duty, had a manifest distaste for sexual relations. The marriage, needless to say, was filled with tensions.

Weber, the eldest child, inherited and experienced these tensions in overflowing measure. As Mitzman convincingly argues, Weber sought to reconcile, intellectually, the capitalist spirit of his father with the pietist ethos of his mother, strong libidinal impulses with the need for ascetic controls, compulsive work with the notion of a "calling." But underlying the intellectual effort was the personal emotional life of Weber himself. Perhaps we can illustrate this relationship with an example provided by Mitzman, from the sphere of sexuality, which, though trivial in itself, opens up a whole world of meaning.

It begins with a typical Victorian situation: a tutor who makes advances to the daughter in the household. The tutor in this case was Gervinus, the historian, and the girl was Helene Fallenstein, later to be Max Weber's mother (Gervinus, incidentally, was married, but childless). As Mitzman tells it, Gervinus, originally a friend of Helene's father, after the latter's death apparently developed "a more than fatherly interest in one of them [the Fallenstein children]." When

Helene was sixteen years old, she was forced to repel his advances, an experience which left her with a permanent distaste for sensual passion" (19). Fleeing from Gervinus, who next tried to marry her to a student of his, she went to live with her sister Ida in Berlin. Ida was married to the liberal historian Hermann Baumgarten, and it was his friend and political colleague, Max Weber, Sr., whom Helene married two years later.

Now, Mitzman himself does not make the comparison, but one cannot help thinking of the case presented to us by Freud as "Dora." Dora, too, as we recall, recoiled from the advances of an older friend of the family, with traumatic results. The case was incredibly complicated, but one aspect of Freud's analysis shows that part of Dora's conscious revulsion was because of the very strength of the positive attraction, which she felt had to be fought off savagely. Is there any reason not to assume a similar ambivalence on the part of Helene Weber?

In any case, the traumatic episode appears to have left her with a permanent distaste for sexual passion. This attitude was clearly conveyed to her son Max, and we can be sure it played a role in his own relations to his wife Marianne. Thus, as promised earlier, the personal detail—Weber's inability to consummate his marriage—spurned by traditional intellectual historians, takes on added resonance, and, as we shall also show later, "intellectual" significance. Before that demonstration, however, a few more comments about the "tutor episode."

There is a curious, inverted, almost compulsive repetition of this episode in Helene's later life. This time, it is she who insists on keeping a tutor for her younger son in the household, against the strong opposition of her husband. Needless to say, there is no hint of the sexual; the tutor, a Herr Voigt, is a highly spiritual young theologian. Nevertheless, Max Weber, Sr. felt threatened by the presence of the young tutor in his household, who was taking his wife away from him "spiritually," and ordered him dismissed. In the words of Marianne Weber, Helene felt this "as unjust to him [the tutor] as well as to her son; it was a long time before she got over it." On this, Mitzman perceptively comments: "It may have taken her eldest son even longer. Thirty-one years later he wrote of Herr Voigt's dismissal: 'The nasty correspondence which resulted from it at the time completely estranged me too from papa'" (46).

What I am suggesting now is that the tutor affair was over-determined. Trivial in itself, it obviously called forth over-reactions on the part of those involved. I have tried to suggest why for Helene and Max Weber, Sr. That Max Weber thirty-one years later would still remember it as completely estranging him from his father is also striking. As Mitzman reminds us, it was a turning point in Weber's growing loathing for his father and "a deep sympathy for his mal-treated mother" (47). What was at stake was the authoritarianism of a father whom Weber could no longer respect, and the dismissal of the tutor struck at Weber's own autonomy as much as at the mother with whom at this point in life he was increasingly becoming identified.

Weber's parental identifications were in constant change and turmoil. Originally a shy and reserved young boy, at the time of going off to university, aged 18, he experimented with being like the father. At the university to study law, as his father had done, Weber quickly became a typical beer-drinking, fraternity-dueling German student (one thinks of Karl Marx's comparable experience). He even changed physically, from a quiet, thin boy to a boisterous, full-bodied man. Helene Weber was dismayed at the change in her beloved son, and did not hesitate to display her displeasure. In a well-known story, as Mitzman retells it, "on his return from Heidelberg, she greeted his bloated, saber-scarred face with a resounding smack" (24).

Why? The picture we have of German fathers always stresses their authoritarianism, and Mitzman supports this view. Yet, one must not underestimate the similar role of the mothers. Though expressing it differently from the father, Helene Weber exercised an enormous moral authoritarianism over the young Max. Her piety formed part of Weber's demanding superego, curtailing and limiting his instinc-tual needs. It was his mother's "influence that kept Max Weber chaste in his Strassburg student days" (33). Worse, it was the mother who set him against his father, and thus against a most important part of himself. In fact, it was Helene Weber who commanded the im-possible, psychologically, of her son: to obey God, the Father, and to rebel against his own, real father (cf. 93–94).

At first, in this turn of his psyche, Weber heeded his mother. He began to despise his father as a philistine and as an authoritarian with clay feet (for in the political arena, Weber now saw his father as prostrating himself supinely before Prussian authoritarianism;

once again a comparison with Marx's life-history is in order). His father's "house" now became for Weber a "house of servitude"—to use a phrase from one of Weber's writings in 1906. It also became a question of who would "rule in the house"; and as any Freudian knows, the "house" also symbolizes the mother. Unable to drive out his father, Weber became desperate to gain his own freedom and financial independence, and to leave; yet, his feelings were probably ambivalent, for he did not make the break until 1894, aged 30!

In 1887, the father had driven the tutor out of the house, symbolically asserting his authority over young Max as well. Surely, that is the real significance of the episode. Ten years later, in 1897, it was the son's turn. Married to Marianne and a precociously successful academician at Heidelberg, Weber invited his mother to visit him. The father insisted on coming along, and on determining the time and duration of her stay. Mitzman summarizes what happened: "When the son saw his father arrive with his mother, the pent-up anger of a decade finally burst forth: such tyranny might still go on in Charlottenburg, but in Max Weber's own house, in his mother's childhood city [Heidelburg], it must stop. If, in 1887, his father had forced Herr Voigt, a spiritual son of Helene Weber if there ever was one, out of his house, now, in excellent conscience, the son by blood would pay him back . . . the old man must leave. The old man did leave, and his wife spent a few guilt-ridden weeks with her son and daughter-in-law" (150).

Max, Jr. had finally done what his mother had asked of him: rebelled against the father. He had separated his parents. Seven weeks later, Max, Sr., estranged from his wife, died suddenly of a stomach hemorrhage. At first, Weber showed no signs of remorse or guilt. In a short while, however, he began to exhibit unusual irritability and nervous exhaustion. A year later, about the anniversary of his father's death—and the way in which Mitzman establishes the correspondence of the dates is a lovely bit of detective work—Weber was overcome by sleeplessness and "functional disturbances." What followed was a complete nervous breakdown, involving an inability to sustain his academic or any other duties. Weber's almost total incapacitation, as we have already noted, lasted until about 1902, reappearing thereafter intermittently, and influencing the rest of his life and career.

The doctors, according to the custom of the times, diagnosed the cause of Weber's breakdown as overwork. Two years later, in 1900, a relatively unknown neuro-pathologist, Sigmund Freud, published his *Interpretation of Dreams,* which advanced a different diagnosis for cases such as Max Weber's. In a preface written a few years after the original publication, Freud commented apropos of a portion of his own dream material, that the most important event in a man's life was the death of his father. Later, he wrote the paper, "Mourning and Melancholia," where he analyzed the sort of delayed reaction found in Weber's case. The overall diagnosis that Freud would have offered for his contemporary, Weber, was of course a classic Oedipal conflict.

Upon his gradual recovery in 1902, Weber inched his way back to scholarly work. Now he began to reject identification with his mother as well as his father, and to search for his own creative synthesis. On one side, he became interested in Marx's explanation of the nature and origin of capitalism. On another side, he manifested an interest in Russian culture, especially Tolstoy, and its challenge to the values of rational and rationalized society. He also involved himself in the George-Kreis, with its glorification of instinct and impulse. In an extraordinary corpus of work—again, one thinks of a famous man, Darwin, who intensely neurasthenic, able to work only for two or three hours a day, turned out a staggering intellectual production—Weber sought to comprehend the elements of the ancient and modern world, and to integrate his comprehension in a true social science.

According to Mitzman, Weber moved intellectually "from asceticism and toward admiration for aristocratic and mystical modes of charisma" (287). His affair with the young lady started about the same time, 1911, and paralleled in its anti-Victorian nature Weber's new intellectual commitments (cf. 287–288). For the rest of his life, Weber's creative intellectual ambivalence and his personal experience of emotion tended to run together. The putative proponent of Western rationalism had come, by the end of his life in 1920, to see and acknowledge the darker hues of existence as well.

Such is part of Mitzman's argument. I have not done justice to his depiction of Weber's life, for the argumentation and detailed knowledge which Mitzman brings to his task need to be encountered by the reader directly. Nor have I indicated that Mitzman is well aware that his hero, or anti-hero, did not exist in an historical vacuum.

Mitzman reminds us of the predicament of liberals in Bismarckian Germany, where, successful in their quest for unification and nationalism, they were not allowed to share power with the man who had pushed through to their aims, though by means they had not intended. He sketches for us, too, the nature of Germany as a "modernizing" society, and the problems of bureaucratization and democracy concomitant with this development. It is in this context that he analyzes the development of Weber's life. Overall, there is no doubt that by his study and depiction of Weber's inner and outer life, Mitzman has enormously deepened our knowledge of the man.

But what of the work? Weber's earlier contemporary, Nietzsche, perceived a crucial aspect of the general relation between a man's life and work when he said: "Most of the conscious thinking of a philosopher is secretly guided by his instinct and forced along certain lines. Even behind logic, and its apparent sovereignty of development stand value judgments, or, to speak more plainly, physiological demands for preserving a certain type of life." Specifically, for Weber, we can see some of his "instincts" and "value judgments" at work in his "conscious thinking" about the East Elbian Question, treated by Mitzman under the heading: "Assault on the Junker Hegemony."

Between 1892 and 1895, Weber analyzed the changing economic and social conditions of the German East, and especially the exodus of German peasants from the East Elbian region and their replacement by Slavic agricultural workers. This analysis foreshadows all his later work. I shall try to summarize Weber's main points. First, world-wide changes in the marketplace—in this case, the grain market—were leading the Junkers toward capitalistic agricultural production. To maximize their profits, that is, in following economic rationality, the Junkers turned from traditional semi-feudal labor to wage contracts on their estates, and to securing tariff protection in the country at large by exercising their political power. The result was paradoxical: ardent patriots, the Junkers were driving semi-independent Germans off their lands and colonizing the East with Slavic workers; vocal anticapitalists, the Junkers were behaving as badly as the most crass capitalist parvenu.

Weber did not rest content with rational economic analysis. He saw that the economic developments which he had analyzed rested on deep psychological foundations. The Junkers were pushed to exploit their holdings more efficiently in order to keep up with the rising standard of living of the urban bourgeoisie (i.e., men like Weber's father), in short, to maintain their status, or "honored" position. The German workers, in turn, were psychologically unable to accept the wage contract system, because it violated their need for personal independence, their growing desire for autonomy from Junker patriarchal control. As Mitzman summarizes it: "the key forces in bringing about this change were not, as Marx might have put it, the development of the forces of production, but psychological motives among both rulers and ruled" (79).

For Weber, the entire development he had described was a disaster. An ardent nationalist, Weber saw Germany being potentially dismembered in the East. A proud liberal bourgeois, he saw his father's generation of middle-class politicians aping the Junker way of life and kowtowing to Junker political domination. Above all, Weber wished economic development to be subordinated to *true* rational control—not the hitherto unintended consequences of seeming economic rationalism—and for Weber this meant *Staatsraison,* that is, rational political control; or such, at least, is my interpretation. It was to this end, I believe, that he worked all his life to create a true social science. Thus, Weber's intense German nationalism, which we may see as a blemish, was an essential motive for his work.

What were some of the other personal motives? Mitzman suggests, and I agree with him, that there was a powerful identification with the German workers' desire for independence and autonomy. As Weber himself put it: "*Psychological* factors of overwhelming power lead both to the flight into the cities and to the disorganization of this labor constitution [sic]" (101). Thus, Weber saw the workers' "psychological factors" as mirroring his own desire to escape from his father's patriarchal domination. I would also argue that Weber was fighting his own temptation to succumb, as his father before him, to the Junker value system and its assumed social superiority. We have already seen his trial identification with these values in his life at the university. His mother's smack recalled him to his own Calvinist inheritance, and a more authentic part of himself. At this point, I suggest, Weber perceived and demonstrated the falseness and weakness—the clay feet—of Junker patriarchalism, and thus of his father's own model.

Weber's personal motives did not determine his findings. They combined with his intellectual developments, his legal and philosophical thinking, and helped supply some of the passion animating his rational analysis. Reinhard Bendix, summarizing Weber's early studies as pointing to all his later work on the sociology of religion, comments from a purely intellectual point of view that

> *His disenchantment with the world in which he lived led him to a search of the past for the origin of the values he prized. As an individualist Weber sought to recover the historical sources of the individualism that prompted the farm workers to prefer the uncertainty of seasonal labor to the security of personal subservience. As a member of the middle class he inquired into the sources of the collectivism and rationality that prompted English and Hanseatic stockbrokers to impose an ethic of trade upon themselves —a practice that stood in marked contrast to the aping of aristocratic ways among his compatriots.*

What Mitzman has done is to supply the unconscious factor to the conscious equation of Weber's work offered us by Bendix.

The breakdown of 1898 dissolved the synthesis worked out in the East Elbian Question. With his gradual recovery after 1902, Weber laboriously set to work to reintegrate himself and the world, but this time on deeper foundations. In 1903, he began work on the "Protestant Ethic," and this led him to a full-scale sociology of religion, and, in fact, to a complete sociology of the modern world. Mitzman summarizes the general dynamics involved when he says:

> *Weber was able to gouge out of his superego and examine critically the commandment of unceasing labor that had been lodged there. Thus, by identifying the work ethic of his mother's Calvinist ancestry as a device which formerly gave evidence of divine grace but now served only as a "housing hard as steel," Weber was focusing his intellect on his own experience in order both to liberate himself from it and to interpret the history of the modern world; he was perceiving the historical dimension of his personal dilemma. (173–174)*

In turn, Mitzman takes the fundamental concepts of Weberian sociology—for example, charisma and bureaucracy, class and status, asceticism and mysticism, rationalism and magic—and seeks to offer an insight into the "personal dilemma" underlying these notions. I have tried to give a hint as to how he proceeds, by drawing on the example of East Elbia. For the full picture, the reader must again go directly to Mitzman's book.

I have already stated my high regard for Mitzman's general presentation. Now, I must pass on to some further reflections which are rather more tendentious and negative. My first comment here is to call attention to the fact that Mitzman simply disregards large aspects of Weber's life and works that might have deepened and broadened the picture offered to us. For example, we are told almost nothing about Weber's sibling relationships, yet these must have been of great significance in affecting his attitudes to other men and women (e.g., sisters as affecting his propensity to fall in love with his cousins). A few lines are given to Weber's brother, Alfred, an important scholar in his own right, but the relationship is not followed out satisfactorily. In short, Weber's father and mother have been allowed to over dominate the scene, without allowing for the psychologically mediating effect of siblings. (If Mitzman was unable to obtain information in this matter, then we should have been so informed.)

Similarly, Weber's experience in the army is almost completely neglected. Gerth and Mills tell us in their brief introduction to *From Max Weber* that he adjusted to the boredom of military life "by having his fill of alcohol in the evening and going through the military routine the next day in the daze of a moderate hang-over" (7). With Mitzman's gift for analysis, I would have expected him to make more of Weber's youthful encounter with stupefying military bureaucratic authority. And then, what of Weber's 1904 visit to the United States? Since Weber drew so many of his examples and so much of his understanding of modernity from the American model, further examination of this personal and intellectual experience would have been useful. Indeed, the intellectual aspects of Weber's encounter with America are shortchanged, as well as, on the other side, an account of Weber's contribution to economic history.

Now Mitzman could respond that he was not trying to present a complete psychological-intellectual analysis of Weber, but only to select certain aspects of the man and his works to illustrate certain theses. This is a perfectly legitimate position; and I suspect it is the one Mitzman would quite properly take. Let me press on then with broader, more methodological considerations. As is well known, the leading theorist and practitioner of psycho-history is Erik H. Erikson. Do his ideas figure in Mitzman's treatment? The only reference to Erikson is a footnote (p. 4), noting his ego-psychology as a branch of post-Freudian theory. Fine; but one wonders why Mitzman does not think it worthwhile to make more use of Erikson's approach to the study of life history? And especially of Erikson's brilliant analysis of the role of the psycho-historian himself, remarked upon earlier, in studying the sources and persons involved with his subject? Thus, in *Gandhi's Truth,* Erikson subjects himself, and his transferences to Gandhi and the informants about Gandhi, to a searching analysis. Only then, does he start on Gandhi per se.

How might this apply to Mitzman's work? In the first instance, one would have wished Mitzman to be more self-conscious about his use of Marianne Weber's *Lebensbild.* Surely, before we can evaluate her revelations, we need to understand *her* more thoroughly as a person. Perhaps Mitzman has done this privately; but we as readers are not allowed to share in his evaluations. More critical still, of course, is the question of Mitzman's own psyche, his own transferences and values (psychically and intellectually). How does *he* feel about parent figures, political authority, technological and scientific society, value-free research? Where are *his* sympathies involved in the pressing social and economic problems of today? How conscious is he of his own psychic processes, as they affect his work?

For example, Mitzman concludes at one point that "the visible danger in *fin de siècle* Europe was by no means a wildly destructive mass breakthrough of the irrational, but the contrary: the permanent victory over human spontaneity and autonomy of the machine, that harsh, material quintessence of the nineteenth-century superego" (251–252). This sounds very present-minded, where those in favor of a radical "aesthetic revolution"—to use the phrase of Herbert Marcuse—see no danger of a "breakthrough of the irrational" but only the terrible pressure of a "rational," mechanized, and thus alienating society. Surely, the danger, then and now, is of *both* kinds. To speak first of *fin de siècle* Europe: was virulent racism not a "visible danger" to those with eyes to see? Was Freud not reacting to the political irrationality he saw around him when he took up a Le Bon-like conservatism in the face of the "mob"? Mitzman mentions Carl E. Schorske's article, "Politics and the Psyche in Fin de Siècle Vienna: Schnitzler and Hofmannsthal," but he does not seem to reckon with Schorske's comment on a novel by Schnitzler: it "shows that instinct has in fact been let loose in the sphere of politics, parliament has become a mere theatre through which the masses are manipulated, sexuality has become liberated from the moral code which contained it" (938).

To pass to another sort of criticism, there is always the temptation to "reduce" thought to the unconscious impulses; to forget that we must seek a *correspondence* of various levels of the human psyche. Occasionally, it seems to me, Mitzman gives way to this temptation, as when he comments apropos of Weber's work on the East Elbian Question: "the most superficial of these realms of consciousness [Mitzman is discussing four such realms] is Weber's broad, scholarly analysis of the social and economic changes occurring in the relationship between Junker landlord and peasant in the German East" (75). Why the word "superficial"? One of its definitions, of course, is simply "on the surface." Another, however, is "not profound; shallow." By his use of a semi-pejorative word, Mitzman risks the sort of implicit reductionism that lurks in psychohistory.

Perhaps I can come to grips more fully with my major caveat to Mitzman's work by a discussion of value-free inquiry. Clearly the context for both Mitzman's and my views is the current debate on the subject between so-called radicals and liberals. Such a debate, for example, forms the core of the interesting book by Hugo Stretton, *The Political Sciences* (Basic Books, 1970), whose thesis is that the social scientist must work by a principle of selection that necessarily involves his values: result, value-free inquiry is impossible and undesirable. Stretton concludes by demanding a clear commitment to values (in his case, activist values).

Like Stretton, Mitzman places the subject of value-free inquiry at the very beginning of his book. His first words in his introduction are:

Max Weber's shadow falls long over the intellectual life of our era. His insistence that a value-free methodology is indispensable to the scientific analysis of society dominates contemporary sociology, often paralyzing the scholar's human commitment and justifying his remoteness and irrelevance. Further, the Weberian vision of modern society as subject to an inexorable rationalization of human activity, and of the modern mind as necessarily disenchanted when it fully comprehends this inexorability, places before us the bleak vistas of universal bureaucratization, the death of art and impulse, the suffocation of instinct . . . our options are far more open than his, our values are more fluid, and our youth determined to wrest control over their fate from impersonal bureaucracies. At the heart of Weber's vision lies only the truth of his epoch, his country and his station, the truth of a bourgeois scholar in Imperial Germany . . . developed under agonizing personal pressures, themselves exerted and maintained by the dilemmas of family, social milieu and historical position. (3; italics added)

The "personal pressures," as Mitzman has explained, came from Weber's parents, threatening Weber with unassimilatable differences. According to Mitzman: "Weber's justification for not taking sides in his parents' quarrels—i.e., for not making a value judgment of them—was, basically, that their notions were set in such different worlds that it was impossible, knowing both, to judge either" (60). Thus, Mitzman concludes; "Weber's methodological presupposition of a rigid separation between the spheres of logical analysis and value judgment serves the critical function of maintaining an equally rigid separation between his attitudes toward his mother on the one hand and his father on the other" (61; and cf. 169–170). Such, then, is Mitzman's etiological explanation of Weber's value-free inquiry.

Now, Mitzman, I suspect, is largely correct in his etiology. However, does the origin of a position in "personal pressures" vitiate its correctness? Is Darwin's theory of evolution any less scientific because we can show how its originator's neurasthenic condition helped him stumble toward it? To answer in the affirmative is simply to commit the etiological fallacy: to mistake a useful explanation of origins for a mischievous judgment as to worth.

What, in fact, is Weber's theory of value-free inquiry? Gerth and Mills, I believe, take us closer to an understanding of Weber's position than does Mitzman. Discussing Weber's reaction to William Ellery Channing, who made a deep impression on him, they state: "Characteristically, Weber does not enter into a theological dispute about the Sermon on the Mount; he keeps at a distance from Channing by locating his perspective in the social and historical situation; he tries thereby to "understand" and, at the same time, he relativizes Channing's position." Thus, Weber went beyond ethical absolutism. As he wrote in one of his letters: "The matter does not appear to me to be so desperate if one does not ask too exclusively (as the Baumgartens, now as often, do): 'Who is morally right and who is morally wrong?' But if one rather asks: 'Given the existing conflict, how can I solve it with the least internal and external damage for all concerned?' " (Gerth and Mills, 8–9).

Weber was a true social ecologist. By that I mean he constantly tried to understand the secondary, the unintended, consequences of actions and motives. That was what social science was about. His analysis of the East Elbian Question, as we have seen, was couched in these terms. Weber's social science was operational science, *Realpolitik* in the best sense of the term, where one recognizes the necessary means to a given end and at least envisions the consequences of these means in systematic fashion.

Whence come the ends, the ultimate values? Weber did not ignore this question; he confronted it first, and then put it to one side. In "Science as a Vocation," Weber quoted Tolstoy to the effect that "Science is meaningless because it gives no answer to our question, the only question important for us: 'What shall we do and how shall we live?' " Weber's answer is mild and thoughtful:

> That science does not give an answer to this is indisputable. The only question that remains is the sense in which science gives "no" answer, and whether or not science might yet be of some use to the one who puts the question correctly. Today one usually speaks of science as "free from presupposition." Is there such a thing? It depends upon what one understands thereby. All scientific work presupposes that the rules of logic and method are valid; these are general foundations of our orientation in the world; and, at least for our special question, these presuppositions are the least problematic aspect of science. Science further presupposes that what is yielded by scientific work is important in the sense that it is "worth being known." In this, obviously, are contained all our problems. For this presupposition cannot be proved by scientific means. It can only be interpreted with reference to its ultimate meaning, which we must reject or accept according to our ultimate position toward life. (Gerth and Mills, 143)

Elsewhere, in *Wirtschaft und Gesellschaft*, Weber went a bit further on the subject of meaning, declaring:

> "Meaning" may be of two kinds. The term may refer first to the actual existing meaning in the given concrete case of a particular actor, or to the average or approximate meaning attributable to a given plurality of

actors; or secondly to the theoretically conceived pure type *[i.e., ideal type] of subjective meaning attributed to the hypothetical actor or actors in a given type of action. In no case does it refer to an objectively "correct" meaning or one which is "true" in some metaphysical sense. It is this which distinguishes the empirical sciences of action, such as sociology and history, from the dogmatic disciplines in that area, such as jurisprudence, logic, ethics, and esthetics, which seek to ascertain the "true" and "valid" meanings associated with the objects of their investigation.*

It is a travesty of Weber to claim that he himself was not an openly committed man, a true activist. One may not like his imperialist or nationalist leanings; but one cannot deny his strenuous public advocacy of these positions. Moreover, it is not for nothing that his journal was called the *Archiv für Sozialwissenschaft und Sozialpolitik*; and I stress the last part of the title. Equally, it would be foolish to contend that, in fact, Weber's activist values did not color and perhaps warp his value-free inquiries. What he sets before us is an ideal type, from which he himself, understandably, often fell short.

Weber's ideal was the construction of the "empirical sciences of action." One can understand, for example, the connection of the Protestant Ethic, or other religious injunctions, with the spirit of capitalism *only* if one seeks to understand the values of the actors of the time without passing "dogmatic" judgment on them. Thus, Weber announced that "the question of the relative values of the cultures which are compared here will not receive a single word," and, more specifically, "in such a study, it may at once be definitely stated, no attempt is made to evaluate the ideas of the Reformation in any sense, whether it concern their social or their religious worth." What Weber has done—and it is of enormous importance— is to take the historicist position and stand it on its head; that is, to place its relativist value position in the service of universalizing social science. I cannot stress the point just made too strongly. In short, Weber's value-freedom is a purely heuristic necessity; to understand unintended consequences, one must first abstain from judging actors.

Thus, to achieve knowledge, an empirical science of action, one must start from a value-free position as *defined by Weber*. Next, *insofar as one is a scholar* one must then offer one's findings objectively to students. Weber detested a Treitschke, who used the scholarly podium as a forum for political propaganda. Equally, he scorned those students who "crave a leader and not a teacher" (Gerth and Mills, 149). Weber's claim was that

> . . . you can take this or that position when concerned with a problem of value. . . . If you take such and such a stand, then, according to scientific experience, you have to use such and such a means in order to carry out your conviction practically. Now, these means are perhaps such that you believe you must reject them. Then you simply must choose between the end and the inevitable means. Does the end "justify" the means? Or does it not? The teacher can confront you with the necessity of this choice. He cannot do more, so long as he wishes to remain a teacher and not to become a demagogue. He can, of course, also tell you that if you want such and such an end, then you must take into the bargain the subsidiary consequences which according to all experience will occur. (Gerth and Mills, 151)

Weber pronounced these words in 1918. To the very end of his life, he held fast to rationality. He knew, as Mitzman has so well shown us, the possible price to be paid: disenchantment of the world, the loss of some kinds of meaning. He also realized that excessive rationality, in the perverted form of over-mechanization of life, could lead to an "iron cage." Weber, however, like Freud, was a rational stoic. In the face of such dangers, he did not lose faith in man's effort at rationality. What was needed, he believed, was more and better rationality: a making intended what was before unintended (or to use the Freudian idiom, conscious what was unconscious). Today, with rationality itself rather than its abuses under attack, Weber's call to attention to the "subsidiary consequences" of seeking a particular end seems especially pertinent.

All in all, Mitzman has done a splendid job in showing us the personal motivations behind Weber's public conceptions. Political positions and sociological theories alike have been illuminated for us. As is obvious, however, I have drawn a slightly different conclusion from Mitzman's work. Of course, much of Weber's achievement is "only the truth of his epoch," but because he tried so desperately to transcend his own limitations, his theories and concepts are frequently "truths" for our time as well. Weber's insights into charisma and status, the Protestant Ethic, and the Spirit of Capitalism may indeed be grounded in the fact that he was "a bourgeois scholar in Imperial Germany," but they reach out far beyond that narrow social terrain.

There is, in fact, a paradox in Mitzman's treatment of Weber. For Mitzman calls upon Freud, a "bourgeois physician in Imperial Austria" (my phrase), to treat Weber, on the assumption that Freud's "truths" transcended his particular setting. Then why not Weber's? In fact, what Mitzman himself has done is to strip away much of the dross surrounding Weber's work, and allow us thereby to see what remains of trans-personal worth. In short, by adding psychology of knowledge to sociology of knowledge, Mitzman has helped to "free" Weber's work of its personal limitations, and, so to speak, has placed before us an "ideal type" of Weberian sociology.

Weber's theories, then, have not been "reduced" to his psychic hang-ups. They have been lifted out of them. Or rather, Weber's theories have been placed in creative tension with his "agonizing personal pressures." Intentionally or unintentionally, Mitzman has given us a Weber, not larger or smaller than life, but truer to life. In spite of any criticisms of the sort I have made earlier, Mitzman's book must take its place among the four or five best works in psycho-history that we now have. It is a powerful instance of how intellectual history can be deepened and made animate with real life. In sum, Mitzman's is not the definite Life and Works of Max Weber—it was never intended as such—but it is a giant step toward that goal.

Suggestions for Additional Reading

Confronted by the constant appearance of more and more works on the various aspects of the Weber thesis controversy, the interested reader is probably best advised to begin by reading more extensively in the works of the authors who have furnished selections for this volume. Fortunately, Weber's collected essays on the sociology of religion, *Gesammelte Aufsätze zur Religionssoziologie,* are now available in English in the following volumes: *The Protestant Ethic and the Spirit of Capitalism,* translated by Talcott Parsons (New York, 1958); *From Max Weber: Essays in Sociology,* translated, edited, and with an introduction by H. H. Gerth and C. Wright Mills (New York, 1946); *The Religion of China: Confucianism and Taoism,* translated by H. H. Gerth, introduction by C. K. Yang (New York, 1964); *The Religion of India: The Sociology of Hinduism and Buddhism,* translated by H. H. Gerth and Don Martindale (New York, 1958); *Ancient Judaism,* translated and with a preface by H. H. Gerth and Don Martindale (New York, 1952). A thoughtful reading of any of these volumes will add to the understanding of a newcomer to the Weber thesis controversy. Those especially interested in Weber as an individual would do well to read more of H. Stuart Hughes' *Consciousness and Society* (New York, 1958) and will find Arthur Mitzman's *The Iron Cage: An Historical Interpretation of Max Weber* (New York, 1970) along with Reinhard Bendix's *Max Weber: An Intellectual Portrait* (New York, 1960) practically indispensable. For those willing to read German, three sources repeatedly cited by authors interested in Weber's life are: Marianne Weber's biography of her husband, *Max Weber: Ein Lebensbild* (Tübingen, 1926); Max Weber's early letters, *Jugendbriefe* (Tübingen, 1936); and Weber's uncle Eduard's account of his brilliant, troubled nephew, Eduard Baumgarten, *Max Weber, Werk und Person* (Tübingen, 1964). Another frequently cited study of Weber's career is Wolfgang Mommsen's *Max Weber und die deutsche Politik* (Tübingen, 1954), which criticizes Weber as influencing German liberalism to turn to *Realpolitik.* A later article by the same author is frequently accepted as a major contribution to the explanation of the historical context of Weber's work, "Universalgeschichtliches und politisches Denken bei Max Weber," *Historische Zeitschrift* 201 (1965): 557–612. Some of the ideas in this long article had been expressed at the 1964 meeting of the German Sociological Association celebrating the centennial anniversary of Weber's birth and found their way into a still longer article in English, "Max Weber Today," *International Social Science Journal* 17 (1965): 9–70, which also includes papers presented at the same meeting by Bendix, Parsons, and Rossi. A famous work frequently associated with Weber's views is Ernst Troeltsch's *The Social Teaching of the Christian Churches,* translated by Olive Wyon (New York, 1950); Troeltsch, a close associate of Weber, seeks to determine to what degree the origin, growth, and modifications in the development of Christianity were sociologically determined. An excellent overview and synopsis of the whole corpus of Weber's work is presented by Julien Freund, *The Sociology of Max Weber,* translated from the French by Mary Ilford (New York, 1968).

For those particularly interested in Weber's methodology, a careful scrutiny of the original fully documented version of R. Stephen Warner's article on Weber's comparative studies of noncapitalist societies will be worthwhile. Also impressive are Rolf E. Roger's *Max Weber's Ideal Type Theory* (New York, 1969) and J. A. Prades, *La Sociologie de la religion chez Max Weber, essai d'analyse et de critique de la méthode,* 2d edition (Paris, 1969). A brief, clear, summary discussion of Weber's methodology is presented by S. Andreski in his article "Method and Substantive Theory in Max Weber," *British Journal of Sociology* 15 (1964): 1–18. Somewhat similar in their interest in the studies of Weber's method are those who are concerned to compare Weber's ideas and methods to Marx's and the alleged sociological roles of Calvinism and Marxism in the societies where they were useful to the established members of the power structure. Such works include: Niles M. Hansen, "The Protestant Ethic as a General Precondition for Economic Development," *Canadian Journal of Economics and Political Science* 29 (1963): 462–474; N. Birnbaum, "Conflicting Interpretations of the Rise of Capitalism: Marx and Weber," *British Journal of Sociology* 4 (1953): 125–141; Robert Stephen Warner, "The Methodology of Marx's Comparative Analysis of Modes of Production," included in *Comparative Methods in Sociology: Essays on Trends and Applications* edited by Ivan Vallier (Berkeley, 1971), 49–74; and Anthony Giddens, *Capitalism and Modern Social Theory: An Analysis of the Writings of Marx, Durkheim and Max Weber* (Cambridge, 1971). A substantial collection of essays ranging over many aspects of the Weber thesis controversy, including the methodologies of Weber and Marx is S. N. Eisenstadt's *The Protestant Ethic and Modernization, a Comparative View* (New York, 1968). The Weber controversy becomes involved in a slightly different way in numerous studies comparing and relating Calvinism and various forms of collectivism; a well-written example of this line of investigation is Thelma McCormack's "The Protestant Ethic and the Spirit of Socialism," *British Journal of Sociology* 20 (1969): 266–276. A somewhat similar emphasis is given by Robert Ashton's "Puritanism and Progress," *Economic History Review* 17 (1964–1965): 577–587. The materialistic emphasis characteristic of Marxist historiography remains somewhat ill at ease with a concept of a "spirit of capitalism." Such a view is presented by Maurice Dobb, *Studies in the Development of Capitalism* (London, 1946). Another Marxist more specifically concerned with the Weber thesis than Dobb is P. C. Gordon Walker whose article, "Capitalism and the Reformation," appears in the November 1937 issue of the *Economic History Review*. Gordon Walker denies the conclusions of both Weber and his critics and asserts that the entire Reformation movement was a product of the price revolution. A truly excellent study of this long-embattled subject is Ingrid Hammarström's "The 'Price Revolution' of the Sixteenth Century: Some Swedish Evidence," *Scandinavian Economic History Review* 19 (1971): 118–154. A widely recognized non-Marxist study of the history of capitalism is Henri Sée, *Modern Capitalism* (New York, 1928); Sée, like Dobb and Gordon Walker, concedes practically nothing to the view of a "capitalist spirit" as a guiding force of economic history. An equally materialistic view of the rise of capitalism will be derived from reading all of H. M. Robertson's *Aspects of the Rise of Economic Individualism* (Cambridge, 1933) including his analyses of the effects of overseas discoveries upon emerging capitalism.

Giving greater emphasis to the closer description of Weber's assertions about Calvinism and conditions and attitudes prevailing from the Renaissance to the eighteenth century are such works as Albert Hyma's *Renaissance to Reformation* (Grand Rapids, 1955) which not only surveys the period but emphasizes the views of Luther and Calvin during their own lifetimes in contrast to some of Weber's assertions. A more recent and very readable work on Calvin in Geneva is W. Fred Graham's *The Constructive Revolutionary: John Calvin and His Socio-Economic Impact* (Richmond, Va., 1971). Amintore Fanfani in *Catholicism, Protestantism and Capitalism* (New York, 1955) takes a broader view of the relationship of religion and economic behavior than Weber and introduces anthropological factors into the emergence of capitalism. In its entirety Kurt Samuelsson's *Religion and Economic Action* (New York, 1961) ranges over the whole time period alluded to by Weber, even finding reason to challenge Weber on the basis of developments in U.S.A. Very brief but well-balanced and informed historical commentaries are provided by Roland H. Bainton's *The Reformation of the Sixteenth Century* (Boston, 1952), pp. 244–256 and by Harold J. Grimm, *The Reformation Era* (New York, 1954), pp. 578–581. Focusing primarily on the British Isles as had Weber in *The Protestant Ethic and the Spirit of Capitalism* is a long list of works which present views conflicting with Weber's in at least some respect. Among the better known or more sharply contrasting with Weber and his partisans are studies such as Charles and Katherine George, *The Protestant Mind of the English Reformation, 1570–1640* (Princeton, 1961); *Essays in the Economic and Social History of Tudor and Stuart England: In Honour of R. H. Tawney,* edited by F. J. Fisher, including an essay by Christopher Hill, "Protestantism and the Rise of Capitalism" (Cambridge, 1961); and Christopher Hill's *Society and Puritanism in Pre-Revolutionary England* (London, 1964). Timothy H. Breen argues that Puritan and Anglican preaching on economic behavior was essentially the same in "The Non-existent Controversy: Puritan and Anglican Attitudes on Work and Wealth, 1600–1640," *Church History* 35 (1966): 273–287; and S. A. Burrell discusses Weber's views with reference to developments in Scotland in "Calvinism, Capitalism, and the Middle Classes: Some Afterthoughts on an Old Problem," *Journal of Modern History* 32 (1960): 129–141.

Still a useful summary of the first forty years of contention is Ephraim Fischoff's "The Protestant Ethic and the Spirit of Capitalism: the History of a Controversy," *Social Research* 11 (1944): 61–77; and a more recent recapitulation of at least the methodological aspects of the long debate is Ehud Sprinzak's "Weber's Thesis as an Historical Explanation," *History and Theory* 11 (1972): 294–320.

Within the last decade more than fifty scholarly journals have published one or more articles on, or at least relevant to, the Weber thesis controversy. The ten journals which seem to give the most attention to the continuing dissension about Weber and his work are (in alphabetical order): *The British Journal of Sociology, Church History, The Economic History Review, History and Theory, The International Social Science Journal, The Journal of Economic History, The Journal of Modern History, Scandinavian Economic History Review, Social Research,* and *Zeitschrift für Nationalökonomie.* This is a rich collection for the reader who wants to dig systematically or browse at will.

2 3 4 5 6 7 8 9 10

APR 0 8 2008		

DEMCO